A History of Old English Literature

Sutton Hoo helmet

A History of Old English Literature
Michael Alexander

broadview press

29582

DEC 1 5 2004

National Library of Canada Cataloguing in Publication Data

Alexander, Michael, 1941-
     A history of Old English literature

Includes bibliographical references.
ISBN 1-55111-322-8

1. English literature — Old English, ca. 450-1100 — History and criticism. 2. Anglo-Saxons — Intellectual life. I. Title.

PR173.A44 2001   829'.09   C2001-900582-2

Broadview Press Ltd. is an independent, international publishing house, incorporated in 1985.

North America:
P.O. Box 1243, Peterborough, Ontario, Canada K9J 7H5
3576 California Road, Orchard Park, NY 14127
TEL: (705) 743-8990; FAX: (705) 743-8353;
E-MAIL: customerservice@broadviewpress.com

United Kingdom:
Thomas Lyster Ltd
Unit 9, Ormskirk Industrial Park
Old Boundary Way, Burscough Road
Ormskirk, Lancashire L39 2YW
TEL: (01695) 575112; FAX: (01695) 570120; E-mail: books@tlyster.co.uk

Australia:
St. Clair Press, P.O. Box 287, Rozelle, NSW 2039
TEL: (02) 818-1942; FAX: (02) 418-1923

www.broadviewpress.com

Broadview Press gratefully acknowledges the financial support of the Book Publishing Industry Development Program, Ministry of Canadian Heritage, Government of Canada.

Book design and composition by George Kirkpatrick

PRINTED IN CANADA

CONTENTS

ACKNOWLEDGEMENTS

THE author and the publisher wish to thank the following who have kindly given permission to quote extended passages from works listed below.

Penguin Books Ltd. for extracts from *The Earliest English Poems*, translated by Michael Alexander (Penguin Classics, 2nd ed., 1977), © Michael Alexander 1966, 1977; *Beowulf*, translated by Michael Alexander (Penguin Classics, 1973), © Michael Alexander 1973.

The Estate of C.L. Wrenn for extracts from *A Study of Old English Literature* (Harrap, 1967).

Sutton Hoo Helmet. The British Museum.
Offa's Penny. © Copyright The British Museum.
Sutton Hoo spoons. © Copyright The British Museum.
Sutton Hoo silver bowls. © Copyright The British Museum.
Sutton Hoo shoulder clasp. © Copyright The British Museum.
Sutton Hoo sceptre. © Copyright The British Museum.
Sutton Hoo sceptre, detail. © Copyright The British Museum.
The Ruthwell Cross. Reprinted by permission of Historic Scotland.

The Lindisfarne Gospels: St. Matthew's Incipit, Cott.Nero.D.IV f27. Reprinted by permission of the British Library

The Lindisfarne Gospels: A Carpet Page, St. Mark, Cott. Nero. D.IV f94v. Reprinted by permission of the British Library.

The Lindisfarne Gospels: St. John, Cott.Nero.D.IV f209v. Reprinted by permission of the British Library.

St. Lawrence, Bradford-on-Avon. © Crown copyright. NMR.

The Franks Casket. © Copyright The British Museum.

The Exeter Book, Folio 103a. Reproduced by permission of the Dean and Chapter of Exeter Cathedral.

The Alfred Jewel. Reprinted by permission of the Ashmolean Museum, Oxford.

St. Dunstan at the feet of Christ, MS.Auct.F.4.32, fol.1. Reprinted by permission of The Bodleian Library, University of Oxford.

Edgar's New Minster Charter (292/41[41]). Reprinted by permission of The Conway Library, Courtauld Institute of Art.

Aethelwold's Benedictional: Entry into Jerusalem, Add.49598 f45v. Reprinted by permission of the British Library.

The Harrowing of Hell. Reprinted by permission of the British Library.

The author and the publisher have made every attempt to locate all copyright holders and would be grateful for information that would allow them to correct any errors or omissions in a subsequent edition of the work.

PREFACE

This is the sort of introductory book I should like to have had available when I first studied Old English as part of a degree in English literature. It provides a simple historical and cultural context for the study of the literature of the Anglo-Saxons, and offers a history, illustrated by many passages in translation, of the whole of the literature that survives.

The literature of the Anglo-Saxons has not always been included in histories of English literature, partly because its language is no longer spoken but has to be learned. Historians of language call the English of the Anglo-Saxons Old English; Middle English begins in the generations after the Norman Conquest of 1066; Modern English begins to appear about 1500. Old English is not a language distinct from English, but one of the varieties of English, like American English, Elizabethan English, or contemporary British English. It is simply early English. As such, it must form part of the history of English literature.

If the language of Old English literature is unfamiliar, so at first is its culture. The ethos of Anglo-Saxon culture between the seventh and the eleventh centuries, although it had absorbed much from Christian and classical culture, differs from that of the high and late Middle Ages. Familiarity with it has to be acquired. Yet this literature is of the greatest interest, not only as part of the genealogy of English culture, but intrinsically. It has great and varied merits.

To most of us the dark ages are dark not because we are happy in our superior enlightenment but because we know so little about them. Ignorance should not lead us to condescend to those who produced the Sutton Hoo treasure, the Lindisfarne Gospels, *Beowulf*, the poetic Elegies or *The Dream of the Rood*. Nor can we neglect the story told in Bede's *Ecclesiastical History* and in the *Anglo-Saxon Chronicle*: the story of how local kingdoms established by conquest were converted and, under threat of Danish invasion, merged into a single Christian kingdom, the survival of which finds a fitting emblem in the survival of the Alfred Jewel in the marshes of Somerset (see page 163). Most students of the matter recognise that the civilised ways and arts of the Anglo-Saxons were superior, except in war, administration, and architecture, to those of the Normans.

This book, originally published in 1984, and revised and rewritten in 2000, attempts to remove one reason for the neglect of Anglo-Saxon England by a simple historical presentation of the main elements in Anglo-Saxon literature, and especially its poetry, in translation. Although its intentions are scholarly, this history of Old English literature is also an illustrative introduction, assuming little knowledge of this period or its surviving products and none of its language. Literary history should be reasonably inclusive, but much Old English literature has been lost, and its scholars have to make their way without the dense grid of authors, titles, dates, and places of later centuries. The extant literature gives a partial and probably misleading impression of what there once was. Several types of literature may have disappeared. In the present volume, writings without literary interest which happen to have survived, such as charms, wills and recipes, are not discussed. The emphasis falls less upon history than on literature, taken as a qualitative rather than merely a descriptive term.

Most of the learned literature of the Anglo-Saxons was, naturally, written in Latin, the language of literacy and of the Church. While such writings in the international language are part of the story, this account focuses on the vernacular, and particularly on Old English verse, which is of greater artistic interest than the prose, and owes less to Latin. The bulk of Old English literary prose consists of sermons and lives of the saints, which gave precious example to the Anglo-Saxons, both to the monks who wrote the manuscripts and their patrons, and to their audience, who heard them read aloud. The monks, who brought letters and learning as well as Christianity to the English, themselves contributed much to the poetry of the native tradition. One of the pleasures of writing this book has been to discover the extent of the variety and interest of Old English religious verse. I should like to record my gratitude to predecessors more learned than I, especially R.W. Chambers, Stanley B. Greenfield, C.W. Kennedy, W.P. Ker, Barbara Raw, T.A. Shippey, J.R.R. Tolkien, Margaret Williams, and C.L. Wrenn, together with the translators, editors, and scholars listed in the bibliography. I would like to thank Professor Felicity Riddy for having read much of the manuscript at a busy time; her suggestions improved it. I am also much obliged to Professor A.N. Jeffares, who originally commissioned the book, and to secretaries at the University of Stirling. Eileen, who rescued me from various follies, has all my gratitude. Finally, I wish to thank Jill Gamble, of St. Andrews, who scanned the 1982 text so that I could revise it for this new edition.

1982, 2001

CHRONOLOGICAL TABLE

DATE	AUTHOR & TITLE	EVENT
43		Conquest of Britain by Claudius
98	Tacitus: *Germania*	
286		St. Alban (*d.*)
312		Milvian Bridge
313		Toleration of Christians
314		Council of Arles
330		Constantinople founded
		St. Helena finds True Cross
384	St. Jerome: Vulgate edition of Bible	
410		Legions recalled from Britain
413	St. Augustine of Hippo: *The City of God*	
417	Orosius: *History of the World*	
429		St. Germanus in Britain
430		St. Patrick in Ireland
		St. Ninian in N. Britain
*c.*431–89	Sidonius Apollinaris	

449		Hengest and Horsa: conquest by Angles, Saxons and Jutes begins
c.500		British resistance: Battle of Mons Badonicus
		St. David in Wales
519		Cedric founds Wessex
521		Hygelac the Geat (d.)
524	Boethius: *Consolation of Philosophy*	
529		St. Benedict founds Monte Cassino
c.547	Gildas: *Conquest of Britain*	
	St. Columba: *Altus Prosator*	
	St. Columbanus	
563	Venantius Fortunatus: Hymns of the Cross	Columba on Iona
577		Battle of Dyrham: British confined to Wales and Dumnonia
	Taliesin	
591	Gregory of Tours: *History of the Franks*	
597	Aneirin: *Y Gododdin*	Gregory sends Augustine to Canterbury
		St. Columba (d.)
c.615		Aethelfrith king of Bernicia defeats Britons at Chester
615–56		Raedwald king of East Anglia
616		Ethelbert king of Kent (d.)
616–32		Edwin king of Northumbria
627		Edwin converted by Paulinus

800	After this date: Cynewulf: *Christ II, Elene, Juliana, Fates of the Apostles*	
802		Egbert king of Wessex
851	(?) *Genesis B*	Danes spend winter in England
865		Danish army in East Anglia
867		Battle of York: eclipse of Northumbria
869		Edmund king of East Anglia killed
871–99	(?) *Andreas*	Alfred king of Wessex,
877		the only kingdom unconquered by Danes
878	Alfredian translations: *Pastoral Care, Ecclesiastical History,* Orosius, Boethius, *Soliloquies; AS Chronicle* begun	
c.886		Bounds of Danelaw agreed
909	*Beowulf* probably composed by this date	St. Dunstan (*b.*)
910		Cluny founded
911–18	(?) *Judith*	Aethelflaed Lady of the Mercians
919	(?) *The Phoenix*	Mercia subject to Wessex
924–39		Athelstan king of Wessex
937	*Brunanburh* in *AS Chronicle*	Battle of Brunanburh: Athelstan defeats Scots and others
954		End of Scandinavian kingdom of York: England united under Wessex
959–75		Reign of Edgar
960–88	Monastic Revival	Dunstan archbishop of Canterbury

961		Oswald bishop of Worcester
963		Aethelwold bishop of Winchester
c.971	*The Blickling Homilies*	
973		Coronation of Edgar
978-1016	The major poetry manuscripts Junius Book, Vercelli Book, Exeter Book, *Beowulf* MS	Reign of Ethelred II
991	(?) *Apollonius of Tyre* *The Battle of Maldon*	Battle of Maldon
990-92	Aelfric: *Catholic Homilies*	
993-98	Aelfric: *Lives of Saints*	
1003-23		Wulfstan archbishop of York
1014	*Sermo Lupi Ad Anglos*	Swein of Denmark king
1017-35		Reign of Cnut
1043-66		Reign of Edward the Confessor
1066		Harold king Battle of Stamford Bridge Battle of Hastings
1066		William I king
1154	End of the Peterborough *Chronicle*	

ONE : PERSPECTIVES

I • WHAT HAS SURVIVED

IF literary criticism is concerned with texts, literary history with contexts, Old English poetry has a very sketchy literary history. There is normally much difficulty in documenting the context of an Old English poetic text. The prose, by contrast, presents less of a problem: prose texts can often be dated, located, even attributed to a specific author, including such well-known figures from Anglo-Saxon history as King Alfred and the leaders of the Benedictine Revival of the late tenth century such as Aelfric and Wulfstan. In his *Martyrdom of Saint Edmund*, for instance, Aelfric tells us that he is translating the account of a named monk of the abbey of Fleury (in France), who had it from St. Dunstan, the Archbishop of Canterbury; who had it from King Athelstan; who had it from Edmund's swordbearer, a witness of the events. Where such precise claims or indications are missing, there is often comparative material, especially for homilies and saints' lives. For documentary prose, such as historical records, the context can be clear, as with charters and wills, or ascertainable, as with the *Anglo-Saxon Chronicle*. Old English prose writing was called into being by King Alfred as an act of policy to fill the gap caused by the Viking destruction of the Latin culture of the kingdoms north of

I

the Thames. In the first place, most Old English prose consisted of translations or adaptations from Latin. Most of the rest had an explicitly stated practical purpose, as in the case of the most celebrated piece of Old English prose, King Alfred's Preface to the *Pastoral Care* of Gregory the Great. Among the many things Alfred writes to the bishop of Worcester, for example, is that he does not think that when he came to the throne (in 871) there was a single man living south of the Thames who could read Latin.

This sort of precise and positive information is not to be found in Old English poetry, even in the late poems on the historical battles of Brunanburgh and Maldon. Both these poems conceive and relate their subjects according to ancient conventions of battle poetry in which the essential ethos of "the glory-trial" is more real than documentary actualities. There may be more in common between *The Battle of Maldon*, composed some time after the battle in 991, and Aneirin's *Y Gododdin*, composed in the language of the defeated Britons some time before 600, than there is between the poetic version of the battle of Maldon and the prose entry in the *Anglo-Saxon Chronicle*. This records that after the defeat it was agreed to pay the Vikings tribute, whereas the emphasis of the poem *The Battle of Maldon* falls upon the heroic conduct of the East-Saxon warriors after their lord's death. So deeply rooted were the conventions expressing the warrior ethos in such poetry that the ideals inspiring the East Saxons at Maldon, though they have a Christian colouring, can be as well understood from the account of Germanic heroism in Tacitus' *Germania*, written in the first century AD, as from contemporary Old English prose. In Old English poetry, then, internal evidence does not usually give much indication of place, date, occasion or author.

Old English verse survives patchily. There are about 31,000 lines of it extant, nearly all of which are to be found in four manuscripts written towards the year 1000 in the late West-Saxon dialect. These are the *Beowulf* manuscript, the Exeter Book, the Vercelli Book, and the Junius Book. An examination of the language of the poems suggests that in most cases they had been composed not in Wessex but to the north of the Thames, in the quite different Anglian dialects of Mercia or Northumbria, one, two or three centuries earlier, and were copied at least once before they reached their present form. Only four of these poems are signed: those by Cynewulf, a person not otherwise known to us. We also have Cædmon's *Hymn*, of nine lines, and Bede's *Death Song*, of five lines. Other poems are anonymous. Most survive in unique copies; where there are two or three copies, texts differ considerably.

We do not, therefore, know when most Old English poems were composed, nor where, nor by whom. Contexts cannot be established, even for the two most studied groups of poems, the heroic poems and the elegies. We are on firmer ground with the religious poetry, since more of it survives; and in the poems of Cynewulf and the poems formerly attributed to Cædmon, we can make comparisons within groups of poems clearly related to each other, to Latin originals, and to periods and areas if not to dates and places. But the shortage of poems comparable with *Beowulf* is limiting. It is certain that there was a tradition of heroic poetry, of which *Beowulf* is the sole surviving substantial early example. Perhaps heroic poems of the heathen period were not often written down. Certainly there was much Old English poetry by clerics which has not survived; both Bede and Aldhelm were noted poets in their mother tongue, but of their work only the five lines of Bede survive (as against a large number of copies of his and Aldhelm's various Latin prose works). Even Cædmon, the unlettered layman who was the first to use the old Germanic alliterative verse for Christian themes, is no longer thought of as the author of the four poems which used to be ascribed to him, but only of his nine-line *Hymn*. If the vernacular works of such revered figures did not survive, what chance of being recorded was there for works less obviously conducive to salvation? The ravages of the Norsemen destroyed many libraries, and during the centuries after the Norman Conquest surviving Old English manuscripts became unintelligible and apparently valueless. The Dissolution of the Monasteries saw merry scenes of the burning of useless monastic books by the agents of the Defender of the Faith. The dangers of accidental destruction and loss are illustrated by the disappearance of the manuscripts of *The Battle of Maldon* and *Finnsburgh* since the eighteenth century, when they had already been considered valuable enough to have been copied. Of the

3

four major old English poetic manuscripts that survive, two are scarred by fire and one has been at Vercelli in Italy since the thirteenth century. Of the three remaining versions and part-versions of *The Dream of the Rood*, none is now in England. The Exeter Book itself, containing the best of the poetry outside *Beowulf*, has a serious burn-mark where a brand or poker rested on its back. This damage may have been accidental; but the manuscript has also been used as a cutting-board and as a beer-mat.

II • SONGS AND SCRIBES

The absence of a detailed historical context for Old English poetry is the result not only of the destruction and dispersal of manuscripts but also of the double distance between the profession of scribe and the old heroic poetry. The scribe's duty, done for eternity in innumerable illuminated Gospels and service-books, was to the word of God, not to secular performances. And the tradition of Germanic alliterative poetry was oral rather than literary — performance, not literature. In preliterate society this poetry was not only recited and transmitted but actually composed orally; it was not meant to be written down. We know that many in holy orders — such as Aldhelm and Bede — liked the old songs. Clerics were rebuked for listening to songs about heathen heroes, by the great English scholar Alcuin, writing from France to their bishop late in the eighth century. Alcuin reminds the bishop that those heathen kings were now in hell: "When priests eat together [*in sacerdotali convivium*]," he writes, "let God's words be read; it is fitting that a reader [*lector*] should be heard there, not a harper [*citharistam*], the sermons of the Fathers [of the Church], not the songs of the pagans. What has Ingeld to do with Christ?" Ingeld was evidently a typical hero of the songs of the heathen; he features in both *Widsith* and *Beowulf*, elements of which must date back to this period. The ultimate irrelevance of pagan literature when compared to the truth of Christian revelation is a familiar theme in Augustine's *Confessions*. Jerome had a nightmare in which Christ himself asked him, "Are you a Ciceronian or a Christian?"

The similar rebuke above, from Alcuin, the schoolmaster of

Charlemagne, is interesting not only for its contrast of the different heroisms of Ingeld and Christ, but for the terms of the
comparisons which lead up to it. The Bible and the sermons of
the Church Fathers are to be *read* by the *lector*; heathen songs are
not to be *sung* by the *harper*. The sacerdotal *convivium*, where clerics sat at table before their spiritual lord, must not revert to the
entertainment in the hall of the temporal lord, which in other
ways it might resemble. Monks were allowed a ration of beer;
Beowulf refers to the hall indifferently as the beer-hall, the mead-
hall, and the wine-hall. The old heroic songs meant something to
the clergy, especially perhaps to communities of monks, just as
many an ex-Christian joins in carol-singing at Christmas. But
although the monks' liking for the old songs was strong enough to
have preserved the Christian *Beowulf* (it was very probably produced in a monastic *scriptorium*), they probably copied very little
pre-Christian poetry, the social context of which was oral and not
literary; nor might it have occurred to monks to write it down.

As a general rule, Old English poems have therefore to provide
their own framework. The heroic poems invariably describe
poetry as being orally composed and sung. Bede's account of
Cædmon's song of Creation assumes that an ability to sing after
supper was a usual social accomplishment, and stresses that the
cowman's gift of composition remained an oral one even when he
had been fed a diet of Old Testament stories. As the Old English
version of Bede puts it, "all that he could learn with his hearing,
that he turned in his mind, and as a clean beast ruminating he
turned it into the sweetest song, and his verses were so winsome
to hear that his teachers themselves learned and wrote from his
mouth" (Margaret Williams, *Word-Hoard*, p. 79). This is a striking
account of oral poetry being written down, as well as of the
appropriation of Germanic verse for Christian narrative. The
convivial context in which the earlier poetry was created is illuminated by internal evidence and by external evidence such as
Bede provides here, but also by the better understanding of the
nature of oral poetry itself, which will be discussed in chapter 3.
Oral literature is a contradiction in terms, and we would not have
the heroic poems if Christian monks had not written them down.
Nevertheless the traditions of the pagan *carmen* (song) and of the
sermo (word) of the Church Fathers were very different, and the

marriage between the two produces a blend, in Old English poetry, which has to be interpreted with care and imagination.

III • THE END OF HEATHENISM

When we imagine the thought-world of the Anglo-Saxons, the nature of their pre-Christian culture is a subject that fascinates but remains speculative. There are relics of their heathenism left at such cardinal points as place-names and the names of days of the week; even the name of the greatest Christian festival is taken from the name of a heathen goddess. But we know no more about her than her name. The sole source here is Bede, who was specially interested in chronology. The English call the fourth month *Eostremonath*, he tells us, after their goddess Eostre, "for whom they were accustomed to hold festivals at that season." Gregory the Great had advised Augustine not to deprive the people of their customary sacrifices of oxen, and to let the old festivals be celebrated on appropriate days as religious feasts. It is in line with this advice that the name of Eostre was retained; as were those of Tiw, Woden and Thor, given to days of the week. These gods roughly correspond to Mars, Mercury and Jove, as Friy did to Venus. Saturn's name was retained for Saturday. But these survivals are modelled on the Roman pagan calendar by permission of the Roman Church; a similar permission may lie behind the retention of some heathen place-names. Gregory at first urged King Ethelbert of Kent to overthrow heathen temples, but on second thoughts suggested to Augustine that he should leave well-built temples standing, replace the idols by relics, and consecrate them as Christian churches. This enlightened Catholic policy may be responsible for the survival of several place-names like Wednesbury (Woden's barrow) and Harrow-on-the-Hill (*hearh*: shrine). And the dynasties of all the Anglo-Saxon kingdoms except that of the East Saxons trace their descent from Woden, whose ancestry is traced back to Noah.

Apart from a handful of charms and spells, that is about the strength of the evidence for the content of Anglo-Saxon paganism. Undoubtedly their religious beliefs in the fifth century corresponded to the beliefs of their cousins whom they left behind on the continent, and to their cousins once removed in Scandinavia. But evidence for Norse beliefs, although extensive, comes from a later period, and is not strictly admissible. *Beowulf* and the earliest English poems are already baptised, and contain only shadows of the old beliefs. They show us with great clarity the plight of men "on Middle Earth," "beneath shifting skies," "heroes under the heavens": that is, the limits of human life and knowledge, and the necessity of a stoic heroism. But of the precise content of Anglo-Saxon heathenism we know next to nothing. The social structure of this Germanic population survived the conversion, however, and it should not be forgotten that the Roman empire itself had been extensively Germanised before its emperors became Christians.

That the old beliefs had great force, that conversion was often not rapid, complete and lasting, is obvious from the apostasies and backslidings recorded in Bede. But the story which, ever since Bede wrote it, has seemed to sum up the moral atmosphere of Anglo-Saxon England at the moment when it encountered Christianity for the first time, is the story of the conversion of Edwin of Northumbria.

Edwin held a meeting of his council, a *witenagemot*, at York in 627, to decide whether to accept Christianity, the faith of his wife. The chief pagan priest of Northumbria, Coifi, began by declaring that since his own devotion to the old religion had not done him much good, his lord the king should give the new faith a good hearing. An anonymous counsellor agreed, and made the following speech:

> Your Majesty, when we compare the present life of man on earth with that time of which we have no knowledge, it seems to me like the swift flight of a single sparrow through the banqueting-hall where you are sitting at dinner on a winter's day with your thanes and counsellors. In the midst there is a comforting fire to warm the hall; outside, the storms of winter rain or snow are raging. The sparrow flies swiftly in through one door of the hall, and out through another. While he is inside, he is safe from the winter storms; but after a few moments of comfort, he vanishes from sight into the wintry world from which he came. Even

so, man appears on earth for a little while; but of what went before this life or of what follows, we know nothing. Therefore, if this new teaching has brought any more certain knowledge, it seems only right that we should follow it.

(Bede, II, 13, trans. Leo Sherley-Price, p. 129)

This speech, which led to the baptism of Edwin, gives a key not only to the success of Christianity but to the conditions and the feel of life in the early Middle Ages. Brevity, uncertainty, and isolation are recurrent themes not only in the heroic world of *Beowulf* but also in the heroic lives of hermits, missionaries, and martyrs, the exemplars of the Christian culture that succeeded it. Many of the typical moments of Anglo-Saxon history find the protagonist on an island: Cuthbert on Lindisfarne, Guthlac in the Cambridgeshire fens, Alfred on Athelney in the Somerset marshes. In Beowulf men are presented as *hæleth under heofenum*, heroes under the heavens, *men on middangeard*, men on middle-earth, *swa hit wæter bebugeth*, surrounded by water, *be sæm tweonum*, between the seas. At the beginning of the poem, Scyld, the founder of the ruling house of the Danes, is a foundling, sent miraculously across the seas to the shore of Denmark. After a heroic life, he is given a magnificent ship-burial: his body, with its arms and armour and royal treasure, is set afloat in a ship. The poet adds:

> Men ne cunnon
> secgan to sothe, sele-rædende,
> hæleth under heofenum, hwa thæm hlæste onfeng.

> Men under heaven's
> shifting skies, though skilled in counsel,
> cannot say surely who unshipped that cargo.

(50–52)

Middangeard, usually translated "middle earth" or "earth," literally means "the enclosure in the middle." The traditional vocabulary and formulas of poetry suggest that *middangeard* was felt to be laterally enclosed by the seas and that man's life was temporally enclosed by an unknown before and after, also symbolised by the seas in the story of Scyld, and, in the speech of the anonymous

counsellor of Edwin, by the darkness of night and storm surrounding the feast of life in the hall.

IV • THE LANGUAGES OF BRITAIN

"The island of Britain is 800 miles long and 200 miles broad; and
here in this island there are five languages: English, British, Scottish, Pictish, and Latin." This, the first sentence of the northern
version of the *Anglo-Saxon Chronicle*, is a category-crumbling
reminder that the literature of Britain between the fifth and the
eleventh centuries was not composed exclusively in the language
of the most recent arrivals, the Angles and Saxons. What little
remains of Pictish, the early language of what is now Scotland, is
undeciphered; it is probably a Celtic language. Literature in the
language of the "Scots" (Gaels from Ireland settled in Argyll and
the Isles) is extant in manuscripts from Scotland only from the
sixteenth century, though in Ireland its writing goes back much
further. But much writing in the language of the Britons, which
we now call Welsh, survives from an earlier period. There is also
much Anglo-Latin (that is, Anglo-Saxon literature in Latin) especially from the age before the Viking destruction of the Latin culture of northern and eastern England in the ninth century. This
collapse of Latin caused King Alfred to put in hand the translation
of the "books most needful for all men to know" from Latin into
the English of Wessex, and so to establish the Old English prose
tradition.

It was in Alfred's reign (871–99) that the *Chronicle* was begun —
the only such vernacular history in western Europe. Professor
Henry Loyn says that "no other part of Europe acquired such a
well-disciplined vernacular literature, prose as well as poetry, so
early." The version of the *Chronicle* kept at Peterborough was to
continue its record of events down to the year 1154. Entries in the
Chronicle for the period before 871 are based on clerical epitomes
of world history, and traditional Anglo-Saxon genealogies and
stories, but chiefly on Bede's *Ecclesiastical History of the English People*, completed in the year 731. The three most flourishing periods
of Old English literature — or so the surviving evidence makes it
now appear — are the lifetime of Bede, the reign of Alfred, and

the period between the accession of Edgar in 959 and the death of Aethelred in 1016. These phases are separated in time but interconnected. The destruction by the Vikings of the golden age of Northumbria caused Alfred to begin his educational programme, which was only to be fulfilled by the Benedictine Revival at the end of the tenth century. Old English literature and English writing in Latin are thus intimately related.

For example, the Old English sentence which begins this section on the languages of Britain condenses a passage of Bede's Latin written a century and a half earlier. Bede's original has been translated:

> At the present time there are in Britain, in harmony with the five books of the divine law, five languages and four nations — English, British, Scots and Picts. Each of these have their own language; but all are united in their study of God's truth by the fifth — Latin — which has become a common medium through the study of the scriptures.
>
> (Bede, trans. Sherley-Price, p. 38)

Bede not only provides a fuller, more historical explanation than the later annalist, but also sees in the relationship between the numbers of nations and languages in Britain an allegorical ratio with the first five books of the Old Testament, the "ecclesiastical history of the Jewish people." In contrast with this speculative truth, Alfred's annalist baldly offers a digest of facts — facts which by this time were perhaps quite well known. He would have been very conscious that by his day some newcomers in the north and east of England spoke a Scandinavian language.

National pride in the antiquity of English vernacular literature has sometimes led to the neglect of writing in Latin even by English and certainly by Celtic writers. Welsh writers in Latin, such as Gildas, author of *Of the Conquest of Britain* (*c.* 547), looked on the Germanic invaders (correctly) as pagan barbarians, in the same way that the Anglo-Saxons were later to regard the Vikings. After Taliesin, the most ancient name in British poetry is that of Aneirin, the author of the heroic poem *Y Gododdin*. It tells how at the battle of Catraeth (Catterick), the Goddodin (Latin Votadini), a British tribe from Dun Edin (Edinburgh) were defeated by the Northumbrians. Of 363 who went to the battle, only four returned. The twenty-first stanza of Clancy's version runs:

> Men went to Catraeth; they were renowned.
> Wine and mead from gold cups was their drink,
> A year in noble ceremonial,
> Three hundred and sixty-three gold-torqued men.
> Of all those who charged, after too much drink,
> But three won free through courage in strife,
> Aeron's two war-hounds and tough Cynon,
> And myself, soaked in blood, for my song's sake.
>
> (Clancy, *The Earliest Welsh Poetry*, p. 40)

The twenty-fourth praises a particular hero:

> Hero, shield firm below his freckled forehead,
>   His stride a young stallion's.
> There was battle's din, there was flame,
> There were keen spears, there was sunlight,
> There was crow's food, a crow's profit.
> Before he was left at the ford,
> As the dew fell, graceful eagle,
> With the wave spreading beside him,
> The world's bards judge him great of heart.
> His warfaring wasted his wealth;
> Wiped out were his leaders and men.
> Before burial beneath Eleirch
> Fre, there was valour in his breast,
> His blood poured over his armour,
> Undaunted Buddfan fab Bleiddfan.
>
> (Clancy, p. 41)

The British heroic world of the late sixth century is not unlike the world of the Old English *Beowulf*, although meetings between the two worlds were hostile, as at Catterick. There is no evidence of the Christian British having tried to convert the heathen Germanic invaders. A large British element remained in the population of England, submerged but pervasive and with an incalculable cultural effect. Proven literary debts are few: Alfred's educational programme was helped by the Welsh bishop of St. David's, Asser, who wrote Alfred's life; and some of the later Old English elegies seem to have been affected by Welsh poetry. There is no doubt, on the other hand, about the Irish contribution to Anglo-Latin writing.

The Angles of the North and Midlands had a great and well documented debt of learning and spirituality to the Irish Church, through Columba, the Irish prince and abbot, who died in 597, the year of Augustine's arrival in Kent. Columba's monastic foundation at Iona was eventually to send to Northumbria such disciples as Aidan, and to form Cuthbert himself, the most revered of Anglo-Saxon saints. Anglo-Saxon manuscript illumination and handwriting derive from these Celtic missions. Bede, in his day perhaps the most learned man in Europe, and a lover of Rome, knew that he owed much to the Irish or "Scottish" tradition of the founders of Lindisfarne. (It must be understood that in the Middle Ages the word "Scot" signified a Gael, whether from Ireland or Scotland.) Some flavour of the early Irish nature poetry composed by the scholar-hermits is communicated in Frank O'Connor's translation of *Pangur Ban*, an Irish poem sometimes attributed to Sedulius Scottus (c. 810–77).

> Each of us pursues his trade,
> I and Pangur my comrade,
> his whole fancy on the hunt,
> and mine for learning ardent.
>
> More than fame I love to be
> among my books and study,
> Pangur does not grudge me it
> content with his own merit.
>
> When—a heavenly time!—we are
> in our small room together
> each of us has his own sport
> and asks no greater comfort.
>
> While he sets his round sharp eye
> on the wall of my study

I turn mine, though lost its edge,
on the great wall of knowledge.

Now a mouse drops in his net
after some mighty onset
while into my bag I cram
some difficult darksome problem.

When a mouse comes to the kill
Pangur exults, a marvel!
I have when some secret's won
my hour of exultation.

Though we work for days and years
neither the other hinders;
each is competent and hence
enjoys his skill in silence.

Master of the death of mice,
he keeps in daily practice,
I too, making dark things clear,
am of my trade a master.

(trans. O'Connor, *Kings, Lords and
Commons*, pp. 14–15)

Such wit and delicate delight in nature make a striking contrast
with the more sombre Old English poetry. Another instructive
contrast can be made between the gravity of *Beowulf* and the
wildness of Irish heroic prose saga. For example, the Ulster hero
Cu Chulainn comes upon the charioteer of one of his enemies:

"What are you doing here?" said Cu Chulainn. "Cutting a
chariot shaft," said the charioteer; "we have broken our char-
iots in hunting that wild doe Cu Chulainn. Help me," said
the charioteer, "but consider whether you will collect the
poles or trim them." "I shall trim them, indeed," said Cu
Chulainn. Then he trimmed the holly poles between his
fingers as the other watched, so that he stripped them
smooth of bark and knots. "This cannot be your proper

13

work that I gave you," said the charioteer; he was terrified. "Who are you?" said Cu Chulainn. "I am the charioteer of Orlamh son of Ailill and Medhbh." "And you?" said the charioteer. "Cu Chulainn is my name," said he. "Woe is me, then!" said the charioteer. "Do not be afraid," said Cu Chulainn; "where is your master?" "He is on the mound over there," said the charioteer. "Come along with me then," said Cu Chulainn, "for I never kill charioteers."

(Jackson, *A Celtic Miscellany*, p. 34)

Though there is boasting in Old English heroic poetry, its characteristic wit takes the form of an understatement that is mild rather than marvellous.

The passage from the *Cattle Raid of Cooley* translated by Jackson above is from a version dated by him to the ninth century, although the background to these stories is older than the coming of Christianity to Ireland in the fifth century—perhaps as old as the very beginning of the Christian era. Nothing in Old English poetry is so definitely pre-Christian in tradition, not even *Widsith* or *Deor*, and certainly not *Beowulf*, though it is set in fifth-century Scandinavia. The date of the literary composition of *Beowulf* is not agreed, but scholars today place it a century or two later than Cædmon's Old English poetic versions of Old Testament narratives. And the bulk—if not the best—of Old English verse is evangelistically Christian, much of it inspired by Latin originals.

V • CONTEXTS

The investigation of the Latin Christian culture from which so much Old English verse sprung has made considerable advances in recent years, and an increasingly Christian interpretation is being suggested for poems which when they were first recovered in the nineteenth century were supposed to be primitively innocent of clerical colouring. Thus, for example, *The Ruin*, a poem in the Exeter Book conjecturally dated to the eighth or ninth centuries, describes the ruins of a Roman city with hot baths, almost certainly Bath. The poem opens:

Well-wrought this wall: Weirds broke it.
The stronghold burst ...

Snapped rooftrees, towers fallen,
The work of the Giants, the stonesmiths,
Mouldereth.
                    Rime scoureth gatetowers
                    Rime on mortar.

Shattered the showershields, roofs ruined,
Age under-ate them.
                    And the wielders and wrights?

Earthgrip holds them — gone, long gone,
Fast in gravesgrasp while fifty fathers
And sons have passed.
                    (Alexander, *The Earliest English Poems*, p. 2)

The archaeology of the period of the Anglo-Saxon invasion, based on the grave-goods found in pagan cemeteries, shows that these cemeteries are related not to Romano-British cemeteries or roads, but to the river-valleys the invaders penetrated. Although the Saxons came to Britain for its land, their exploitation of it was not primarily based on Romano-British villas or estates. Contrasting this discontinuity with the situation in Visigothic Roman Gaul, Peter Brown remarks, "while in Britain not a single Roman estate-name survived the Saxon invasion, the villages of the Garonne and the Auvergne bear to this day the names of the families that owned them in the fifth century" (*The World of Late Antiquity*, p. 129). Indeed, Old English contains hardly any words borrowed from Roman Britain.

This avoidance of things Roman is strikingly borne out by the way that Roman buildings in stone, conspicuously massive and secure in the wet, wild and wooded landscape of Britain, are referred to in Old English poetry as "the work of the Giants." The invaders did not build in stone but in wood, and did not live in cities but in villages. An incomprehension of Roman things is suggested also by the Old English poet's thought that the builders

of this city have been in the earth for "a hundred generations" —
although these may be poetic numbers. Given this background, it
seems natural to take *The Ruin* as an awed reaction to this monument of a race expert at massive construction in stone but evidently extinct. But some recent commentators agree in linking it
not with archaeology but with eschatology. The early Church's
belief that the end of the world was imminent found acceptance
in the minds of men in the insecure conditions of the earlier
Middle Ages. The Fall of Rome provoked Augustine of Hippo to
write his *City of God*. A counsellor at the Northumbrian court of
Edwin advised his king to become Christian because Christians
knew what followed after death. More specifically, there is much
in the Fathers of the Church on the end of the world, picturing
ruined cities and moralising on the folly of glory and pride in
wealth and possession. *The Ruin*, according to scholars who refer
its composition to a patristic rather than an actual context, is not
so much about Bath as about Babylon; for Babylon, like other
earthly empires, is to be destroyed—unlike the New Jerusalem
seen by St. John in his vision of the end of the world, known as
the Apocalypse in the mediaeval Vulgate, and Revelations in the
Authorised Version of the Bible. The poet of *The Ruin* may have
known Latin poems on the fall of other proud cities, poems
coloured by this apocalyptic feeling. His tone, however, is one of
regret rather than zeal.

TWO : ENGLAND 449–1066 : A SKETCH

This chapter offers an elementary sketch of the cultural history of the period 449–1066, with particular reference to its literature. The Chronological Table (pages xiv–xviii) supplements the information given here, and should be consulted. Such tables came to the west through the example of Eusebius of Caesarea, the historian of the Council of Nicaea (325). Eusebius' *Ecclesiastical History* offered a model to the doctor of chronology, Bede, in his *Ecclesiastical History of the English People*. It is due to Bede that we reckon years from the nativity of Christ; for although he did not invent the system, it was his reasoning and example, as H.P.R. Finberg says, that led to its rapid adoption throughout Christendom (*The Formation of England*, p. 90).

According to Bede the invasion of Britain began in the Year of Grace 449, when the British king Vortigern invited Germanic mercenaries under Hengest and Horsa to help to protect Britain against the Picts and Irish. In this Vortigern followed imperial practice; indeed, Roman history and archaeology show that there had been Saxon settlement on the east coast — "the Saxon shore" — for two hundred years before Hengest and Horsa. The Roman army had withdrawn from Britannia in 410, the year of the sack of Rome by the Goths. The mercenaries stayed, of course, and summoned their continental friends. The Jutes took Kent and the Isle of Wight, the Saxons the Thames valley and south of it, the Angles the Midlands and North. All over Europe the Germanic peoples were moving into the Roman empire: the conquest of Britain took a century and a half.

The Saxon invasion and settlement, the first phase of this story, was complete by the year 597, the year which saw the death of Columba, the father of the Irish mission, on Iona and, on another island at the opposite corner of Britain, the landing of the Roman missionary, Augustine, on Thanet. The second phase, of consolidation and civilisation, is the period of the conversion of the Anglo-Saxon kingdoms and their eventual unification under the kings of Wessex. The primacy of the kingdoms passed southward in the eighth century from Northumbria to Mercia, and then, after the death of Offa, to Wessex. Offa, who ruled Mercia 757–96, called himself *rex totius Anglorum patriae* (King of the whole fatherland of the English), and treated Charlemagne as an equal. Some of his successors in Wessex during the next two centuries, such as Alfred (871–99) and Athelstan (924–39), were more conspicuously gifted rulers, but after Offa's death Anglo-Saxon England, under the Wessex dynasty, was often seriously threatened by the Vikings.

The *Chronicle* entry for 793 reads:

In this year terrible portents appeared in Northumbria, and miserably afflicted the inhabitants: there were exceptional flashes of lightning, and fiery dragons were seen flying in the air, and soon followed a great famine, and after that in the same year the harrying of the heathen miserably destroyed God's church in Lindisfarne by rapine and slaughter. (Garmonsway, *The Anglo-Saxon Chronicle*, pp. 54–56)

In 855 a Danish host first wintered in England, on the Isle of Sheppey at the mouth of the Thames. From 878 the Danes were confined by Alfred in the northern and eastern third of England, later known as the Danelaw. After 939 they again gave trouble to Wessex, and in the next century the English throne passed to a Dane, Cnut, and, eventually, to a Norman. This third and last phase, 793–1066, the Scandinavian phase, was thus a period of more and less successful maintenance, defence, and development of the English Christian polity established in the seventh and eighth centuries.

I • OLD ENGLISH

The Old English language was scarcely written before 597, when professional clerks were first welcomed by an Anglo-Saxon king, who was persuaded that they should write down his laws. But English had certainly been spoken, and presumably sung, in boats crossing the North Sea for centuries before that. This Old English language survives largely in the form of West Saxon, which became the official and literary language from the 890s until the Norman Conquest in 1066; but texts in the Anglian dialects of Northumbria and Mercia, and in the Kentish dialect, also survive. Old English is the western representative of the Germanic group of languages, a branch of the Indo-European family, of which Latin is also a branch, as are the two kinds of Celtic spoken in Britain. These are British (or Brythonic), spoken now in Wales, formerly in Cornwall, and, in the Anglo-Saxon period, in Strathclyde; and Gaelic (or Goidelic), spoken in Ireland and western Scotland. It is possible that it was in Latin that in 449 the Britons treated with Hengest on Thanet, and likely that King Ethelbert of Kent greeted Augustine on the same island in 597 in the same language — through a Frankish bishop attendant upon Ethelred's Frankish Queen, Bertha. In 603 Augustine, meeting the British bishops, offended them by failing to rise to his feet (he was unwell), and the breach that the Saxon invasion had made between Rome and the ancient British Church was not healed. The preliminaries at this legendary meeting surely took place in Latin. And we know of these incidents primarily through Bede's Latin history. Thus "Anglo-Saxon" history (the awkward epithet is borrowed directly into modern English from Latin) was in reality transacted very often in languages other than Old English. The *Oxford English Dictionary* gives 1610 as the date of the first occurrence of the word "Anglo-Saxon" in English. It was under Elizabeth I that the study of Old English began, out of a nationalist interest in the origins of the English Church. (The chief manuscript of the *Anglo-Saxon Chronicle* belonged to Parker, archbishop of Canterbury under Elizabeth.) A historical patriotism also enshrined the study of the Old English language as the foundation of the study of modern English literature in the late nineteenth century at Oxford.

The word "English" derives from *anglisc*, the speech of the Angles, who settled in Mercia and Northumbria. From the Anglian dialect derive both Middle English and Middle Scots: Scots from the Anglian dialect spoken by the Northumbrian inhabitants of Lothian, English from the Anglian dialect of the south-east Midlands spoken in London in the fourteenth century. The London variety of Middle English used by Chaucer was full of French, the language of the conquerors, whereas the language in which Old English literature is preserved — the West Saxon of Alfred's time and later — is a language purely Germanic. The linguistic situation in England in 600 contrasts with that existing in Gaul. The Angles, Saxons, and Jutes (together with the Frisians and Franks who came over with them) still spoke their own closely related languages, whereas the continental Franks, equally Germanic, had adopted Latin, incorporating into it many Germanic words. All the Anglo-Saxon invaders seem to have taken from the Latin or Celtic languages is a few names—such as the Celtic names of the rivers by which they penetrated the country. The words Avon and Derwent mean "river." Likewise, Chester, Worcester, Doncaster, and Caister were *castra*—Roman forts or towns, the anglicisation varying with the dialect. Illustrating the impact of Rome on Britain, two of the rare Latin contributions to Old English are *weall*, from *vallum*, a wall or rampart, and *stræt*, from *strata*, street.

Offa's penny

II • CONQUEST

The invaders came piecemeal, in small bands, in small boats, under individual leaders. They spread inland, overcoming British resistance and settling the valleys. From individual small settlements a mosaic of small tribal kingdoms emerged, of which there were far more than the seven commemorated in the name given to the period in the seventh and eighth centuries, the Heptarchy. The chief kingdoms at the end of this process were Northumbria, Mercia, Wessex and, for a period, Kent and East Anglia. But life remained very local. Many place-names ending in -*ing* mark settlements of the followers or kindred of one man. Sir Frank Stenton remarks that "fifty years before the Norman Conquest the *Hæstingas* [the people of Hastings] and the South Saxons [the people of Sussex] were regarded as two separate folks" (*Anglo-Saxon England*, p. 18). *The Anglo-Saxon Chronicle* account of the invasion and settlement is a series of separate tribal histories and legends; the unification of England was at first ecclesiastical. The title of Bede's history suggests that the Saxons could be considered as part of the people of the Angles. Overlordship of the Angles was claimed by Offa of Mercia in the eighth century, and exercised by the descendants of Alfred in the tenth.

The name of England derives from *Engla-land*, the land of the Angles, a term which appears toward the end of our period. Before the ascendancy of Wessex over the rest of Engla-land in the tenth century, there is occasional mention of *Angelcynn*, the kindred or people of the Angles. But an English national consciousness, like the widespread use of written English, is something which began to crystallise only with Alfred's resistance to the Danes. Unusually powerful kings whose overlordship was recognised for the period of their lifetimes were in the early period known as *Bretwalda*, ruler of Britain; but the Bretwaldaship resided in these individuals rather than in dynasties, tribes or institutions.

One of the most powerful war-leaders among the early kings was Aethelfrith of Bernicia, the more northerly of the two Northumbrian kingdoms. He married the daughter of Aelle, king of the more southerly Deira, and united Northumbria. Aethelfrith was almost certainly the leader of the Angles at the battle of

Catterick, when the British "Gododdin" were defeated, as we have seen from Aneirin's poem. In 603 he defeated the Irish, or "Scots," advancing from Argyll, and ten years later he routed the Britons at Chester, having first slaughtered a large company of British monks who had come to pray for victory. The battle of Chester, with the West Saxon victory of Bedcan ford in 571, marks the confining of independent British strength to Wales, and the virtual completion of the conquest of what is now England. Around the year 500, with the battle of Mons Badonicus, the Britons had made a successful resistance, later associated with the name of Arthur. But one hundred years later the ascendancy of the invaders had become irreversible.

III • CONVERSION

It was at this stage, when pagan English had triumphed over Christian Britons, that the Roman mission arrived in Thanet. How it was that Gregory resolved to send a mission is told in a traditional story recounted by Bede. Twenty years earlier, the future pope had seen some boys put up for sale in the Roman market, slave boys with white bodies, fair faces, and beautiful hair. On learning that they came from Britain, he asked whether those islanders were Christians or still ignorant heathens. On hearing that they were pagans, he lamented that the Author of Darkness should possess men so bright of face. He asked the name of their people, and on being told that they were Angles, said that it was right, for they had angelic faces and should jointly share in the inheritance of the angels in heaven.

> "And what is the name of the province from which they have been brought?" "Deira," was the reply. "Good. They shall indeed be snatched from wrath — De ira — and called to the mercy of Christ. And what is the name of their king?" "Aelle," he was told. "Then," said Gregory, playing on the name, "it is right that their land should echo with the praise of God our Creator in the word Alleluia." (Bede, trans. Stevens, p. 64)

Aethelfrith married Aelle's daughter, and Edwin was Aelle's son, so Gregory's triple conversion of English names was to come true. If the Pope could pun thus, it might be thought that the dark ages had indeed arrived. Although the story may be presumed to have an English origin, Stenton sees no reason to doubt its truth. St. Peter's successors knew the biblical precedents for changing the meaning of names.

The Roman mission was, notably, the very first that the papacy had sent to a pagan people. Thanks to Bede we have some of the letters of instruction that Gregory sent to Augustine and we know the progress of the conversion much better than we can know that of the invasion. It was remarkably successful: by 680 all the Anglo-Saxon kingdoms were ruled by Christian kings, the golden age of Northumbria had begun, and English missionaries were converting the southern Germans. Heathen religion must have been well rooted in England, but it seems to have put up only a sporadic resistance; we know of no martyrs on either side. Augustine was made welcome by Ethelred of Kent, partly because the queen, a Frank, was a Christian, and the court soon converted. Though Ethelred's son lapsed into heathenism, he eventually reconverted.

This Kentish pattern was repeated with interesting variations in the case of Rædwald, king of the East Angles, the next *Bretwalda* after Ethelbert. Rædwald was baptised in Kent but, says Bede,

> on his return home his wife and certain perverse advisers persuaded him to apostatise from the true Faith. So his last state was worse than the first: for, like the ancient Samaritans, he tried to serve both Christ and the ancient gods, and he had in the same temple an altar for the holy Sacrifice of Christ side by side with an altar on which victims were offered to devils. (Bede, II, 15, trans. Sherley-Price, p. 133)

Most of Rædwald's sons were, however, Christians.

Rædwald had at his court the exiled Edwin, son of Aelle and rightful king of Deira, whom Aethelfrith had excluded. Rædwald was persuaded by his wife to support his guest Edwin against Aethelfrith, who fell in battle against them in 616. Edwin succeeded to the kingdom of Northumbria, and, as we have seen, was converted in 627 by Paulinus of York. Again, his wife, the daughter of Ethelbert of Kent and Bertha of Paris, was already a Christian. After a glorious reign, Edwin was killed in battle by Cadwalla, king of Gwynedd, in alliance with the pagan Penda of Mercia. In 641 Penda killed King Oswald of Northumbria, but in 654 was himself killed by Oswy of Bernicia. Penda was the last pagan war lord. He had no objection to his sons becoming Christians. This violently unstable period of political and religious history has been thus rapidly summarised to give the temper of the times, times so warlike that clerics often retired from the fray. But religion mattered more to the Christian kings than to their pagan opponents.

There is an aspect to the conversion which is often forgotten, even by those English who like to regard King Arthur as an honorary Englishman, namely that Britain was Christian before the Anglo-Saxon invasion, and that no "conversion" was required in Wales. Tertullian states that the Gospel was preached in parts of the island which the arms of Rome had not yet (in about 200) penetrated. The Pater Noster inscription found at Corinium (Cirencester) is of the same date. There were British Christian martyrs, like St. Alban, before Constantine's recognition of Christianity in 313, and three British bishops attended the Council of Arles in 314. Archaeology reveals the extent of Romano-British Christianity: a recent excavation at Dorchester shows a fourth-century Christian graveyard with four thousand graves. The British heretic Pelagius, in Rome in 410, fled to North Africa before the advancing Goths; his views on free will seemed to deny the priority of Grace and were so influential throughout the Christian world that they provoked Augustine of Hippo into a major refutation. Pelagius also collected the comment from St. Jerome that he was a corpulent dog weighed down with Scottish porridge. St. Germanus of Auxerre later made two visits to Britain to combat Pelagianism. Ireland itself was introduced to Christianity by a Briton, St. Patrick. However, it seems clear that the Britons made no effort to convert their conquerors. In consequence the heathen Anglo-Saxons lay as a land barrier between Rome and the Welsh and the Irish Churches, behind which these two different Churches, though pious, learned, Catholic, and orthodox, each grew insular and out of step with the universal Church. The result of this British failure to convert the Saxon was that when the Roman mission succeeded, the Scottish party in the English Church had at the Synod of Whitby to accept the Roman computation of Easter, imposed upon them by the superior scholarship and authority of the recently converted Saxons. Ireland and Wales followed, and Iona eventually came into line.

It has been shown that we know little of the pagan religion of the Anglo-Saxons. The figure of Rædwald, who maintained both a pagan and a Christian altar, is representative of the transition for Bede, and so for us. Rædwald has been raised to even greater representative significance by his association with the famous ship burial found in 1939 at Sutton Hoo, Suffolk, with its royal treasure, now exhibited in the British Museum. The Museum Handbook written by Rupert Bruce-Mitford identifies the king for whom this burial was made as Rædwald. It is a pagan burial and yet it contains Christian symbols, notably a pair of baptismal spoons marked SAULOS and PAULOS in Greek, and a set of bowls adorned with crosses.

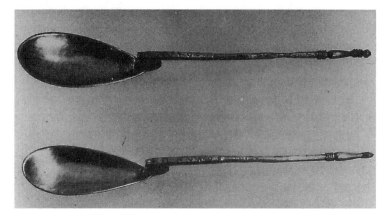

Sutton Hoo spoons

*Sutton Hoo
silver bowls*

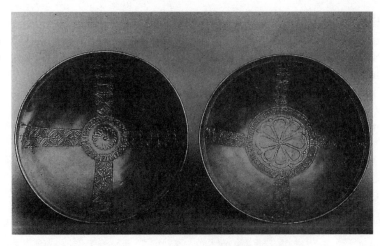

IV • SUTTON HOO AND WARRIOR SOCIETY

The Sutton Hoo ship burial, whether Rædwald's or not, is of supreme interest as the prime exhibit of the material culture of the pagan period and of the Germanic heroic age as described in *Beowulf*. *Beowulf* begins with the burial of Scyld, the founder of the royal house of the Danes, in a ship:

> At the hour shaped for him Scyld departed,
> The hero crossed into the keeping of his Lord.
> They carried him out to the edge of the sea,
> His sworn arms-fellows, as he had himself desired them
> While he wielded his words, Warden of the Scyldings,
> Beloved folk-founder; long had he ruled.
>
> A boat with a ringed neck rode in the haven,
> Icy, out-eager, the aetheling's vessel,
> And there they laid out their lord and master,
> Dealer of wound gold, in the waist of the ship,
> In majesty by the mast. A mound of treasures
> From far countries was fetched aboard her,
> And it is said that no boat was ever more bravely fitted out

Sutton Hoo shoulder clasp

With the weapons of a warrior, war accoutrement,
Swords and body-armour; on his breast were set
Treasures and trappings to travel with him
On his far faring into the flood's sway.
This hoard was not less great than the gifts he had had
From those who at the outset had adventured him
Over seas, alone, a small child.

High over head they hoisted and fixed
A gold signum; gave him to the flood,
Let the seas take him, with sour hearts
And mourning mood. Men under heaven's
Shifting skies, though skilled in counsel,
Cannot say surely who unshipped that cargo.

(26–52)

Similar ceremonies must have occurred at the burial of funeral ships on shore such as have been found in Sweden, and now in Britain. In a large barrow at Sutton Hoo, about 600 yards from the waters of the Deben estuary near Woodbridge in Suffolk, a burial chamber was discovered, amidst a buried ship 30 metres long. The chamber contained what Rupert Bruce-Mitford calls "the richest treasure ever dug from British soil, and the most important archaeological document yet found in Europe for the era of the migration of the Germanic peoples" (*The Sutton Hoo Ship Burial*, p. 21). Where the body would have lain are a standard and a sceptre; shield, sword, helmet and armour; silver and bronze bowls for eating and drinking, a lyre, and drinking horns. The conspicuous personal honorifics, laid along the keel-line, are wholly or partly of gold: the great buckle, the shoulder-clasps (see p. 27), the purse-lid and the forty Merovingian coins dating from before 625. There is much else in the hoard, but the burial is clearly princely or royal, by the symbolism of the sceptre and the standard and by the spectacular union in its parts of wealth in the materials, artistry in their manufacture and variety in their provenance: Byzantine, Coptic, Swedish, Frankish and Celtic as well as Anglian. Apart from the artistic quality of the items of local manufacture (of an awesome refinement previously quite unsuspected by the art historians of this period), Sutton Hoo shows the truth-

Sutton Hoo sceptre

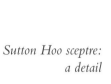

Sutton Hoo sceptre:
a detail

fulness of the descriptions of heroic life in *Beowulf,* and equally their applicability to conditions in an obscure corner of seventh-century England.

The material culture of the Wuffing dynasty of the East Angles revealed at Sutton Hoo is a very rich one, and symbolically rich also, telling of the role of the lord in that society. The lord's authority is declared in the sceptre (see p. 29) and the standard, which was perhaps like the *vexillum* described by Bede as carried before King Edwin. This authority was the result of strength in war: the principal personal belongings which are to travel with the buried lord are warlike; the jewels are part of his armour; and the lyre, the drinking horns, and the coins testify to an heroic glory based on war. The feasting vessels tell of the lord's liberality to his companions, but that too is based on success in war. And virtually throughout the treasure, not only in its armour, the majority of the images are of ferocious animals: hart, dragon, boar, and bird of prey. Exceptions to this are the swivelling bronze fish which "swam" in the Celtic hanging-bowl; the classical female head in the silver bowl; and the baptismal spoons (see p. 25). The ship burial itself suggests the place of the sea in the minds of the East Angles after a century of settlement.

Beowulf orders his own burial, together with the gold he has won from the dragon's hoard, as follows:

> "Bid men of battle build me a tomb
> Fair after fire, on the foreland by the sea
> That shall stand as a reminder of me to my people,
> Towering high above Hronesness
> So that ocean travellers shall afterwards name it
> Beowulf's barrow, bending in the distance
> Their masted ships through the mists upon the sea."
>
> (2802–8)

Military power mattered vitally throughout the Anglo-Saxon period and supremely in the phase of invasion and settlement when the heroic values of warrior society had no challenge from Christianity. The laws of King Ine and the agriculture of the early settlers show that the Angles had interests other than war, but Sutton Hoo and *Beowulf* show heroic ideals as central. The early poetry—*Widsith, Deor, Waldere,* and *Finnsburh*—is that of an heroic society with the values of courage, strength, and honour described by Tacitus in *Germania*. The drinking horns found at Sutton Hoo, six inches across at the mouth, are made from the horns of the aurochs, hunted by the Germans in Julius Caesar's day. As he said in his *Gallic War,* Book VI, "The Germans collect them eagerly, encase their edges in silver, and use them as beakers at their most magnificent banquets" (see Bruce-Mitford, p. 55). In its essential symbolism, Sutton Hoo speaks directly of an heroic and pagan past which seems archaic but which was to remain powerful despite the changes inaugurated by Gregory the Great.

V • CONVERSION AND ACCOMMODATION

The name of Saul of Tarsus, together with his Christian name, is cut in Greek letters on the baptismal spoons at Sutton Hoo. The hoard also contains a silver plate known as the Anastasius dish because its control stamps show that it was assayed at Constantinople in the reign of Anastasius I (491–518). These reminders of continuities of empire and of trade in the Age of Migration are salutary, yet the reincorporation of the island's settlers into Christian and Latin Europe brought immense changes. The "more certain knowledge ... of what went before this life or of what follows" promised by the "new teaching" of Paulinus transformed the perspectives of the heroic world. Rædwald's Christian altar would have had sealed into it the relics of a saint or martyr, one who sat at the feast in the kingdom of heaven. The honour, glory, and security represented by the gold in the Sutton Hoo burial chamber was of a kind specifically denied by the gospel. Apostles such as Aidan and Cuthbert, bishops such as Theodore and Wilfrid, and abbots such as Benedict Biscop had immense and lasting effects on their society, not only by their personal example and teaching but through the institutions they introduced, both in the episcopal hierarchy itself and in the monastery, where the Catholic liturgy, the religious rule of life, the library, and the *scriptorium* created a striking microcosm of the new metaphysical order. Only a reading of Bede can show this side of seventh-century England.

One aspect of the interaction of the old heroic world and the new Christian teaching is a consequence of the conversion of kings first and people afterward — namely, an accommodation of all points of both systems that were not absolutely incompatible. The Mercian prince St. Guthlac might give up a heroic campaigning life and become a hermit, and there were many noblemen and women who retired, like him, from the world. But Christianity was not only an established but also a conquering religion. Roman emperors of the fourth century were successful soldiers of barbarian stock. The Emperor Constantine, converted in 312, told Eusebius of Caesarea that on campaign he had seen the Cross against the midday sun inscribed with the words "In this sign thou shalt conquer." His soldiers used the Chi-Rho monogram of Christ's name on their standards. This militant aspect is not evident in the peaceful advance of Augustine and his monks on Thanet in 597 "carrying a silver cross as their standard and the likeness of our Lord and Saviour painted on a board." Nor is earthly victory the message of the Ruthwell Cross (see p. 33), erected in Bede's time in Dumfriesshire, with lines from *The Dream of the Rood* carved upon it in runic letters. Crosses were used for preaching before Churches were built. But the Cross was the sign by which King Oswald triumphed over the Briton Cadwalla at the battle of Heavenfield in 634, as told in the second chapter of Bede's third book:

> When King Oswald was about to give battle to the heathen, he set up the sign of the holy cross and, kneeling down, asked God that He would grant his heavenly aid to those who trusted in Him in their dire need. The place is pointed out to this day and held in great veneration. It is told that, when the cross had been hurriedly made and a hole dug to receive it, the devout king with ardent faith took the cross and placed it in position, holding it upright with his own hands until the soldiers had thrown in the earth and it stood firm. This done he summoned his army with a loud shout, crying, "Let us all kneel together, and ask the true and living God Almighty of His mercy to protect us from the arrogant savagery of our enemies, since He knows that we fight in a just cause to save our nation." The whole army did as he

The Ruthwell Cross

ordered and, advancing against the enemy at the first light of dawn, won the victory that their faith deserved. At this spot where the king prayed, innumerable miracles of healing are known to have been performed, which serve as a reminder and a proof of the King's faith. Even to this day many folk take splinters of wood from this holy cross, which they put into water, and when any sick men or beasts drink of it or are sprinkled with it, they are at once restored to health.

(Bede, III, 2, trans. Sherley-Price, pp. 144–45)

Conversion narratives often include miracle-combats, very similar to those between Elijah and the priests of Baal in the Book of Kings, by which Christ's Cross and priests are proved stronger than the Devil's idols and worshippers. By a natural progression, worldly success is seen, as with the kings of Israel, to follow upon faith, and worldly failure is the result of apostasy. Martyrs such as King Edmund, killed by invading Danes in 870, or St. Boniface, hacked to pieces by Frisians in 755, are exceptional in Old English history. Bede writes warmly of the reign of King Edwin of Northumbria, whose conversion was followed by that of his people: Paulinus baptised in the River Glen continuously for 36 days. In the peaceful days of Edwin, according to Bede, a woman could carry her new-born baby across the island from sea to sea with no fear of harm. Where there were springs by the side of the roads Edwin had posts put up with brass bowls hanging from them so that travellers could drink. Everywhere that Edwin went, even on foot, the royal standard was carried in front of him. Although the Christian King Edwin was inexplicably killed by the Christian Cadwalla and the pagan Penda (both Britons), Bede regards the blessings of his reign as the reward of faith. This natural perspective for a Christian historian suggests that if paganism and Christianity are incompatible, heroism and Christendom are not.

The friendship between Edwin and Paulinus was repeated when Christianity returned to Northumbria after the victory at Heavenfield. Oswald had been in exile among the Scots, and when he gained the throne he asked the Scots for a bishop. Aidan came from Iona to Lindisfarne, and close relations between kings and monks resumed.

VI • BEDE'S NORTHUMBRIA

Bede's *Ecclesiastical History* is the best-known monument, literary and otherwise, of the golden age of Northumbria, but the illuminated gospel-books of his day provide more intense and overwhelming evidence of their remarkable new civilisation, so antithetical to that of Sutton Hoo yet drawing on the same human stock and some of the same artistic traditions. Aidan brought to Lindisfarne the Irish tradition of decorative illumination practised in Iona, and this gradually fused with Roman traditions of human representation in the set of Anglo-Saxon gospel-books from the late seventh century, of which the best known are the Book of Durrow, the Codex Amiatinus, the Lindisfarne Gospels, and the Echternach Gospels. The Codex Amiatinus directly imitates manuscripts brought from Rome by Benedict Biscop for his new monastery of Monkwearmouth. In the Lindisfarne Gospels, written by Eadfrith, bishop of Lindisfarne 698–721, these traditions combine most fruitfully. The "carpet" page (see p. 38) shows Celtic interlace, while the image of St. John (see p. 39) gives us a human figure in the Roman tradition; both are, however, recognisably Northumbrian.

Augustine was sent by Gregory from the monastery of St. Andrew the Apostle on the Coelian Hill in Rome from which Gregory himself had been called to the chair of Peter. The personal apostolic tradition from St. Peter and St. Paul, martyred in Rome, was vividly present in the minds of the missionaries to England. Augustine's monks "brought with them everything necessary for the worship and service of the Church, including sacred vessels, altar coverings, church ornaments, vestments for priests and clergy, relics of the holy Apostles and martyrs and many books." The liturgy of the universal Church must have announced itself as a thing of power even to unbelieving Anglo-Saxons. But of the physical objects brought by the missionaries (apart from the Cross and the icon of Christ which they carried before them), the last two in Bede's list must have contributed most to their authority: relics of the apostles, and many books. Books were regarded with awe, and certain gospel-books had in the dark ages a power which latter ages found in images and relics. St. Columba's psalter, the *Cathach* (Battler), was enough when paraded in procession to put armies to flight. And the relatively sceptical Bede, who had many books and was not for the Irish in all things, says in his first chapter: "I have seen that folk suffering from snake-bite have drunk water in which scrapings from the leaves of books from Ireland had been steeped, and that this remedy checked the spreading poison and reduced the swelling."

The language of the gospels was reinforced in educated missionaries by a training in classical rhetoric, and in such men as Theodore of Canterbury and Wilfrid by a formidable expertise in theology and in ecclesiastical administration. Quite apart from the apostolic simplicity of the monks, they carried letters such as the one Pope Boniface wrote to King Edwin of Northumbria.

> To the illustrious Edwin, King of the English, Boniface, Bishop, servant of the servants of God.
>
> The words of man can never express the power of the supreme Divinity, abiding in His own greatness, invisible, inscrutable, eternal, such that no human intelligence can understand or define how great it is. Nevertheless, God's humanity having opened the doors of man's heart to admit Him, mercifully infuses into their minds by secret inspiration some knowledge of Himself. Accordingly, we have undertaken to extend our priestly responsibility to disclose to you the fullness of the Christian Faith, in order that we may impart to your senses also the Gospel of Christ, which our Saviour commanded to be preached to all nations, and may offer you the medicine of salvation. (Bede, II, 10, trans. Sherley-Price, p. 120)

The letter goes on to recommend Edwin to renounce idols and embrace the salvation of the Cross from the king of kings. This is the language of authority and was perhaps recognised as such by a king who had his standard carried before him wherever he went. But even after more than thirteen centuries, in an age less confident of faith, it also reads as the language of an august civilisation — philosophical, measured, eloquent, and lucid.

Northumbria owed the early richness of its culture to the mingling of this Mediterranean Christian civilisation, confident in its

The Lindisfarne Gospels: St. Matthew

The Lindisfarne Gospels: a Carpet Page

The Lindisfarne Gospels: St. John

absorbed classicism, with the Celtic Christianity of Aidan, deriving from Iona; there may also have been a Celtic culture in the area previously. But if there was a Celtic-Roman blend in Northumbria, there was also a settling of differences between continental and insular traditions at the Synod of Whitby in 663. This celebrated row, the significance of which has too often been distorted by post-Reformation and post-imperial perspectives, resulted in victory for the Roman party, led by Wilfrid. At issue was the method of computing the date of Easter: Bede relates that when King Oswy had finished Lent and was celebrating Easter, Queen Eanfled was still fasting and keeping Palm Sunday. The king followed the Scots custom kept at Lindisfarne, the queen the Roman use followed in her native Kent. (To this day, the eastern Orthodox Easter is held a week later than the Easter of the Catholic Church and its western offshoots.) The king was persuaded by the forceful speech of Wilfrid (repeated verbatim by Bede) and especially by the winning argument that, whatever St. Columba may have done, the usage of the universal church had been first established by St. Peter, the keeper of the keys of heaven. The Celtic party withdrew to Iona. However, the ascetic saintliness of the followers of Columba illustrates many pages of Bede, and efforts to apportion credit for the evangelisation (or art) of Northumbria on nationalistic or even sectarian grounds are worse than pointless. It is clear that the different ecclesiastical organisation of the two traditions (Irish abbots were senior to their bishops) was due to the different social needs of an Ireland without urban centres and a centralised empire organised in dioceses.

Easter was properly to be celebrated on the first Sunday following the first full moon after the spring equinox — ideally a day of uninterrupted light. This was agreed at the abbey of Streonaeshalch (Whitby), a British name which means the Bay of the Beacon. The abbess of this double monastery was Hilda, a member of the royal family of Northumbria, who had been converted by the Italian Paulinus but became a nun when Aidan was bishop of Lindisfarne. She was a supporter of the Celtic Easter; yet Wilfrid, the champion of the Roman usage, began as a monk in her monastery. A lay brother at the monastery called by the British name of Cædmon became the first Christian poet in Old English.

Bede's account of Cædmon, mentioned in chapter 1, is given and discussed later, but the above circumstances briefly illustrate how inextricable "Celtic" and "Roman" were in Northumbria.

VII • THEODORE AND A LEARNED CHURCH

The golden age was not confined to the north. The key figure was Theodore of Tarsus, chosen by Pope Vitalian to fill the see of Canterbury in 664 when he was 66 years old. Assisted by Abbot Hadrian, an African scholar, this venerable Greek sailed from Rome to Massilia (modern Marseilles), then went via Arles to Agilbert, bishop of Paris (who had been present at the Synod of Whitby). Bede writes that:

> Theodore arrived in his see on Sunday May 27th in the second year after his consecration, and held it for twenty-one years, three months, and twenty-six days. Soon after his arrival, he visited every part of the island occupied by the English peoples, and received a ready welcome and hearing everywhere. He was accompanied and assisted throughout his journey by Hadrian, and he taught the Christian way of life and the canonical method of keeping Easter. Theodore was the first archbishop whom the entire Church of the English obeyed, and since, as I have observed, both he and Hadrian were men of learning both in sacred and in secular literature, they attracted a large number of students into whose minds they poured the waters of wholesome knowledge day by day. In addition to instructing them in the holy Scriptures, they also taught their pupils poetry, astronomy, and the calculation of the church calendar. In proof of this, some of their students still alive today are as proficient in Latin and Greek as in their native tongue. Never had there been such happy times as these since the English settled in Britain; for the Christian kings were so strong that they daunted all the barbarous tribes. The people eagerly sought the new-found joys of the kingdom of heaven, and all who wished for instruction in the reading of the Scriptures found teachers ready at hand.

The knowledge of sacred music, hitherto limited to Kent, now began to spread to all the churches of the English. With the exception of the deacon James, already mentioned, the first singing-master in the Northumbrian churches was Eddi, known as Stephen, who was invited from Kent by the most reverend Wilfrid, the first bishop of English blood to teach the churches of the English the Catholic way of life. (Bede, IV, 2, trans. Sherley-Price, p. 205)

While Theodore was thus putting the Church in order in the seven English kingdoms, scholars in Wessex were studying

the fourfold revelation of the Gospel story, set forth in the mystic commentaries of the Catholic Fathers and spiritually revealed to their very marrow, and digested according to the fourfold rule of ecclesiastical tradition, that is, the historical, the allegorical, the tropological, the analogical, skilfully investigated; now the primitive tales of historians, and the successions of chroniclers, who, with tenacious memories, have handed down in writing the fortuitous permutations of the days of old, rightly searched into; now the rules of grammarians and the drillings of orthographers, balanced in pitch and rhythm, put together in poetic feet, with colons and commas, that is, divided into penthemimerin and heptemimerin, and again distinguished, by careful scrutiny, into one hundred different species of metre. (Williams, p. 181)

The man who could write in this style was St. Aldhelm (*c.* 639–709), a relative of King Ine, first abbot of Malmesbury and bishop of Sherborne. He was, says Bede, "A man most learned in all respects, for he had a brilliant style, and was remarkable for both sacred and liberal erudition."

Aldhelm's erudition was not gleaned, as was long believed, from the Irish hermit Maeldhub after whom Malmesbury was called, but from study with Abbot Hadrian at Canterbury. As Margaret Williams writes (p. 182), "To read Aldhelm is to be back in a time when the potent name of Virgil still acted like an incantation on a mind to which Latin was not a fossilised but an active speech, capable of combining with Greek to form a new luxuriance of words." Aldhelm wrote his treatise on Virginity (for the nuns at Barking) twice, once in prose and once in verse. He also wrote verse sermons, and an epistle on Metrics to King Aldfrith of Northumbria which is full of acrostics and riddles. His own collection of riddles is signed with a double acrostic on his name. A modest sample of his ornate style is his reproach to an Englishman who had gone to Ireland:

> The fields of Ireland are rich and green with learners, and with numerous readers, grazing there like flocks, even as the pivots of the poles are brilliant with the starry quivering of the shining constellations. Yet, Britain, placed, if you like, almost at the extreme edge of the western clime, has also its flaming sun and its lucid moon.... (Williams, p. 186)

It has, as he goes on to explain, Theodore and Hadrian. Aldhelm's very Roman Church at Bradford-on-Avon (see below), and his new diocese of Sherborne, were on the western frontier of Anglo-Saxon England.

St. Lawrence, Bradford-on-Avon

More Roman than Bradford-on-Avon was the monastery of Monkwearmouth, founded by Benedict Biscop in 674; and more Roman (and English) than Aldhelm was St. Bede himself, whose lifetime (673–735) defines the golden age. Both men lived in a period of spectacular literacy, indeed bookishness, in the English Church. The example and memory of this literacy were inspiring for subsequent vernacular literature. There is a sense in which it is true to say that the English Church was never again to be quite so interested in the Word, and in words, as it was at the beginning. Bede and Aldhelm also composed verse in English, as did the illiterate Cædmon and doubtless many more. *Beowulf* itself, much the greatest Old English poem, is often thought to have been largely composed in the later eighth century, and much of the rest of Old English verse may have been composed in the same century, though Old English non-legal prose begins only in Alfred's reign. Until then Latin did most jobs adequately.

Clerks used writing not only for the many essential tasks of the Church but also for learned recreation. Among leading clerics of the year 700 it was almost obligatory to have written a few Latin riddles. Some of the Old English riddles in the Exeter Book must go back to this period. The Gospel Book riddle is an example of the genre:

> I am the scalp of myself, skinned by my foeman:
> Robbed of my strength, he steeped and soaked me,
> Dipped me in water, whipped me out again,
> Set me in the sun. I soon lost there
> The hairs I had had.
>
>   The hard edge
> Of a keen-ground knife cuts me now,
> Fingers fold me, and a fowl's pride
> Drives its treasure trail across me,
> Bounds again over the brown rim,
> Sucks the wood-dye, steps again on me,
> Makes his black marks.
>   A man then hides me
> Between stout shield-boards stretched with hide,
> Fits me with gold. There glows on me

The jewelsmith's handiwork held with wires.
Let these royal enrichments and this red dye
And splendid settings spread the glory
Of the Protector of peoples — and not plague the fool.
If the sons of men will make use of me
They shall be the safer and the surer of victory,
The wiser in soul, the sounder in heart,
The happier in mind. They shall have the more friends,
Loving and kinsmanlike, kind and loyal,
Good ones and true, who will gladly increase
Their honour and happiness, and, heaping upon them
Graces and blessings, in the embraces of love
Will clasp them firmly. Find out how I am called,
My celebrated name, who in myself am holy,
Am of such service, and salutary to men.

(*Old English Riddles from the Exeter Book*, p. 28)

The production of a book required the scraping, dressing and cutting of animal skins; the collection and preparation of lamp black for ink, and reeds or goose-quills for pens; hours of concentrated labour by a skilled hand. Books were an extreme instance of the fact that everything had to be done by hand, that is, by modern standards, very slowly. Only monasteries offered the necessary order, peace, time, and motive. And even for monasteries peace could only be guaranteed in a secure kingdom like Edwin's Northumbria and a well-governed church like Theodore's — united two-and-a-half centuries before England became a united state.

The peace of Northumbria did not last beyond the middle of the eighth century, although the tradition of learning continued at Wilfred's school at York and contributed to the continental revival of learning at Charlemagne's court, the Carolingian renaissance. Bede ends his *Ecclesiastical History* by remarking that Ethelbald of Mercia was (in 731) the ruler of all England south of the Humber. Bede's last work is a prophetic letter of remonstrance to Bishop Egbert of York at

The connivance of Church and state which permitted local magnates to turn their establishments into sham monasteries

45

and thus to evade their public liabilities. (Finberg, p. 92)

Monasteries were exempt from the three common dues: man-power for building bridges and defences, and men for the *fyrd* or militia. Ethelbald of Mercia put these exemptions to an end, and in 798 Cenwulf of Wessex succeeded in obtaining the pope's permission to turn Glastonbury, the holiest minster in Wessex and the burial place of her kings, into a "proprietary church" — the private and heritable fief of his son Kenelm. Monasteries were evidently not what they had been, even before the Viking sack of Lindisfarne, and kings were more powerful.

VIII   •   WESSEX

The ascendancy of Offa of Mercia was so great that he persuaded the pope to create a third English archbishopric at Lichfield, the see of Mercia, where he secured his succession by having his son consecrated as king, the first king in England to be anointed. The style of Offa's coinage (p. 20) was followed until after the Norman Conquest. But his most daunting memorial was the 120-mile Dyke against the Welsh which still bears his name. Coincidentally, his ancestor in the twelfth generation, Offa I, who ruled over Angeln (Schleswig-Holstein) in the fifth century, is reputed to have personally fixed the boundary between the continental Angles and their neighbours — or so it says in *Widsith*. This Offa I of Angeln is also introduced into *Beowulf*, which has suggested that one stage of the poem's composition may have been at Offa's court, or that a diplomatic compliment is being paid. Offa's dynastic pride was such that he refused Charlemagne's tender of his son as a husband for one of Offa's daughters unless Charlemagne's daughter should also be given to his son Egfrith, a condition which led to relations being broken off. Offa was the first king of all the Angles.

The power of Mercia did not long survive Offa, however, and it was to Wessex that the ascendancy passed in the ninth century in the person of Egbert, who ruled from 802 to 839. He conquered Cornwall, Kent, and Mercia, and was recognised in Northumbria. In the last years of his reign the Archbishop of

Canterbury entered into a concordat of perpetual friendship with the dynasty of Wessex. In the same years the Isle of Sheppey was raided by Scandinavian pirates.

"Wessex against the Vikings" is the general rubric for the military history of the next century and more. The story of Alfred's resistance told in the *Anglo-Saxon Chronicle* receives separate consideration in chapter 7, as do the educational reforms of Alfred, which involved the institution of Old English prose. Effectively, however, even after Alfred's victories, the Danes remained in possession of East Anglia, the east Midlands, and modern Yorkshire after 877. The Old English language was written in only half of Alfred's England. His son Edward the Elder regained the overlordship of England and all the kings of Britain submitted to him. Edward's son Athelstan called himself king of Britain, a title he justified by the famous victory of 937 commemorated in the poem *Brunanburh*. The power of the house of Wessex, and its support of the church and of education, was maintained by Athelstan's successor Edmund — the fourth great king in succession. He was succeeded by four minors.

IX • THE BENEDICTINE REVIVAL

English monasticism, and indeed clerical celibacy in general, had fallen into disrepair, and the Rule of St. Benedict was reintroduced into a dilapidated Glastonbury only by Abbot Dunstan, a product of Alfred's old school there, in 940. These Benedictines educated the young Edgar, and when Edgar succeeded to the throne as a boy in 957, their influence was profound. Dunstan became Archbishop of Canterbury in 959, and with Oswald bishop of Worcester and Aethelwold bishop of Winchester, policy was dominated for the eighteen-year reign by three followers of the reformed Benedictine tradition of Fleury-sur-Loire. The monastic party was strong again when the boy Ethelred II (known as the Unready) came to the throne in 978. But magnates who disliked the ascendancy of the monks were not disposed to obey Ethelred as they had his formidable predecessors, and the Scandinavian threat revived.

The end of the tenth century, like the end of the ninth, was however a most productive period for literature in the vernacular, and for all the arts to which the church was patron. The Benedictine Revival had begun originally at Cluny in 910, and at Cluny and Fleury-sur-Loire the tradition was one of the most solemn, austere, and yet resplendent celebration of the liturgy and the monastic hours. Service-books were produced, music elaborated, churches and minsters enlarged and rebuilt in stone. The Gregorian chant was refined and perfected; the organ at Winchester had 400 pipes. Aethelwold, like Dunstan, was a skilled craftsman in gold, and the decorative arts flourished. The most conspicuous memorial of all this is the number of splendid illuminated manuscripts of the Winchester school (see pp. 232–33). The manuscripts in which Old English poetry is preserved come from the *scriptoria* of this period, as do the seven different manuscripts of the *Chronicle*, which takes on new life at this time, and perseveres in one local continuation until long after the Conquest. This too is the time of Aelfric, the most graceful and productive of writers in Old English, and the most influential. He wrote two cycles of sermons, widely imitated, and a series of lives of the saints, and translated some books of the Old Testament. From Aelfric's period comes the widest spectrum of Old English prose, including the writing on chronology of Byrhtferth of Ramsey. The Byrhtnorth who fell at the battle of Maldon was a champion of monasteries, which may be why the poem on this battle was composed and/or preserved. Old English verse and Latin prose have, however, little to show after the year 1000. The popular sermon was the medium of Old English literature which had the most active life after the Conquest, although much Old English saga material appears in the Norman chroniclers.

The last name in Old English literature is that of Wulfstan, archbishop of York, whose *Sermo Lupi Ad Anglos* of 1014 denounces the disasters befalling England at the hands of the Danes as the wrath of God, more purposefully than Gildas had bewailed the sorrows of the Britons. Although the administrative system survived well enough for the unhappy Ethelred to extract tribute after tribute to pay the Danegeld, disunity was rife and the Danish succession was at hand. After the reigns of Cnut and his son, Edward the Confessor was welcome, but he was not able to strengthen the political unity or the military system of the country. When Harold heard that William had landed at Hastings, the *Chronicle* records, he

> gathered together a great host, and came to oppose him at the grey apple-tree, and William came upon him unexpectedly before his army was set in order. Nevertheless the king fought against him most resolutely with those men who wished to stand by him, and there was great slaughter on both sides. King Harold was slain, and Leofwine, his brother, and earl Gurth, his brother, and many good men. The French had possession of the place of slaughter, as God granted them because of the nation's sins. (Garmonsway, p. 199)

The Franks Casket

THREE : HEROIC POETRY INCLUDING

BEOWULF

THE *Chronicle* says of the Normans at Hastings that after the battle they "possessed the place of slaughter." This phrase was the traditional way for an Old English poet to indicate the outcome of a battle. The *Chronicle* had also said of the Vikings at Maldon: *hy thone ealdorman thær ofslogon and wælstowe geweald ahtan* (they slew the ealdorman there and had possession of the place of slaughter). In the poem on the battle of Maldon the ealdorman Byrhtnoth calls out to the Vikings over the cold water:

> "Nu eow is gerymed: gath ricene to us
> guman to guthe. God ana wat
> hwa thære wælstowe wealdan mote."
>
> (93–95)

Literally, line for line:

> "Now room has been made for you: come quickly to us,
> Warriors to battle. God alone knows
> Who may possess this place of slaughter."

The phrase *wælstowe wealdan* is typical of the two-stress alliterative combinations common in Old English verse. It occurs incidentally in *Beowulf* as follows:

> tha him gerymed wearth
> thær hie wælstowe wealdan moston.
>
> (2983–84)

> when room had been made for them
> Where they might possess the place of slaughter.

By a recurrent habitual attraction between such phrases, *gerymed* also appears here as in *Maldon*. At *Beowulf* 2051 the phrase is found in its most economical form occupying the first half of the line: *weoldon wælstowe* (they possessed the place of slaughter). One could translate more prosaically: "they controlled the battlefield" or "they held the field." *Stow* means "place" (as in many place-names) and *wæl* means "corpse, the slain," as in Valkyrie "chooser of the slain," one of the twelve war-demons who bore corpses from the battlefield to the Scandinavian military heaven, Valhalla, the "hall of the slain." In the *Chronicle* for 1066 the etymology of *wælstow* may be inert enough for one to translate "battlefield." But in his fine translation Garmonsway, a lexicographer, preserves "place of slaughter": the *Chronicle* has specifically commemorated by name those who were slain. In *The Battle of Maldon* the line following *hwa thære wælstowe wealdan mote* begins *wodon tha wæl-wulfas*: "The slaughterous wolves [that is, the Vikings] advanced." Here the idea of *wæl* is poetically active, and in identifying the Vikings as wolves (who with ravens and eagles are the scavengers of battlefields in Old English poetry) a demonic association may be insinuated. In the lines quoted above from *Maldon*, the phrase *guman to guthe* is also a formula: neither *guma* nor *guth* is found outside poetry, though both are common in Old English verse, which has a traditional vocabulary peculiar to itself. This repertory gives the old poetry an archaic clang peculiar to itself and virtually inimitable in Modern English.

A consideration of the *wælstow* of Hastings thus catches many facets of heroic poetry. This kind of poetry comes first in any history of Old English literature because most other Old English verse grows out of it in vocabulary and form, and also, since the medium is itself conservative, in its view of the world—even when the metaphysics of the later world-view are quite different. Not only is the heroic poetry ancestral to Old English verse in general, it also informs much in Old English prose, as the *wælstow* of Hastings testifies.

A chief reason why heroic poetry retained its ascendancy for so long was that the conditions of life renewed its force: in 1066 "the King fought against him most resolutely with those men who wished to stand by him." Early in *Beowulf* it is said that

> In youth an atheling should so use his virtue,
> Give with a free hand while in his father's house,
> That in old age when enemies gather,
> Established friends may stand by him
> And serve him gladly. It is by glorious action
> That a man comes by honour in any people.
>
> (20–25)

But at the end of the poem only one of the Geats, Wiglaf, comes forward to help the aged Beowulf against the Dragon. Afterwards Wiglaf upbraids the companions who had stood idly by:

A man who would speak the truth may say with justice
That the lord of men who allowed you those treasures,
Who bestowed on you the trappings that you stand there in—
As, the ale-bench, he would often give
To those who sat in hall both helmet and mail-shirt
As a lord to his thanes, and things of the most worth
That he was able to find anywhere in the world—
That he had quite thrown away and wasted cruelly
All that battle-harness when the battle came upon him.
The king of our people had no cause to boast
Of his companions of the guard. Yet God vouchsafed him,
The Master of Victories, that he should avenge himself
When courage was wanted, by his weapon single-handed.
I was little equipped to act as body-guard
For him in the battle, but, above my own strength,
I began all the same to support my kinsman.

Our deadly enemy grew ever the weaker—
When I had struck him with my sword—less strongly welled
The fire from his head. Too few supporters
Flocked to our prince when affliction came.
Now there shall cease for your race the receiving of treasure,
The bestowal of swords, all satisfaction of ownership,
All comfort of home. Your kinsmen every one,
Shall become wanderers without land-rights
As soon as athelings over the world
Shall hear the report of how you fled,
A deed of ill fame. Death is better
For any earl than an existence of disgrace!

(2864–91)

That sets out the obligations of a thane to a lord under the heroic code: Beowulf had given with a free hand but the members of the *heorthwerod*, the hearth-companions, did not wish to stand by him. The speech of Aelfwine in *The Battle of Maldon* after Bryhtnoth has fallen is similar:

Remember the speeches spoken over mead,
Battle-vows on the bench, the boasts we vaunted,
Heroes in hall, against the harsh war-trial!
Now shall be proven the prowess of the man.
I would that you all hear my high descendance:
Know that in Mercia I am of mighty kin,
That my grandfather was the great Ealhelm,
Wise Earl, world-blessed man.
Shall the princes of that people reproach Aelfwine
That he broke from the banded bulwark of the Angles
To seek his own land, with his lord lying
Felled on the field? Fiercest of griefs!
Beside that he was my lord he was allied to me in blood.

(212–24)

This speech is followed by those of Offa, Leofsunu, Dunnere, and Byrhtwold, the last three of whom were not nobles. Leofsunu says:

I swear that from this spot not one foot's space
Of ground shall I give up. I shall go onwards,
In the fight avenge my friend and lord.
My deeds shall give no warrant for words of blame
To steadfast men on Stour, now he is stretched lifeless,
— that I left the battlefield a lordless man,
Turned for home. The irons shall take me,
Point or edge.

(246–53)

Tacitus says in chapter 6 of his *Germania*: "men have often survived battle only to end their shame by hanging themselves." The great historian was describing the customs of the Germani for the benefit of his imperial Roman audience of the end of the first century, somewhat as British imperial servants might admire the warrior tradition among Pathans or Zulus. The hardy and stern virtues of Livy's Roman republic are implicitly recommended to soft citizens of the Empire via these noble barbarians north of the Rhine. In Tacitus' *Agricola* the British resistance of Boudicca gets the same idealistic treatment. Although there is a propaganda element in the account of the Germani, the number of correspondences between the warlike code described there and the code observed in Old English (and other northern) heroic poetry and saga is too great to allow one to dismiss Tacitus as a fictionalist. The continuity of the Germanic system of values is unmistakable. The ideally loyal *comitatus* of *Germania* is the *heorthwerod* of *Beowulf*. There are also many correspondences between the world of *Beowulf* and that of the *Iliad*, as was pointed out by W.P. Ker in *Epic and Romance* (1896), still the best introduction to the medieval narrative literature of north-western Europe in the Middle Ages. Literary historians have elaborated the notion of the heroic age, a phase found in the evolution of many cultures. Described fully in H. M. Chadwick's *The Heroic Age* (1912), it was already part of the accepted lore of Hesiod in the eighth century BC. The lord's conspicuous hospitality in peace was to be repaid by the loyalty of his *geneatas* or *gesithas* in war. Heroic society was last seen in Britain in the Scottish Highlands, and survives in some parts of the world today.

The function of heroic literature, or rather heroic song, was to celebrate and so perpetuate heroic conduct. The heroes themselves tell of their adventures, like Beowulf or Odysseus, and the poets entertain the heroes at the banquet by tales of past deeds; Germanic heroes at the meadbench boast of the past and vow for the future. Honour and glory were potently realised in the giving of rings, mead, and armour to retinue; shame and disgrace led to defeat and exile or enslavement, to which death was indeed preferable. There are complications of the code brought about by conflicting loyalties to lord or kindred or host or guest or friend; but the code was a social institution, an ethical reality enforced by life-or-death sanctions, and not some private dream of chivalric honour. Although aristocratic, in that there is in *Beowulf* no mention of the economy, of food or farming, such as we find in Homer, it is also adhered to by the churl Dunnere at Maldon. As Ker says, there was a considerable identity of practical interest between lord and man; there was no exclusive noble caste such as develops in late medieval French romances. (Anglo-Saxon society was however by no means the village-green yeoman democracy projected by nineteenth-century Whig historians.)

Tacitus says of the Germans that their songs are the only kind of history they possess. A fascinating glimpse of this history at work is provided by Sidonius Apollinaris. He tells how his soul was vexed at the barbarous songs of his long-haired Burgundian neighbours, how he had to suppress his disgust, and praise these Germans lays, though with a wry face (R.W. Chambers, *Widsith*, pp. 2–3). Sidonius had become bishop of Clermont in 471. A provincial Gallo-Roman aristocrat, and so a representative of the *ancien régime*, he was diplomatic enough to lose at backgammon whenever he played against the Visigothic king Theodoric at Toulouse, and, at wild Burgundian banquets, to praise what was sung by his hosts. He describes the Burgundian as a seven-foot high, long-haired eater of onions, who smeared his locks with rancid butter. "What the Burgundian sang" must have included the destruction in 436 of the Burgundians under their prince Gundahari, keeper of the Nibelung treasure, by Attila the Hun. This event was to inspire many tales throughout Europe from the

Caspian to Greenland, for the Germanic peoples adopted each others' histories as their own, even making their enemies the Huns into honorary Germans, rather as the English were later to adopt their legendary enemy King Arthur. The heroes of this period of the Wandering of the Peoples include Eormanric and Theodoric the Ostrogoths, Ongentheow the Swede, Offa the Angle, Ingeld the Heathobard, Finn the Frisian, Hrothgar the Dane, Albion the Lombard, and Guthere, Hagen and Waldere from the Burgundian cycle. All these figure at least once in the Old English heroic corpus: *Deor, Widsith, Beowulf, Finnsburh,* and *Waldere.* These poems name only one man ever supposed to have been in England: the name of the Saxon leader in Kent, Hengest. But though he appears in *Beowulf* and *Finnsburh,* Hengest the Half-Dane or Dane is not mentioned there in an English connection. His opponent, Finn the Frisian or Jute, appears, however, in a Mercian genealogy of the ninth century, as does Offa the Angle. These are the only apparent links with England in what is usually taken to be the earliest English verse. Yet these last west-Germanic names, together with some others in the poems, must have been of a more ancestral interest in England than those of Eormanric, Attila, Guthere, and others of the remoter Germanic past.

It is, nevertheless, striking that the heroic poems celebrate only continental Germans. This does not mean that they must be, in the forms we have them, very early in date, for in the eighth century the Anglo-Saxons considered themselves to be Germans, as the writings of Aldhelm, Bede, and Boniface attest. Dorothy Whitelock says that

> this strong sense of kinship with the Germanic tribes on the Continent led the Anglo-Saxons to attempt their conversion even before the last strongholds of heathenism in England had fallen.
>
> (*The Beginnings of English Society,* p. 12)

The heroic poems were naturally of special interest to those to whom heroic status was accorded and of whom heroic conduct was expected: the rulers of the Anglo-Saxon kingdoms. Whoever was buried at Sutton Hoo would have found the burials of Scyld and Beowulf "worthy to drawen to memorie"—as Chaucer's *gentil* pilgrims say of the *Knight's Tale*. The creator of Offa's Dyke would have been pleased to remember Offa the Angle, who established the boundary of continental Angeln.

> Offa ruled Angel, Alewih the Danes;
> He was of all these men the most courageous,
> Yet he did not outdo Offa in valour:
> Before all men Offa stands,
> Having in boyhood won the broadest of kingdoms;
> No youngster did work worthier of an earl.
> With single sword he struck the boundary
> Against the Myrgings where it marches now,
> Fixed it at Fifeldor. Thenceforward it has stood
> Between Angles and Swaefe where Offa set it.
>
> (*Widsith*, 35–44)

King Alfred himself loved to learn the old Saxon songs by heart. The social function of the heroic songs was exemplary: in poetry as in life, courage and loyalty lead to glory for a king and, often, to success for his warriors. Although this is a crude reduction of the heroic poetry to its central motive, and *Beowulf* itself embodies a much more complex understanding than such a formulation might imply, the Old English heroic poems do celebrate outstanding examples of the conduct that created and preserved barbarian society. It was for the same reason of morale that the Norman *jongleur* Taillefer is said to have sung the *Chanson de Roland* before going into battle at Hastings.

Song had another function, to provide a livelihood for the singer. Widsith is a wandering minstrel (as his name "wide-adventure" implies), and as well as listing all the heroes he has visited on his journeys over some thousands of miles (and over several centuries), he offers several advertisements for his own role:

> This is the testimony of Widsith,
> traveller through
> Kindreds and countries;
> in courts he stood often,
> Knelt for the lovely stone,
> no living man more often.

Unlocks his word-hoard.

(1–4)

And I was with Eormanric all the days
That the Goth King was kind towards me:
Lord over cities and they who lived in them.
Six hundred shillings' worth of sheer gold
Were wound into the ring he reached to my hand.

(88–92)

… when the name was asked of the noblest girl,
Gold-hung queen, gift-dealer,
Beneath the sky's shifting — the most shining lady —
I sang Ealhhild; in every land
I spoke her name, spread her fame.
When we struck up the lay before our lord in war,
Shilling and I, with sheer-rising voices,
The song swelling to the sweet-touched harp,
Many men there of unmelting hearts,
Who well knew, worded their thought,
Said this was the best song sung in their hearing.

(99–109)

The poem ends with a more complete picture of relationship between fame and poetry:

The makar's weird is to be a wanderer:
The poets of mankind go through the many countries,
Speak their needs, say their thanks,
Always they meet with someone, in the south lands
      or the north,
Who understands their art, an open-handed man
Who would not have his fame fail among the guard
Nor rest from an earl's deeds before the end cuts off
Light and life together. Lasting honour shall be his,
A name that shall never die beneath the heavens.

These scenes apart, *Widsith* has historical and geographical value, as a roll-call of the Germanic tribes of the migration period and their most famous chiefs. Despite its fictive framework, it is an encyclopaedic catalogue poem of the same kind as the Catalogue of Ships in the *Iliad*.

The role of the Old English *scop* (poet) is more tellingly dramatised in *Deor*. Deor is, like Widsith, a wanderer, but he has lost his position.

DEOR

Wayland knew the wanderer's fate:
That single-willed earl suffered agonies,
Sorrow and longing the sole companions
Of his ice-cold exile. Anxieties bit
When Nithhad put a knife to his hamstrings,
Laid clever bonds on the better man.

    That went by, this may too.

Beadohild mourned her murdered brothers:
But her own plight pained her more
— Her womb grew great with child.
When she knew that, she could never hold
Steady before her wit what was to happen.

    That went by; this may too.

All have heard of Hild's ravishing:
The Geat's lust was ungovernable,
Their bitter love banished sleep.

    That went by; this may too.

Thirty winters Theodric ruled
The Maering city: and many knew it.

    That went by; this may too.

We all know that Eormanric
Had a wolf's wit. Wide Gothland

Lay in the grasp of that grim king,
And through it many sat, by sorrows environed,
Foreseeing only sorrow; sighed for the downfall
And thorough overthrow of the thrall-maker.

That went by; this may too.

When each gladness has gone, gathering sorrow
May cloud the brain; and in his breast a man
Can not then see how his sorrows shall end.
But he may think how throughout this world
It is the way of God, who is wise, to deal
To the most part of men much favour
And a flourishing fame; to a few the sorrow-share.

Of myself in this regard I shall say this only:
That in the hall of the Heodenings I held long the makarship,
Lived dear to my prince, Deor my name;
Many winters I held this happy place
And my lord was kind. Then came Heorrenda,
Whose lays were skilful; the lord of fighting-men
Settled on him the estate bestowed once on me.

That went by; this may too.

  In its series of compressed allusions to well-known stories, *Deor*
resembles the other heroic poems and the Old Icelandic Poetic
Edda; these allusions to yesterday's headlines make today's footnotes.[1] But in its intensification of the plight of the speaker as a

---

1 Deor seems an invented character, but the examples of wrongs endured
   with which he makes his consolation bear famous Germanic names.
   Wayland (or Weland) was the smith of the gods, the northern Vulcan. He
   was captured by Nithhad and hamstrung. He escaped, nevertheless, having killed Nithhad's two sons and turned their skulls into bowls. He can
   be seen on one side of the Franks Casket (see p.49) presenting such a
   bowl to Nithhad as an example of his art. On the right of this scene is a
   figure who may represent Beadohild, whom Wayland ravished. The
   offspring of this union was Widia, a famous hero; later his parents were
   reconciled. The story behind the third strophe cannot be identified,
   though it seems that the woman's sorrow may, again, turn to something

lordless and landless exile, *Deor* resembles Old English elegies such as *The Wanderer*. Equally characteristic of the elegies is the stoicism to which the refrain aspires, although the use of strophic form with a refrain is unique in Old English verse.

III • VERSIFICATION

Old English verse is remarkably uniform in its versification. The Old English poetic line is a balance of two half-lines, notionally equal in prosody; and the half-lines themselves likewise contain two units, normally with a stressed and an unstressed syllable. This metrical line, though varying in the number of syllables, is notably symmetrical in its ideal form, being evenly divided by a firm medial caesura, like a lot of pre-Chaucerian octosyllabics but unlike the five-foot line which—after Chaucer—succeeded it. This basic stress-pattern is a more profound distinguishing mark than the alliteration which links the half-lines together and gives rise to the name "alliterative measure." The first stressed syllable of the second half-line has to begin with the same sound as one or both of the stressed syllables in the first half-line; the final stress in the line must not alliterate. Thus:

> One or other   of the opening stresses
> Must alliterate   with the leading syllable
> In the second half-line;   sometimes both do,
> In triple front-rhyme;   the fourth does not.

All vowels alliterate with each other, and it is the initial sound of the stressed syllable which is involved (thus "alliterate" alliterates on "l" not "a"). Old English, unlike Modern English, is a synthetic rather than an analytic language, incorporating into the

---

sweeter. Theodoric might be either the Ostrogoth who ruled Merano for only thirty years before being exiled by Eormanric; or the Frank who was exiled to Merano and ruled it unhappily for thirty years. Eormanric (in the fifth strophe) was the king of the Goths who died in 375; in legend he was a tyrant. Finally, Deor himself has been discarded by King Heoden in favour of Heorrenda, a singer and harper with the skill to win the heart of the beauty Hild for his new master.

inflexions and endings of words the information now conveyed by separate articles and prepositions. Old English verse of the classical period of *Beowulf* has no need of "of the," "with the," and "in the" in the above mnemonic, and is thus much more economical of syllables. Nevertheless the number of unstressed syllables in a half-line often exceeds the two allowed for in this simple account. So long as these unstressed syllables have little natural stress, the metre can swallow them without distracting from the salience of the long stressed syllables, which are the root syllables of words such as nouns, adjectives, and verbs. This metre, although an artificial selection from the patterns naturally occurring in Old English, is well suited to the accentual character of the language. When English resurfaced as the chief literary language in the late fourteenth century, it had lost much of its synthetic accidence; the alliterative measure of *Piers Plowman* or *Sir Gawain and the Green Knight* is overburdened with short words and lacks metrical economy and precision, though such looseness allows different possibilities. This relaxation has already begun to show by the time of *The Battle of Maldon* (991).

Old English prose, especially the "performance" prose of the writers of homilies, and of Wulfstan in particular, often exhibits this recurrence of two-stress phrases, though in looser form. It is sometimes maintained that this pattern can be heard both in modern English blank verse and also in public speaking, so engrained is it in the language. Early editors were not sure whether to print some of these homilies as verse or as prose; Old English scribes wrote out verse continuously, as if it were prose. Indeed, since Old English verse (with the exception of *The Rhyming Poem*) is blank, and does not, except in *Deor*, use stanzas, its only distinguishing formal feature is its metre.

IV • POETIC DICTION

The diction, however, of Old English verse is distinctive, and sometimes peculiar to itself. In the glossary to his great edition of *Beowulf*, Klaeber lists hosts of words which are found in poetry only, and a considerable number which occur only in *Beowulf*. These words, often compound words, are what give the heroic poetry its elevated character, as in the first two lines of the poem:

Hwæt, we Gar-Dena in geardagum,
theodcyninga thrym gefrunon.

Literally, "What! we have heard of the glory of the kings of the people of the Spear-Danes in days of yore." The "Spear-Danes" are in *Beowulf* also called "Bright-Danes" and "Ring-Danes" (and "Scyldings," for which there are several epithets, and "Friends of Ing"). *Theodcyning* (king of the people) is a word found only in poetry, though a compound of two common words; *geardagas* is a somewhat poetic word; and *"Hwæt, we … gefrunon"* is an entirely poetic and oral opening.

The vocabulary of Old English heroic poetry is sufficiently specialised for it to be recognised as a true poetic diction—not the refined poetic diction of which Wordsworth complained in Pope and Gray, but the language proper to traditional poetry, like the language of Homer. The Homeric heroes and deities are almost invariably accompanied by their faithful standard epithets: wide-ruling Agamemnon, well-greaved Hector, Odysseus of the great war-cry, white-armed Hera, cloud-gathering Zeus. Qualification by a standard attribute is characteristic of many other features in the Homeric world: rosy-fingered Dawn, Troy of wide streets, the wine-dark sea, swift-running horses. This kind of standard, often compound, poetic epithet is so prominent in Homer that it is known as the Homeric epithet. And the example of Homer laid down what became almost an adjectival policy for most classical poets, and classically educated European poets. Milton is the major exponent in English, with his "green-eyed Neptune," "half-regained Eurydice" and "two-handed engine." It was the too automatic and attenuated echo of this adjectival tradition that irritated Wordsworth in his predecessors among nature poets of the eighteenth century. "The finny tribe," a common periphrasis for fish in eighteenth-century verse, is a clichéd example of the feeble poetic epithet.

The habit of mind and language revealed by the Homeric epithet goes much further in the Homeric poems themselves. Not only are individual men and gods and single natural features presented by means of a typifying attribute—the whole Homeric world is conceived in this generic and almost systematic manner. For example, speeches in Homer are announced and back-announced by standard formulas. This too has long been imitated: "thus spake Zarathustra." The same feature is found in *Beowulf,* where "Thus spoke Beowulf, son of Edgetheow" is a recurrent line. The battles or banquets or assemblies at which such speeches are made in the old heroic poems are standardised in construction, as are such narrative elements as voyages, sacrifices, encounters, even boasts, or ways of dying. Folklorists have identified in traditional literature not only such type-scenes but also tale-types: the structures of the stories themselves have been listed and categorised. If such an approach can be reductive, it can in the right hands be productive.

V   •   FORMULAIC COMPOSITION

Milman Parry, in *The Making of Homeric Verse,* demonstrated that the entire structure of Homer's poetic language is formulaic, and that the thousands of hexameters are composed of standard elements and phrases. Parry defined the formula as "a group of words which is regularly employed under the same metrical conditions to express a given essential idea," and showed that for each idea the number of formulas was only as large as was necessary to fit the different grammatical inflexions of the words composing the formula into the metrical patterns of the hexameter. His elegant demonstration of the economy of Homeric formulaic composition was a radical contribution to the subject.

In so far as Parry's investigation of the Homeric texts was merely more thorough, systematic, and statistical than earlier ones, it was at first resisted, in much the same way as Darwin was resisted, for seeming to reduce Homer to a mechanical manipulator of a ready-made vocabulary. This reaction, based on a false idea of originality, has evaporated. More awkward for the academic regard for Homer's text as a supreme literary achievement was Parry's demonstration that the economy which matched formulaic phrase with grammatical and metrical exigencies in Homer was to be found exactly paralleled in the living tradition of oral composition in Yugoslavia. For the logical corollary of this parallel was that Homer's poems were not merely recited from memory but were in a strict sense orally composed, like the remarkable perfor- mances of early twentieth-century Yugoslav illiterates. In extem- pore oral composition it is a functional necessity that the verbal and metrical components of lines should lie ready to hand in the singer's word-hoard—*cliché*, in its original French sense of "minted." For the making of the monumental Homeric poems the number of these formulas had to be as small as was consistent with the complex and precise requirements of the hexameter. But for the Old English *scop*, the demands of a metre not based on syllable-count were more easily met: for example, the change of a noun-and-adjective combination from the subjective case to the objective case would not, as it would in the Greek dactylic hexa- meter, require it to be rejected from a particular metrical position. It may be as a consequence of this less strict exigency that although formulas are often repeated in the 31,000 lines of Old English verse, there is no economy in their use. Indeed, the abun- dance of parallel and alternative expressions for given essential ideas is one of the most noticeable features of Old English verse, and a notorious problem for the translator. An extreme example is one of the two surviving Old English poems which are known to have been orally composed, *Cædmon's Hymn*. The other is *Bede's Death-Song*. In reply to the angel's command to "sing the Creation," Cædmon sang (this is the earlier, Northumbrian, version):

> Nu scylun hergan hefaenricaes uard,
> metudæs maecti end his modgidanc,
> uerc uuldurfadur, sue he uundra gihuaes,
> eci dryctin, or astelidæ.
> He aerist scop aelda barnum
> heben til hrofe, haleg scepen;
> tha middungeard moncynnæs uard,
> eci dryctin, aefter tiadæ,
> firum foldu, frea allmectig.
>
> (J.C. Pope, *Seven Old English Poems*, p. 3)

Word for word:

Now we must praise the Keeper of Heaven's Kingdom,
The Maker's might, and His conception,
The deed of the Father of Glory; as He of all wonders—
The Eternal Lord—established the beginning.
He first created for the children of men
Heaven as a roof, the Holy Shaper;
Then Middle Earth (did) Mankind's Keeper,
The Eternal Lord, afterward ordain,
The earth for men, the Almighty Lord.

Although God is a special case, and has many names in the
Bible and in Latin hymns, it is striking that there is a periphrasis of
His name in eight of these nine lines. One of the formulas (*eci
dryctin*) is repeated within five lines, and others echo elements of
each other. There are also two formulas for "men" in these lines,
and here one of the apparent disadvantages of a heavily formulaic
style arises, for one of these formulas might seem logically inappropriate: the men for whom heaven is created as a roof are called
ælda barnum, the children of men. In West Saxon versions this
phrase became *eorthan bearnum*, the children of earth. Rationalistic
objections might not have bothered Cædmon any more than they
would have bothered Moses. The idea of heaven makes little sense
without the idea of earth, and the formula "heaven and earth" is
found in the common poetic stock of the Germanic languages.
Likewise men were "the children of men" even if God had just
created them. The expression *ælda barnum* must, if Bede's account
of Cædmon is trusted, have been familiar to its hearers at Streonaeshalch, embodying the traditional Germanic conception of men
in terms of their generations on Middle Earth and in the order of
things; likewise, the Old English *weorold* (world) derives from *wer*,
man. In Englishing the story of Creation, Cædmon inevitably
used terms from the old Germanic cosmology, such as heaven and
hell; Easter and Yule were baptised in the same way. The traditional content of the formulaic language of Old English poetry is
of more significance than the terminological and statistical argument about whether it is "oral" or "literary." Of the formulaic
nature of the original Old English verse vocabulary there can be
no doubt; nor is there any doubt that in its genesis and nature it is
an "oral" style. Of course, some later Old English poems were

literary translations from Latin: the *Paris Psalter*, the *Metres of Boethius*, and *The Phoenix*, from Lactantius. Cynewulf carefully signed some of his poems, also largely based on Latin, with a runic acrostic. And verse composition must increasingly have been affected by the prevalence of the new culture brought by writing as well as the inhibiting process of the verse being written down verbatim. The inhibition given to oral improvisation by the presence of a transcriber is so severe that, according to A. B. Lord, Parry's assistant, in his *The Singer of Tales*, the text is either oral or literary; there can be no transitional stage. But the situation of the *scop* differs from that of the Yugoslav bard whose performance has been recorded on tape, and from that of Homer, whose text seems to have crystallised into a stable form before being written down. Bede makes it clear that Cædmon's poems were orally composed, and implies (what his Old English translator says) that they were then written down by scribes. Their mastery of books enabled them to pass on the Creation story to him. His mastery in vernacular extempore composition enabled him to dictate the poems to them.

The word-for-word gloss of Cædmon's *Hymn* provided above pretends to literalness rather than literacy, but even the most resourceful translator would be embarrassed by having to render such an accumulation of near-synonyms in apposition. Unlike Homer, the Yugoslav singers, and the author of *La Chanson de Roland*, Cædmon moves forward very slowly. Richness rather than rapidity is his delight. And this is also true of straight narrative poems on contemporary events, even of the late *Maldon*. Parallelism and variation can be used with more propriety and skill than Cædmon shows here. In *Beowulf* the opening of Hrothgar's hall Heorot is celebrated by a poet singing the story of Creation:

> There was the music of the harp,
> The clear song of the poet, perfect in his telling
> Of the remote first making of man's race.
> He told how, long ago, the Lord formed Earth,
> A plain bright to look on, locked in ocean,
> Exulting established the sun and the moon
> As lights to illumine the land-dwellers
> And furnished forth the face of Earth

With limbs and leaves. Life He then granted
To each kind of creature that creeps and moves.

(89-98)

That this habit of variation was appreciated may be gleaned from another passage describing a poetic performance in *Beowulf*. After the story of Creation has been sung in the new hall, Heorot, "the company of men lived a careless life." The monster Grendel then attacks the hall and terrorises the Danes; eventually Beowulf the Geat overcomes him and he flees to his lair mortally wounded. Next morning the Danes follow Grendel's tracks to the Mere to make sure he is dead:

Then the older retainers turned back on the way
Journeyed with much joy; joined by the young men,
The warriors on white horses wheeled away from the Mere
In bold mood. Beowulf's feat
Was much spoken of, and many said
That between the seas, south or north
Over earth's stretch no other man
Beneath the sky's shifting excelled Beowulf,
Of all who wielded the sword he was worthiest to rule.
In saying this they did not slight in the least
The gracious Hrothgar, for he was a good king.

Where, as they went, their way broadened
They would match their mounts, making them leap
Along the best stretches, the striving riders
On their fallow horses. Or a fellow of the king's
Whose head was a storehouse of the storied verse
Whose tongue gave gold to the language
Of the treasured repertory, wrought a new lay
Made in the measure. The man struck up
Found the phrase, framed rightly
The deed of Beowulf, drove the tale,
Rang word-changes.

Of Waels's great son,
Sigemund, he spoke then, spelling out to them

All he had heard of that hero's strife,
His fights, strange feats, far wanderings,
The feuds and the blood spilt....

(853–78)

This scene is memorable not least for showing tradition in action: a great deed is the natural occasion for immediately improvised composition of poetry. Horseback composition, which may recur at Beowulf's funeral, was evidently not extraordinary: the king's thane knew the old poems, the old stories, the language, and the measure: he knew how to go about it, as Haydn knew how to compose a symphony. Having sung Beowulf's feat, he turns to the greatest of dragon-slayers, Sigemund, better known as Sigurd the Volsung or (in Wagner) as Siegfried.

The half-line immediately preceding the comparison with Sigemund is *wordum wrixlan*, "rang word-changes," almost certainly an allusion to the practice of variation. (The word *wrixlan* is also used in a riddle in the Exeter Book about the warbling song of a bird, an *eald æfensceop*, "old evening-singer.") This is the culminating phrase of the most valuable passage in Old English poetry on the points of the art. *Wrixlan* can also mean "wrestle," which adds an element of strenuousness to the idea of musical and verbal variety. Some of the pleasure of listening to oral composition must have been in the sense of a sustained feat, of difficulty mastered.

VI • THE USES OF POETRY

The incidence of poetry in *Beowulf* affords valuable illustration of its context and uses in heroic times. Heroic story, as in the lay of Sigemund, often takes the form of tribal history. When Beowulf arrives at Heorot, Hrothgar's welcome ends with these words:

"Yet sit now to the banquet, where you may soon attend,
Should the mood so take you, some tale of victory."

A bench was then cleared for the company of Geats
There in the beer-hall, for the whole band together,

The stout-hearted warriors went to their places,
Bore their strength proudly. Prompt in his office,
The man who held the horn of bright mead
Poured out its sweetness. The song of the poet
Again rang in Heorot. The heroes laughed loud
In the great gathering of the Geats and the Danes.

(489–98)

The "tale of victory" is not specified here, although bench, beer, mead, music, and subsequent laughter create the classic context for poetry.

After Beowulf's victory over Grendel, however, Hrothgar provides more mead, together with gifts:

> Then string and song sounded together
> Before Healfdene's Helper-in-battle: *i.e. Hrothgar*
> The lyre was taken up and tales recited
> When Hrothgar's bard was bidden to sing
> A hall-song for men on the mead-benches.
> It was how disaster came to the sons of Finn....

(1063–68)

This is a "tale of victory" for the Danes, of a successful vengeance on the Frisians carried out by Hengest. By a fortunate coincidence, the complicated story summarised allusively at this point in *Beowulf* is made clearer by the preservation in an early eighteenth-century transcript of *Finnsburh*, a vivid 48-line fragment of a lay on the same subject, perhaps known to the audience of *Beowulf*, which gives us an idea of the poem Hrothgar's *scop* sang. In *Finnsburh* the Danes are guests at Finn's *burh*, settlement, sleeping in their hall at night, when the fragment opens with a question to Hnæf, the Danish leader, by a man on guard at the hall door. The reply is:

> "It is not the eaves aflame, nor in the east yet
> Does day break; no dragon flies this way.
> It is the soft clashing of claymores you hear
> That they carry to the house.
>   Soon shall be the cough of birds,
> Hoar wolf's howl, hard wood-talk,

Shield's answer to shaft.
　　　　Now shines the moon,
Welkin-wanderer. The woes at hand
Shall bring to the full this folk's hatred for us.

Awake! on your feet! who fights for me?
Hold your lindens right, hitch up your courage,
Think bravely, be with me at the doors!"

Finnsburh is an exciting sample of the heroic poem of action. Unfortunately our other examples, *Waldere* and *Maldon*, are incomplete also, and the only extended heroic poem which is complete is the great, long, elegiac, and complex *Beowulf*.

At the end of the recital in *Beowulf* we read:

　　　　　　　Thus the story was sung,
The gleeman's lay. Gladness mounted,
Bench-mirth rang out, the bearers gave
Wine from wonderful vessels.

(1159–62)

The function of poetry, and its social context, is sufficiently indicated by noticing that the word *gleo* (glee) occurs four times in *Beowulf*, first here as part of *gleo-man* (gleeman, singer). The second is at 2105: *Þær wæs gidd and gleo*—"There was music and laughter, lays were sung." The third is at 2263 as part of *gleobeam* (joy-wood, musical instrument). The fourth is at 3031, as part of *gleodream* (mirth, joy). In both later instances *gleo* is coupled with *gamen* (games). Poetry was an art to make glad the heart of man, taking its place at the centre of what are commonly summed up as "hall-joys."

However, poetry could also be used to express grief: in all four instances of *gleo* in *Beowulf*, a hint of sorrows to come is also present. At 2105 Beowulf tells his king Hygelac of the feast at Heorot after Grendel was killed:

There was music and laughter, lays were sung:
The veteran of the Scyldings, versed in the sagas,
Would himself fetch back far-off times to us

The daring-in-battle would address the harp,
The joy-wood, delighting; or deliver a reckoning
Both true and sad; or he would tell us the story
Of some wonderful adventure, valiant-hearted king.
Or the seasoned warrior, wrapped in age,
Would again fall to fabling of his youth
And the days of his battle-strength; his breast was troubled
As his mind filled with the memories of those years.

(2105-14)

The reckoning Hrothgar made was *soth and sarlic*, both true and sad. Earlier in the poem Grendel's persecution of the Danes "was not hidden / From the sons of men, but was made known / In grieving songs." At the end of the poem at Beowulf's funeral pyre the Geats "uttered their sorrow at the slaughter of their lord." Then

A woman of the Geats in grief sang out
The lament for his death. Loudly she sang,
Her hair bound up, the burden of her fear
That evil days were destined her—
Troops cut down, terror of armies,
Bondage, humiliation. Heaven swallowed the smoke.

(3150-55)

So poetry and song (a modern distinction which does not seem to apply, though we know nothing of the styles of chanting or of accompaniment) were used to mark occasions of joy and sorrow, royal recreation and public entertainment, tribal history and the praise of God.

But quite apart from all special occasions, no Anglo-Saxon feast seems to have been complete without poetry: after drink, poetry was the means by which the past and the future were made endurable and the present enjoyable. (The drinking of beer, mead or wine—the word used in poetry being governed largely by the demands of alliteration—was a central part of a warrior's life. Even monks were permitted, by the English *Regularis Concordia* of the late tenth century, a good quantity of beer per day.) But the traditional function of poetry was to communicate heroism. Literature, according to Ezra Pound, is news that stays news, and the most welcome news in the heroic age was of human heroism, new or old. This is the message of the end of *Beowulf*:

> Then the warriors rode around the barrow
> Twelve of them in all, athelings' sons.
> They recited a dirge to declare their grief,
> Spoke of the man, mourned their King.
> They praised his manhood and the prowess of his hands,
> They raised his name; it is right a man
> Should be lavish in honouring his lord and friend,
> Should love him in his heart when the leading-forth
> From the house of flesh befalls him at last.
> This was the manner of the mourning of the men of
>   the Geats,
> Sharers in the feast, at the fall of their lord:
> They said that he was of all the world's kings
> The gentlest of men, and the most gracious
> The kindest to his people, the keenest for fame.

(3169–82)

The poem begins *We ... thrym gefrunon*, "we have heard of the glory," and ends *lof-geornost*, "most eager for fame."

As this poem of 3182 lines represents precisely the "fame" of the man after whom it is named, it is right that its last word should mean "most eager for fame," though as the supreme compliment this may come oddly to our ears on the heels of three tributes to Beowulf's care for others. But for a Germanic lord, reputation was to be gained by showing liberality toward and responsibility for retainers, as well as by the deeds of valour which directly earned fame (and might express responsibility and permit liberality). The softening or civilising of the heroic ideal offered in the figure of Beowulf owes something to Christianity, but our understanding of Christianity has some difficulty reconciling *lof-geornost* with religious humility. This difficulty, of knowing what to the original audience may have seemed compatible with what, is a frequent aspect of the verbal detail of Old English poetry. Another instance will show how an awareness of the formulaic element in composition may contribute to understanding such issues.

The classically-educated W. P. Ker liked the scenes of Beowulf's humane reception at the court of Hrothgar the Dane, and drew the parallel with Odysseus' entertainment at the court of Alcinous. But he disapproved of the way in which at the end of *Beowulf* "the hero and the dragon, under the influence of literary convention, pass together from 'this transitory life'" (*The Dark Ages*, p. 258). Ker scorns the incongruous application of the phrase *lænan lifes*, from transitory life, to the dragon, which lived for over 300 years. The phrase reflects the medieval sense of life's brevity (*læne* literally means "on loan"), probably with the Christian homilist's connotation of the transitoriness of this life as compared with eternal life. In so far as the phrase is Christian, it is literary and was to become conventional in Ker's derogatory sense. But Parry's work casts another light on such issues, for in formulaic composition the propriety of an epithet is general and generic, applying to the noun it qualifies rather than to a precise sense of the situation in which the noun may find itself. "Life" in general is "on loan," and the mortality of these exceptional opponents invokes the poet's formula for this general truth. Oral-formulaic habits of composition have their own providence, of which the results may not have the nicety of application of a more considered literary word-choice, but the authority accrued in these crystallisations of human experience can be compensation enough. Sometimes the providence of the formula is hard to understand, as when it is said that when Beowulf fails to return to the bloodstained surface of the Mere, the *hwate Scyldingas* abandoned the Geats — their guests — to wait for him. *Hwate* means brisk, bold, keen; a sarcasm is not inconceivable: the Danes are quick to give up. There is irony elsewhere in *Beowulf*, both structural and verbal, at the expense of the Danes; yet the interpretation of *hwate* remains problematic. In general, however, the use of formulaic poetic epithets and traditional diction is a great moral strength in *Beowulf*, as Dr. Johnson's Imlac says in *Rasselas*, "the business of the poet is to examine, not the individual, but the species."

VII • *BEOWULF*

Beowulf defines the species of heroic poetry in Old English. It dominates the extant verse literature to an extent that defeats perspective—as Shakespeare does in English Renaissance drama or *Paradise Lost* does with the epic poem in English. A tenth of the lines of Old English verse are to be found in *Beowulf*, as are most of the memorable lines, scenes, and sentiments. This pre-eminence has been recognised ever since the full Old English corpus became available to readers, but many of the difficulties attendant upon the poem have cleared only in the last three generations. Mastering enough of the language to enjoy *Beowulf* properly, however, demands a great deal of time.

Only since J.R.R. Tolkien's 1936 British Academy Lecture "*Beowulf*: the Monsters and the Critics" has an intelligible general view of the poem prevailed. Previously the poem had to some extent been obscured by the excavations of Germanic philologists and historians. These had illuminated the language, the background, and the allusions, and Klaeber's third edition (1950) is a monument to that formidable but necessary scholarship: 628 pages for 3182 lines of text. As English studies evolved, C.L. Wrenn in 1953 was in a position to reverse old priorities: "The purpose of this edition," he begins, "is mainly twofold—to present *Beowulf* in its proper setting as a great *poem* to university students, and to make available in a readable and manageable form the more significant results of recent scholarship." Since then the art and unity of the poem have been vindicated, it has disengaged itself from its background, and is ready to become a classic.

Old English literature, however, is, like other literature demanding study, more often an optional than a compulsory part of a degree course in English literature, so *Beowulf* will be more often read in translations. With the exception of the Bible, it has perhaps been translated more often than any other text in the last two hundred years, often by poets. Seventy Modern English versions have appeared, together with translations into 22 foreign languages, eight into Japanese. *Beowulf* now seems a less heathen poem than it did to the Victorian poet William Morris, who translated it in 1897. It is a Christian poem for an English audience about their ancestors, when these ancestors were heathen and lived across the North Sea. What it shares with the Vulgate Bible and with other Christian literature in Latin has sharply corrected our awareness of its kinship to the Germanic past with which it is concerned. Where nineteenth-century scholars, in the wake of Wolf and Grimm, mythologised the poem, modern commentators have established how deeply it is indebted to Christianity. There remains an empirical English resistance to a thoroughly allegorical interpretation. The monsters are what cause the problem.

Beowulf is the story of a monster-slayer, Beowulf the Geat, nephew of King Hygelac of Geatland in the southern tip of what is now Sweden. Hygelac is recorded in the sixth-century historian Gregory of Tours, and by others, as having died in about 521 in a raid on Frankish peoples at the mouth of the Rhine — an event mentioned four times in the poem. The Danes Hrothgar and Hrothulf and the leading Swedes are also known to history. The wars between Swedes and Geats in the background of the second part of the poem seem historically authentic; and archaeology confirms the reliability of the descriptions of heroic life in the poem in such things as armour, gold rings, and burial practices. The setting of the poem in southern Scandinavia of the fifth and sixth centuries is, then, historical enough.

Many of the persons mentioned more fleetingly in the poem are historical but known to us from heroic legend — Eormanric, Offa, Ingeld, Finn, Hengest, Widia and Hama. More shadowy is Scyld, founder of the Scyldings. Purely legendary are Wayland the Smith and the Brising fire-dwarves, makers of armour and jewellery. Only the central characters of the poem, Beowulf and the monsters, are not to be found in history. Beowulf is unknown outside the poem, as are Grendel, Grendel's mother, and the dragon, although there are folk-lore analogues to Beowulf's fights both with the monsters and with the dragon, and the name of Grendel survives in some placenames.

Since the Renaissance, monsters, giants, dwarves, and dragons have gone out of fashion in serious literature, which today prefers any heroes to be tarnished. The fairytale basis of the central story of *Beowulf* has undoubtedly been an embarrassment to its admirers. W. P. Ker thought Grendel "a lumpish ogre" and that Beowulf was demeaned by having to fight subhuman enemies rather than

someone like Hector. J.R.R.Tolkien reversed this humanist ver-
dict, and Beowulfians have marched on after him, resolutely not
turning back. Positivism and rationalism are not what they were
before the world wars, and rationalists can no longer be confident
that human nature is simply good; but the educated Western
mentality is likely to remain resistant to that universal belief in the
everyday reality of invisible powers, especially of demons, so characteristic of the dark ages. This is not to say that Grendel is not
frightening or that Beowulf's death is the less fearful because it
comes through the dragon. The story of *Beowulf* is not history but
historical legend with a mythical dimension, or perhaps a myth in
a historical setting. The poem attains the stature of myth rather
than folk-tale by subordinating grotesque detail and by creating a
human hero representative of the heroic age itself—a figure who,
against the dragon, assumes a sacrificial role. *Beowulf* is a true epic
poem, containing elements of legend, but it also embodies a
myth.

A summary of the central action of *Beowulf* has some use,
although critics vary in how far they dwell on this action. Most
might agree with Shippey that the folk-tale basis of the story, with
its fantasy and brutality, has all but disappeared; and some with
Tolkien that in conception Beowulf's last opponent is dragon-
hood rather than a dragon. Yet it could not be said of any early
epic, as it could of the novel at a sophisticated stage of its history,
"Yes, oh dear, yes, the novel tells a story." The action of *Beowulf*,
however unmodern or prehumanist, bears much of the significance of the poem, even if this significance is modified by the
many stories of historical and legendary human feuds which
accompany it. Beowulf the Geat kills Grendel, a monster who for
twelve years has nightly possessed the hall of Hrothgar the Dane.
Grendel's death is avenged by his mother, who kills Hrothgar's
counsellor in a raid on Heorot. Beowulf then kills Grendel's
mother in the monsters' hellish lair at the bottom of the Mere.
Returning home, Beowulf eventually becomes king of the Geats,
whom he rules for fifty years. The Geats are attacked by a fire-
breathing dragon whose hoard has been robbed. In the final fight
Beowulf and the dragon are killed.

The main story, simple enough in reading as it is in summary,
stands out against a historical background of much complexity,

involving directly or indirectly the ruling houses of the continental coasts of north-west Europe over the generations either side of the death of Hygelac the Geat in 521. The final outlook for the Geats (as by implication for the Danes earlier) is bad: destruction and treachery will overwhelm both peoples.

The foreground of the poem, however, is occupied by Beowulf and his deeds. He performs other feats, notably of swimming, but is mentioned as killing only one named person in the poem (the champion of the Franks, who had killed Hygelac). Despite the superhuman strength of his hands (equal to that of thirty men, so that swords broke when he used them), Beowulf is a peaceable man who is cast in the role of a slayer of monsters and dragons. He is (by the standards of Germanic heroes) exceptionally modest, gracious, generous, and magnanimous. He declines the throne of Geatland for as long as he can, and does not make enemies. That Beowulf is an ideal rather than an actual historical figure is confirmed by the fact that his name does not, as was customary, alliterate with that of his father. All we know of Edgetheow is that having married the only daughter of King Hrethel he had to go into exile because he killed a man whose *wergild* (legal compensation paid to the family) was too great for the Geats to pay. Hrothgar the Dane handsomely paid the *wergild* for him, creating an obligation for Edgetheow's son Beowulf. For the purposes of the story this obligation to Hrothgar matters more than Beowulf's ancestry. Beowulf has no son and heir, and no wife is mentioned for him. He is thus an oddly unattached man, although by his father's marriage a member of the Geat royal family and eventually, after the death of Hygelac's son, king. Everything that happens in the poem emphasises Beowulf's uniqueness. His name is derived from "bee-wolf," that is, an animal which is the enemy of the bee, a bear. And "bear," as R.W. Chambers wrote,

> is an excellent name for a hero of story. The O.E. *beorn*, "warrior, hero, prince" seems originally to have meant simply "bear." The bear, says Grimm, "is regarded, in the belief of the Old Norse, Slavonic, Finnish and Lapp peoples, as an exalted and holy being, endowed with human understanding and the strength of twelve men." (*Beowulf, An Introduction*, p.368)

This interpretation is borne out by Beowulf's bear-like habit of hugging his adversaries to death, ordinary swords being of no use to him. Beowulf's sluggish youth and his first two fights with a house-troll and a water-hag conform to a folk-tale type known as the Bear's Son tale, of which there are over two hundred examples. A notable analogue to Beowulf's fights is to be found in the Saga of Grettir the Strong, an historical eleventh-century Icelandic outlaw. That Beowulf's fights in Denmark have an archetype in folklore is not in doubt, although the poem both raises his story to an epic myth and turns him into a very gentle bear. Both these developments are most visible after Beowulf's return to Geatland: his character as thane and king is shown to be lacking in the headstrong qualities of the usual northern hero; and his sacrificial role in killing the dragon gives the poem a mythical though still human depth. The earlier part of the poem, especially the Grendel episode, is simpler and more vivid as narrative and as adventure; yet it lacks the grandeur, horror, pathos, and human complexity of the end.

The monsters are the other half of the main story. All are called *aglæca*: "wretch, monster, demon, fiend" (Klaeber). The word is, strikingly, also used of Sigemund and, twice, of Beowulf, where it is somewhat pallidly glossed "warrior, hero" by Klaeber; and once, in the plural, of Beowulf and the dragon together: the terrible ones. What exactly are Beowulf's enemies? This is an awkward question for modern readers unaccustomed to trolls, elves, monsters, giants, and dragons, not to mention demons. We do not recognise Grendel, his mother or the dragon; we cannot even guess their species, though we feel some of the horror they inspire. We conceive our fears differently and seek to deal with them by psychology and drugs rather than with our bare hands. In Scandinavia Grendel was a troll, but in Christian England he belongs to the kindred of Cain: from the elder son of Adam and the first killer of kin descend all monsters, elves, goblins, and giants. He is introduced into the poem anonymously, as a mighty spirit dwelling in the darkness surrounding Heorot, listening to the above-quoted hymn of Creation being sung at the feast within. This menace is introduced directly after an anticipatory reference to the hostile fire that will as the result of a treacherous feud eventually consume Heorot. Thus the descendant of Cain is wait-

ing outside the hall of the feast, much as in *Paradise Lost* it is
through Satan's eyes that we see the fragile happiness of the Garden of Eden.

> So the company of men led a careless life,
> All was well with them: until One began
> To encompass evil, an enemy from hell.
> *Grendel* they called this cruel spirit,
> The fell and fen his fastness was,
> The march his haunt. This unhappy being
> Had long lived in the land of monsters
> Since the Creator cast them out
> As kindred of *Cain*. For that killing of Abel
> The eternal Lord took vengeance.
> There was no joy of that feud: far from mankind
> God drove him out for his deed of shame!
> From Cain came down all kinds misbegotten —
> Ogres and elves and evil shades —
> As also the Giants, who joined in long
> Wars with God. He gave them their reward.
>
> With the coming of night came Grendel also,
> Sought the great house and how the Ring-Danes
> Held their hall when the horn had gone round.
> He found in Heorot the force of nobles
> Slept after supper, sorrow forgotten,
> The condition of men. Maddening with rage,
> He struck quickly, creature of evil:
> Grim and greedy, he grasped on their pallets
> Thirty warriors, and away he was out of there,
> Thrilled with his catch: he carried off homeward
> His glut of slaughter, sought his own halls.
> As the day broke, with the dawn's light
> Grendel's outrage was openly to be seen:
> Night's table-laughter turned to morning's
> Lamentation. Lord Hrothgar
> Sat silent then, the strong man mourned,
> Glorious king, he grieved for his thanes
> As they read the traces of a terrible foe,

A cursed fiend. That was too cruel a feud,
Too long, too hard!

(99-134)

Grendel is therefore both a troll and a devil, not merely terrifying or nasty, but evil. The existence of the kind of evil that Grendel betokens is not to be disposed of by his own removal. This realisation is more sinister than his various folklorique characteristics: a hellish light shines out of his eyes, he has a *glof* or bag of devils' skins in which he puts his prey, and fingernails like steel. He is also a solitary, a cannibal, an animal exclusively nocturnal, and is likened variously to a man, a giant, a ghost and a fiend. He is not only "the enemy of mankind" but "God's adversary."

His next appearance is at his advance on the hall, now guarded by Beowulf:

Gliding through the shadows came
The walker in the night. The warriors slept
Whose task was to hold the horned building
All except one. It was well-known to men
That the demon could not drag them to the shades
Without God's willing it; yet the one man kept
Unblinking watch. He awaited, heart swelling
With anger against his foe, the ordeal of battle.
Down off the moorlands' misting fells came
Grendel stalking; God's brand was on him.
The spoiler meant to snatch away
From the high hall some of human race.
He came on under the clouds, clearly saw at last
The gold-hall of men, the mead-drinking place
Nailed with gold plates. That was not the first visit
He had paid to the hall of Hrothgar the Dane:
He never before and never after
Harder luck nor hall-guards found.

Walking to the hall came this warlike creature
Condemned to agony. The door gave way,
Toughened with iron, at the touch of those hands.
Rage-inflamed, wreckage-bent, he ripped open
The jaws of the hall. Hastening on,

82

The foe then stepped onto the unstained floor,
Angrily advanced: out of his eyes stood
An unlovely light like that of fire.
He saw then in the hall a host of young soldiers,
A company of kinsmen caught away in sleep,
A whole warrior-band. In his heart he laughed then,
Horrible monster, his hopes swelling
To a gluttonous meal. He meant to wrench
The life from each body that lay in the place
Before night was done. It was not to be;
He was no longer to feast on the flesh of mankind
After that night.

(702-36)

After Beowulf's victory and the banquet at Heorot at which the story of the successful Danish revenge upon Finn has been sung, the Danes drink deep.

Then they sank into sleep. A savage penalty
One paid for his night's rest! It was no new thing for
      that people
Since Grendel had settled in the gold-giving hall,
Working his evil, until the end came,
Death for his misdeeds. It was declared then to men,
And received by every ear, that for all this time
A survivor had been living, an avenger for their foe
And his grim life's-leaving: *Grendel's Mother* herself,
A monstrous ogress, was ailing for her loss.
She had been doomed to dwell in the dread waters,
In the chilling currents, because of that blow
Whereby Cain became the killer of his brother,
His own father's son. He stole away, branded,
Marked for his murder, from all that men delight in,
To inhabit the wastelands.

(1251-65)

It comes as a surprise to the reader, as well as to the Danes, to find that Grendel has a mother. Some older translators try to dampen the sympathy aroused by bereaved motherhood by calling her

83

"Grendel's dam." That chivalry would be misplaced is shown later by the undignified picture of her sitting on the chest of her "hall-guest." (She is also described as a *secg*, a word applied only to masculine warriors.) Her "hall" is a cave at the bottom of a lake—the Mere—into which Beowulf has to dive to get at her. The hellish region in which she lives is perhaps the most frightening thing about this water-hag. Hrothgar tells Beowulf what he has heard of the monsters:

> I have heard it said by subjects of mine
> Who live in the country, counsellors in this hall,
> That they have seen such a pair
> Of huge wayfarers haunting the moors,
> Otherworldly ones; and one of them,
> So far as they might make it out,
> Was in woman's shape; but the shape of a man,
> Though twisted, trod also the tracks of exile –
> Save that he was more huge than any human being.
> The country people have called him from of old
> By the name of Grendel; they know of no father
>   for him,
> Nor whether there have been such beings before
> Among the monster-race.
>   Mysterious is the region
> They live in—of wolf-fells, wind-picked moors
> And treacherous fen-paths: a torrent of water
> Pours down dark cliffs and plunges into the earth,
> An underground flood. It is not far from here,
> In terms of miles, that the Mere lies,
> Overcast with dark, crag-rooted trees
> That hang in groves hoary with frost.
> An uncanny sight may be seen at night there—
> The fire in the water! The wit of living men
> Is not enough to know its bottom.
> The hart that roams the heath, when hounds have
>   pressed him
> Long and hard, may hide in the forest
> His antlered head; but the hart will die there
> Sooner than swim and save his life;

He will sell it on the brink there, for it is not a safe place.
And the wind can stir up wicked storms there,
Whipping the swirling waters up
Till they climb the clouds and clog the air,
Making the skies weep.

(1345-75)

Beowulf only escapes from the clutches of Grendel's mother
with the help of a giant-sword provided to him by God. The victorious hero then returns to Heorot with the hilt of this sword
and presents it to Hrothgar:

Then the golden hilt was given into the hand
Of the older warrior, the white-haired leader.
A Giant had forged it. With the fall of the demons
It passed into the possession of the prince of the Danes,
This work of wonder-smiths. The world was rid
Of that invidious enemy of God
And his mother also, with their murders upon them;
And the hilt now belonged to the best of the kings
Who ruled the earth in all the North
And distributed treasure between the seas.
Hrothgar looked on that long-treasured hilt
Before he spoke. The spring was cut on it
Of the primal strife, with the destruction at last
Of the race of Giants by the rushing Flood,
A terrible end. Estranged was that race
From the Lord of Eternity: the tide of water
Was the final reward that the Ruler sent them.
On clear gold labels let into the cross-piece
It was rightly told in runic letters,
Set down and sealed, for whose sake it was
That the sword was first forged, that finest of iron,
Spiral-hilted, serpent-bladed.

(1677-98)

The Giants and the Flood come, like Cain, from the early chapters
of Genesis. It seems that monsters who live under water and survived the Flood may be regarded as giants. The "primal strife"

85

repeats and repeats in the pre-Christian world of *Beowulf*. If country people do not know whether there have been such creatures as Grendel before among the monster-race, there is no reason why there may not be other kinds of monsters in store for mankind in the future, for the monstrous is a mutation of the human. This, however, is the moment of Beowulf's triumph: he has cleansed Denmark of its infestation, and in the flush of his sunlit success he is reminded by the aged Hrothgar to avoid complacency, pride, and meanness.

Beowulf returns home, tells his tale and is gloriously rewarded with great estates by his king Hygelac. Then, as happens constantly throughout the poem, things change with great suddenness.

> But it fell out after, in other days,
> Among the hurl of battle—when Hygelac lay dead
> And the bills of battle had dealt death to his Heardred
> Despite the shield's shelter, when the Scyldings
> > found him
> Amid his conquering people, and those keen war-wolves
> Grimly hemmed in Hereric's nephew —
> That the broad kingdom came by this turn
> Into Beowulf's hands.
> > Half a century
> He ruled it, well: until One began—
> The king had grown grey in the guardianship
> > of the land —
> To put forth his power in the pitch-black night-times—
> The hoard-guarding *Dragon* of a high barrow
> Raised above the moor.
>
> > > > (2201-13)

The introduction of Grendel is very similar:

> So the company of men led a careless life
> All was well with them: until One began
> To encompass evil, an enemy from hell.
>
> > > > (99-101)

Oththæt an ongan (until One began) is common to both appearances, as is the element of darkness. This helps to link the dragon
with Grendel and his mother: great happiness seems almost to
invite its opposite. The unpredictability of life is a medieval commonplace, characteristically expressed by Chaucer:

> Thanked be Fortune, and hir false wheel,
> That noon estaat assureth to be weel.
>
> (*The Knight's Tale*, 66–67)

But reversal of fortune in *Beowulf* is more fatal, abrupt and, in
human terms, unintelligible. The poet assures us that God has
ruled the affairs of men from the beginning. But a trust in His
providential ordering, such as Boethius attains in his *De Consolatione*, is not available to anyone in this tale set centuries back in the
heathen past and in places which remained heathen at the time
that *Beowulf* was copied into the manuscript in which it now survives, in about 1010. Whatever the significance of the dragon, it
comes in here as a further embodiment of destructive malignity.
In itself the dragon is a beast of a different sort to the manlike
Grendel, and belongs in a less provincial world. The slaying of a
dragon was a supreme feat for heroes in classical myth and
remained so for Germanic heroes such as Sigemund the Volsung.
From the earlier comparison to Sigemund in the lay composed
about Beowulf's slaying of Grendel, it is clear that a dragonish fate
remained for Beowulf also. In Indian mythology the world itself is
created through the god's killing of the world-serpent. Some distant reflex of this may remain in Beowulf's killing of the dragon
and winning of the hoard of gold. The gold in the barrow in
Beowulf has a peculiarly complex history, having first been buried
by noble princes with a curse upon it, then discovered and used
by a warrior race. The last survivor of this race, which has perished, perhaps through the curse, then reburies it in the barrow,
described by the poet as "new." Elsewhere the terms he uses make
it clear that the barrow resembles a chambered megalithic construction. The hoard is then discovered by the flying dragon, who
guards it for three hundred years. The gold itself, when Wiglaf
brings it out of the barrow, looks as if it had rested for "a thousand

winters in the womb of earth." The hoard is then carried to Beowulf's funeral pyre and finally reburied in Beowulf's newly built funeral mound, where it lies in the earth "as useless to [or unusable by] men as it was before."

Whatever the hoard of gold represented in earlier myth, in *Beowulf* it has become grave goods—specifically those goods of the battlefield and meadhall that heroic society found most glorious. The curse that attaches to all buried gold and grave-goods is given a Christian turn, although it is particularly said that Beowulf had not looked upon the gold "too greedily."

Dragons were traditionally the jealous guardians of gold: in the Old English *Gnomic Verses* or *Maxims* it is said that "the dragon dwells in a barrow, ancient, proud of treasures." It is this possessiveness which make *Beowulf*'s dragon take revenge on men, after a man (a fugitive slave who wanted something to appease his master) has robbed the hoard of a cup. Breathing fire at night (it may be the first fire-breathing dragon in western vernacular literature), it destroys Beowulf's hall and the dwellings of his people. Beowulf goes out to challenge the dragon. His spirit is described as "gloomy, death-eager, wandering"; yet his final words to his companions are

> "This affair is not for you,
> Nor is it measured to any man but myself alone
> To match strength with this monstrous being,
> Attempt this deed. By daring will I
> Win this gold; war otherwise
> Shall take your king, terrible life's-bane!"
>
> (2532-37)

Age was no barrier to active leadership in war, as we see from Ongentheow, the king of the Swedes in *Beowulf*, and Byrhtnoth in *Maldon*, although Hrothgar seems to have lost his nerve. The last words of the above speech recall Hrothgar's earlier warning against pride:

> "Beloved Beowulf, best of warriors
> Resist this deadly taint, take what is better,
> Your lasting profit. Put away arrogance,

> Noble fighter! The noon of your strength
> Shall last for a while now, but in a little time
> Sickness or a sword will strip it from you:
> Either enfolding flame or a flood's billow
> Or a knife-stab or the stoop of a spear
> Or the ugliness of age; or your eyes' brightness
> Lessens and grows dim. Death shall soon
> Have beaten you then, O brave warrior!"
>
> (1758-68)

The arrogance of Beowulf here is not the sort Hrothgar warns against — it is, on the contrary, Beowulf's final generosity towards his people. Without the sacrifice of Beowulf's life, the dragon would not die. Wiglaf gives the first wound (in the belly, a dragon's only vulnerable spot), but it is Beowulf who kills the dragon. It is difficult not to recognise in the resonance of Beowulf's superb defiance of death the essence and the splendour of heroism:

> Passion filled the prince of the Geats:
> He allowed a cry to utter from his breast,
> Roared from his stout heart: as the horn clear in battle
> His voice re-echoed through the vault of grey stone.
> The hoard-guard recognized a human voice,
> And there was no more time for talk of friendship:
> Hatred stirred. Straightaway
> The breath of the dragon billowed from the rock
> In a hissing gust; the ground boomed.
>
> (2550-58)

The consequence of Beowulf's death, it later becomes clear, is that his people will be overrun by the Swedes or by the Franks. The Geats seem to disappear from history in the sixth century. The gold which Beowulf gains, the sight of which allows him to die more calmly, is of use only in glorifying his funeral. But the dragon is dead, and we are clearly not to say that the struggle naught availeth.

In Christian tradition the devil is often conceived as a dragon, following many hints in the Bible, from the serpent of Eden to the dragon of the Apocalypse. Although there are more Satanic epithets applied to Grendel than to the dragon, the dragon is Beowulf's supreme antagonist. This raises the apparent logical difficulty that if the dragon in any way suggests Satan, Beowulf is by the same process assimilated to the Christ whose victory over Satan in the Harrowing of Hell episode was so popular a feature of medieval Christian belief. The fifteenth-century Scottish priest William Dunbar began his poem on the triumph of the Resurrection with the line "Done is a battell on the dragon blak." But medieval allegory is not, as it is in Bunyan's *Pilgrim's Progress*, simple, consistent, and systematic; it can be local and symbolic. Beowulf may be a saviour-figure, and his soul seems to go to "the judgement of the righteous." This seems to be the meaning of the poet's comment, though it is not unambiguous. But the final note at Beowulf's funeral is a dignified acceptance of the inscrutability of *wyrd* or fate: "Heaven swallowed the smoke." Beowulf, a good young hero, and a good old king, was a gentler man than the Northumbrian Aethelfrid, of whom Bede said "that he might well be compared to Saul the King of Israel, except of course that he was ignorant of true religion."

Beowulf, however, is neither a theological work nor an allegory, though it can be read allegorically. Its significance is chiefly to be found at the level of its own story, the story of a deliverer stronger and nobler than other men but subject to mortality, who made of mortality as fine a thing as could be made. The Christian perspective created by the song of Creation and by Grendel's descent from Cain, and implicit or explicit in some of the poet's comments, shows the limitations of the morality of the heroic age, not least by the way that the hero himself rises as far as possible above the ethic of the blood-feud and is ready to sacrifice himself for his people. What is glory? What is honour? These are questions that the funerals of Scyld and Beowulf raise. But the end of the heroic age signalled by the death of Beowulf is something to be mourned.

FOUR : THE WORLD'S WONDER: RIDDLES

GEORGE HERBERT's *Virtue* concludes:

> Only a sweet and virtuous soul,
> Like seasoned timber never gives;
> But though the whole world turn to coal,
> Then chiefly lives.

Our "world" descends from the Old English *weorold*, which is related to *wer*, a man, itself a cousin of the Latin *vir* from which the word *virtue* is derived. A man in the heroic world of Old English poetry was virtuous in so far as he acted heroically. When Beowulf was aroused the morning after the visit of Grendel's mother, and summoned to see Hrothgar in Heorot, he enquired of his host "whether the night had been quiet after a call so urgent."

Hrothgar spoke, the Helmet of the Scyldings:

"Do not ask about our welfare! Woe has returned
To the Danish people with the death of Ashhere,
The elder brother of Yrmenlaf.
He was my closest counsellor, he was keeper of my thoughts,

He stood at my shoulder when we struck for our lives
At the crashing together of companies of foot,
When blows rained on boar-crests. Men of birth and merit
All should be as Ashhere was!"

(1321-29)

Hrothgar now tells of Grendel's mother and her lair in the Mere
and asks Beowulf's aid.

Beowulf spoke, son of Edgetheow:

"Bear your grief, wise one ! It is better for a man
To avenge his friend than to refresh his sorrow.
As we must all expect to leave
Our life on this earth, we must earn some renown,
If we can, before death; daring is the thing
For a fighting man to be remembered by ...."

(1383-89)

Beowulf's opening words here are *Ne sorga, snotor guma*, literally "Do not sorrow, wise man." This bracing piece of comfort decisively expresses the instinct of heroic virtue that the thing to do is to act, not to mope. Beowulf's more reflective justification of his instinctive reaction is also typical of Old English poetry; he has an old head on his young shoulders. But it is heroic initiative which had moved him—to seek out Hrothgar in the first place, to ask if he may defend Heorot, to forego the use of a sword, to dive into the Mere without waiting for an answer, and to go out against the dragon. A hero is a man who knows what to do. When Hrunting, the sword Unferth lends to Beowulf, fails to wound Grendel's mother,

Determined still, intent on fame,
The nephew of Hygelac renewed his courage.
Furious, the warrior flung it to the ground,
Spiral-patterned, precious in its clasps,
Stiff and steel-edged; his own strength would suffice him,
The might of his hands. A man must act so

When he means in a fight to frame himself
A long-lasting glory; it is not life he thinks of.

(1529-36)

Swa sceal man don: a man must act so. This imperative still governs
Beowulf in old age:

The strong champion stood up beside his shield
Brave beneath helmet, he bore his mail-shirt
To the rocky cliff's foot, confident in his strength,
A single man; such is not the coward's way.

(2538-41)

Strengo getruwode anes mannes: literally, "he trusted to the strength
of a single man." When he has to fight, Beowulf does not think
about life. In the end he loses his life, of course, as the hero must if
he is human; for, as the poet says with true Anglo-Saxon deliberation and understatement:

To elude death
Is not easy: attempt it who will,
He shall go to the place prepared for each
Of the sons of men, the soul-bearers
Dwelling on earth, ordained them by fate:
Laid fast in that bed, the body shall sleep
When the feast is done.

Death is a limit and challenge to heroic virtue, its test not its
refutation. Without it the myth of Beowulf's life would lose its
meaning. The nobility and simplicity of Beowulf's nature are not
unthinking. When the dragon burns down Beowulf's hall and
gift-stool,

Grief then struck
Into his ample heart with anguished keenness.
The chieftain supposed he had sorely angered
The Ruler of all, the eternal Lord,
By breach of ancient law. His breast was thronged

93

With dark, unaccustomed care-filled thoughts.

(2327-32)

The Danes in similar circumstances after Grendel's attack resort to heathen sacrifices, but Beowulf still knows what to do. He leads his companions to meet the dragon, keeping his misgivings from them.

The stern war-king sat on the headland,
Spoke encouraging words to the companions of his hearth,
The gold-friend of the Geats. Gloomy was his spirit though,
Death-eager, wandering; the weird was at hand
That was to overcome the old man there.

(2416-20)

Beowulf now recalls much of his life, and more than half of the rest of the poem is given over to speeches of retrospection. There is as much speech as action in *Beowulf*, framing the man's struggle against monsters with many stories of man against man. Though he now resolutely advances into battle, Beowulf's seated position on the headland (where his barrow is later to stand) is a reminder of his isolation in time of trial. Similar doubts and cares have afflicted Hrothgar and are soon to come to Wiglaf. Hrothgar's counsellors, seeing blood rising to the surface of the Mere, gave up hope for Beowulf, "abandoning the cliff-head."

Seasoned warriors,
Grey-headed, experienced, they spoke together,
Said it seemed unlikely that they would see once more
The prince returning triumphant to seek out
Their famous master.

(1594-8)

Though ironical here, the association of experience with wisdom is normative in Old English poetry: the elders of the tribe sit in council. Equally characteristic is the association of deep thought with individual isolation, something we may take for granted but a new and critical phenomenon in so communal a culture as that of the mead-hall. The last survivor of the race who placed the gold in the barrow has a soliloquy, also on the headland. The Old English Elegies are likewise soliloquies. The most complete of them, *The Wanderer*, introduces its conclusion with the words *Swa cwæth snottor on mode, gesæt him sundor æt rune*: "So spoke the wise man in his heart; he sat apart in secret thought." This position — reminiscent of Rodin's *Le Penseur*—is that of the young Edwin in Bede's account of the vision which came to him in exile at the court of Rædwald: "His friend being gone, Edwin remained alone without, and, sitting with heavy heart before the palace, began to be overwhelmed with many thoughts, not knowing what to do, or which way to turn himself" (Bede II.12, trans. Stevens, p. 88). The impression left by the poem *Beowulf* is very much due to the combination of the directly presented heroic world, where thought and deed are ideally one, with a more reflective moral commentary, such as the remarks above beginning "But to elude death /Is not easy." These comments are at times so impersonal that they are almost part of the narrative, as where it is said of Scyld: *thæt wæs god cyning* (that was a good king). Or they can come from a character, as with Beowulf's *Ne sorga, snotor guma* to Hrothgar. But many narrative paragraphs in the poem end with a sententious comment from the poet, unexceptional in sentiment but pointed in style. "To elude death is not easy" is not a truism, for "not easy" means (by understatement) "impossible." And the development of this sentiment, for example, has the gravity of Samuel Johnson and the sublimity of a simpler age. To a modern reader, they can at first seem of a tribal simplicity or on the contrary too obtrusively editorial, as when the heathen sacrifices of the Danes are historically explained:

> Such was their practice,
> A heathen hope; Hell possessed
> Their hearts and minds: the Maker was unknown to them.
>
> (178-80)

Yet the cumulative effect of the commentary is not only to deepen the tone of the poem but to make it more complex: it becomes more meditative without becoming less dramatic. Heroic virtue is exemplified and enforced, and yet at the same time the code of heroism, while magnificent, is not quite enough. Beowulf is uniquely continent, but the iron code of loyalty requires that he avenge Hygelac, and also support his king's guests in their wars. The quarrel started by Cain continues. And the glory Beowulf wins is as "useless to men" as the gold.

Whatever may seem to be the point of balance amid the many strains of the poem — and in this account the blood-stained complexities of the poem's many digressions are neglected — its final effect is a profound awe before the mysterious nature of life and death. The poem opens and closes with funerals. As heaven swallows the smoke from Beowulf's funeral pyre, we may recall that no man knows who sent Scyld Shefing or who unloaded his boat. Of the many deaths in the poem none is foreseen. God, we are often told, "has ruled the affairs of the race of men / Thus from the beginning." There is a dignified acceptance of the inscrutability of *Weird* (Fate, the way things happen) and, behind *Weird*, of God's intentions.

The religious awe which is the ground of *Beowulf*, and the wisdom of the poem's commentary on its events, are features of much Old English verse. These related qualities, of respect for the workings of the universe and of a love of wisdom, are part of the traditional Germanic view of the world, pre-dating the influence of Christianity. They harmonise well, however, with much in the Old Testament, especially the Psalms, the Wisdom books, and some of the Prophets.

I • RIDDLES

This pondering side of Old English poetry is most attractively encountered in the Riddles of the Exeter Book. Here is the first of them, *Storm*:

> What man so quick and clever of wit
> To divine who it is who drives me on my course
> When I arise in my strength and sudden fury
> Threatening hugely, throwing myself about,
> Bursting across country, burning men's houses
> And sacking their dwellings? Dark smoke
> Rises above the roofs. Roaring is on the earth,

The sudden death of men. When I move the forest,
The flourishing groves, I fell the trees;
The powers above dispatch me to wander
Far on my range, roofed in with the waters.
I have on my back what buried the forms
Of dwellers on earth deep in ocean,
Body and soul. Say who hides me
Or how I am called who carry these burdens.

The penultimate sentence of this riddle expresses the idea, familiar from Genesis, of "the waters above the firmament," and of the Flood; which also appears in *Beowulf*, on the hilt of the sword with which the hero killed the giantess under the water:

The spring was cut on it
Of the primal strife, with the destruction at last
Of the race of Giants by the rushing Flood,
A terrible end.

Even more exalted is the third and longest of the Riddles, so grand that a long extract is reproduced here, the second half of the poem. It again describes a storm.

Sometimes I rush through what rides on my back,
The dark moisture-bearers, drive them asunder
With their bellying waters; or bring them once more
Sliding together. The greatest of sounds is it
The ear-splitting clap of thunder overhead
When one cloud sharply encounters another,
Edge against edge. These umber creatures
Go sweeping over the peoples, sweating flame,
White fire. They forge on above men,
Black thunder-clouds, bellowing loudly,
Ramping and lowering. They allow dark raindrops
To come pattering down, drop from their breast,
Distil from their bellies. Braying onward come
Their terrible troops: disaster stalks
Among mankind, commotion and fear
Spread through the cities, as the spectres stray

And darkly shoot their sharp weapons.
The fool fears not these fatal darts,
Yet if the true Lord allows an arrow,
A tearing shaft from the tumult above,
To streak down straight through the rain,
He dies nevertheless. Not many live
Once the swift foeman's weapon has touched them.
I bring about the beginning of that conflict
When among the clash of clouds I go up
To thrust with power through the thickest of it
Above the cloud tops, where battalions
Deafen the heavens. Then I descend again
Below the cloud-cover close to the land
And, moved once more by my mighty Lord,
Hoist onto my back what I have to carry.

Thus I, a strong servant, stir wars by turns:
Sometimes under the earth, sometimes under the waves
Descending low; or I disturb the waters
Of ocean from above; or ascending high
I gather the cloud-wrack, career far
In my strength and swiftness. Say what I am called,
Or who arouses me when I must rest no more,
Or when I am still who stays me then.

The final questions are similar to those put by Chaucer's Man of
Law about the preservation of Constance:

since / *slain*	Now sith she was nat at the feeste yslawe,
	Who kepte hire fro the drenchyng in the see?
	Who kepte Jonas in the fysshes mawe
	Til he was spouted up at Nynyvee?
	Wel may men knowe it was no wight but he
Hebrew / *their*	That kepte peple Ebrayk from hir drenchynge,
	With drye feet throughout the see passynge.

(484-90)

But the Old English questions have no answer given; their formulation is deliberately enigmatic, as befits riddles. Their purpose is

not simply the vindication of Providence but equally the expression of awe. Other cosmological riddles have no theological reference, for example *Moon and Sun*:

A curious and wonderful creature I saw,
— Bright air-grail, brave artefact —
Homing from a raid with its haul of silver
Brimming precarious crescent horns.

To build itself a hideaway high up in the city,
A room in a tower, timbered with art,
Was all it aimed at, if only it might.

Then over the wall rose a wonder familiar
To the earth-race, to everyone known.

It gathered to itself the hoard, and to its home drove off
That unhappy outcast. Onward it coursed,
Wandered westward with wasting heart.

Dust rose to the skies, dew fell to the earth,
Night was no more. No man knew
Along what ways it wandered after.

That final awareness of the limits of human knowledge is a standard element in riddles. Most of the ninety-two Exeter Book examples have less elevated subjects, and some have more cunning than wonder in them.

I'm the world's wonder, for I make women happy
— A boon to the neighbourhood, a bane to no one,
Though I may perhaps prick the one who picks me.

I am set well up, stand in a bed,
Have a roughish root. Rarely (though it happens)
A churl's daughter more daring than the rest
— And far lovelier! —lays hold of me,
Rushes my red top, wrenches at my head,
And lays me in the larder.

> She learns soon enough,
> The curly-haired creature who clamps me so,
> Of my meeting with her: moist is her eye!

The answer scholars supply to this (the manuscript gives no answers) is Onion, although a less decent possibility is meant to come to mind. There are a number of such *double entendre* riddles but it is not only in them that the game of language half conceals and half reveals the object. Old English poetic diction, as we have seen earlier, "rang word-changes" not only in the well-known *kennings* such as "the world's candle" and "the sky's jewel" for sun, but constantly. The borrowing by critics of the Old Norse term *kenning* to describe such expressions is misleading if it suggests that "the gannet's bath" or "the whale's acre" are examples of a special technique for forming a figure of speech, for much of the texture of the verse language is figurative. Thus ingenuity and awe go hand in hand, in a way which a still popular idea of poetry, opposing artifice to sincerity, does not lead us to expect. Some of the riddles are, like the Gospel Book in chapter 2, just poems which need little or no thought to solve:

> Their dark bodies, dun-coated,
> When the breeze bears them up over the backs of the hills
> Are black, diminutive.
> > Bold singers,
> They go in companies, call out loudly;
> They tread the timbered cliff, and at times the eaves
> Of men's houses.
> > How do they call themselves?

Natural things are easier to identify than manmade objects. Scarcely more difficult than those Swallows or Martins is this bird:

> When it is earth I tread, make tracks upon water
> Or keep the houses, hushed is my clothing,
> Clothing that can hoist me above house-ridges,
> At times toss me into the tall heaven
> Where the strong cloud-wind carries me on

The Exeter Book

Over cities and countries; accoutrements that
Throb out sound, thrilling strokes,
Deep-soughing song, as I sail alone
Over field and flood, faring on,
Resting nowhere. My name is —.

After the reference to this bird's heavy wing-beat, the missing rhyme imported into the translation at the end is a simple clue. So is the end of the previous poem, which literally means "they name themselves."

At the other extreme from these natural poems is the fantastic number 85:

Many were met, men of discretion
Wisdom and wit, when in there walked ....

Two ears it had, and one eye solo,
Two feet and twelve hundred heads,
Back, belly, a brace of hands
A pair of sides and shoulders and arms
And one neck. Name, please.

The answer, A One-Eyed Garlic-Seller, is scarcely obvious. The poem is derived from a Latin riddle by the obscure Roman Symphosius, whose collection of 100 three-line riddles was known to the Anglo-Saxons. His *Luscus allium vendens*—Symphosius provides titles—also has 1200 heads, and clearly gave the idea for this one, as his *Flumen et Piscis* (River and Fish) did for number 84:

My home is not silent: I myself am not loud.
The Lord has provided for the pair of us
A joint expedition. I am speedier than he
And sometimes stronger; he stays the course better.
Sometimes I rest, but he runs on.
For as long as I live I live in him
If we leave one another it is I who must die.

Symphosius' riddle *Arundo* (*Reed*) also suggested riddle 60 in the Exeter Book:

I was by the sand at the sea-wall once:
Where the tide comes I kept my dwelling
Fast in my first seat. There were few indeed
Of human kind who cared to behold
My homeland in that lonely place,
But in every dawning the dark wave
Lapped about me. Little did I think
That early or late I ever should
Speak across the meadbench, mouthless as I am,
Compose a message. It is a mysterious thing,
Dark to the mind that does not know
How a knife's point and a clever hand,
A man's purpose and a point also,
Have pressed upon me to the purpose that
I might fearlessly announce, for none but us two,
A message to you, so that no man beside
Might spread abroad what is spoken between us.

To show how greatly the English poet has naturalised and
expanded his original, the original is given, with Wyatt's translation in brackets:

> Dulcis amica Dei, ripis vicina profundis,
> Suave canens Musis, nigro perfusa colore,
> Nuntia sum linguae, digitis stipata magistri.

> (I, the god's dear mistress, that dwell near the deep
> banks, sweetly singing to the Muses, overspread with
> black hue, I am the herald of my master's tongue
> when pressed light between his fingers.)

The *Reed* or *Reed Pen* is often taken as one of the most "Anglo-
Saxon" of the riddles; it certainly seems far away from the story in
Ovid's *Metamorphoses*, which lies behind the riddle of Symphosius,
of the nymph Syrinx who was turned into a reed to save her from
the unwanted attentions of the god Pan. Another very "Germanic" poem is number 35:

> The womb of the wold, wet and cold,

103

Bore me at first, brought me forth.
I know in my mind my making was not
Through skill with fells or fleeces of wool;
There was no winding of wefts, there is no woof in me,
No thread thrumming under the thrash of strokes,
No whirring shuttle steered through me,
No weaver's reed rapped my sides.
The worms that braid the broidered silk
With Weird cunning did not weave me;
Yet anywhere over the earth's breadth
Men will attest me a trustworthy garment.

Say truly, supple-minded man,
Wise in words, what my name is.

Yet this is derived from a Latin original *De Lorica* (*Mailshirt*) by the Anglo-Saxon monk, St. Aldhelm. These last examples illustrate the danger of always associating what is animistic and heathen with the Old English tradition and what is sophisticated and Christian with the Latin. There were supple-minded men, wise in words, in Britain and in Anglo-Saxon England before the advent of Theodore and Hadrian.

Cædmon himself was a cowman, and it was on his way to look after the cows that the angel appeared to him. It may be because of his humble occupation that Bede uses a ruminative analogy in speaking of his process of composition:

> They explained to him a passage of scriptural history or doctrine and asked him to render it into verse if he could. He ... returned next morning with excellent verses.... Cædmon stored up in his memory all that he had learned, and like one of the clean animals chewing the cud turned it into such melodious verse that his delightful renderings turned his instructors into auditors.
>
> (Bede, trans. Sherley-Price, p. 252)

Milton tells us that *Paradise Lost* was composed in a not dissimilar way; according to his nephew, the blind poet could be found in the garden in the morning calling "Milk me" to his daughters, who were to write the night's verses down.

The stable, the kitchen, the garden, the ploughed field, the woods, the sky, the table, and the study supply many of the subjects of the riddles. The monks who copied them and presumably composed some of them were surrounded by natural sights and sounds, like all other men of that age, and wrote of them with the same familiar observation and imaginative inwardness as did the Dorset poet, William Barnes, in the nineteenth century, and the old Irish monk who wrote in the margin of the manuscript of Cassiodorus on the Psalms that he was copying: "Pleasant is the glittering of the sun today upon these margins because it flickers so" (Nora Chadwick, *The Celts*, p. 258).

Aldhelm, Bede, his abbot Eusebius, Tatwine the archbishop of Canterbury, St. Boniface, and Alcuin all wrote riddles in Latin in a kind of clerical *conversazione*. These are among the greatest names of the Old English Church of the eighth century. Critics judge, however, that the riddles in Old English are richer as poems; in view of the inherited strengths of the medium of their composition, this is not surprising. Here are two which relate to the practice of writing, to give an idea of the physical circumstances in which our manuscripts were copied:

> I heard of a wonder, of words moth-eaten;
> That is a strange thing, I thought, weird
> That a man's song be swallowed by a worm,
> His binded sentences, his bedside stand-by
> Rustled in the night — and the robber-guest
> Not one whit the wiser for the words he had mumbled.

Then,

> I saw four fine creatures
> Travelling in company; their tracks were dark,
> Their trail very black. The bird that floats
> In the air swoops less swiftly than their leader;
> He dived beneath the wave. Drudgery was it
> For the fellow that taught all four of them their ways
> On their ceaseless visits to the vessel of gold.

The first is a Bookworm, the second a Hand Writing. Books were of skin, inkwells usually of horn—the subject of more than one riddle, part of one of which (number 92) follows:

> I catch in my mouth now
> Black wood and water; my belly contains
> Some dark thing that drops down upon me
> As I stand here on my single foot.
> Now my hoard is preyed on by a pilfering foe
> Who once carried far the comrade of the wolf.

The last allusion is to the quill of the raven, traditionally the comrade of the wolf (and of the eagle), after a battle. The habit of poetic circumlocution here also occurs memorably in another horn riddle, where the horn says it has "carried in his heart the hollow tree's fruit." The "hollow tree's fruit" is honey, used in the making of mead.

Bees are heard again in number 27:

> Men are fond of me. I am found everywhere,
> Brought in from the woods and the beetling cliffs,
> From down and from dale. In the daylight wings
> Raised me aloft, then into a roof's shade
> Swung me in sweetly. Sweltered then
> By men in a bath, I am a binder now,
> Soon a thrasher, a thrower next:
> I'll put an old fellow flat on the ground.
> A man who tries to take me on,
> Tests my strength, soon finds out,
> If his silly plan doesn't pall on him,
> That it is his back that will hit the dust.
> Loud in words, he has lost control
> Of his hands and feet, and his head doesn't work:
> His strength has gone. Guess my name
> Who have such mastery of men on earth
> That I knock them about in broad daylight.

This seems to be a traditional riddle, as is number 28, Barley:

Part of the earth is prepared fittingly
With what is hardest and what is sharpest
And what is least merciful of what men possess.
Cut down, rubbed out, rolled out, dried out,
Bound and twisted, blanched and sodden,
Decked and dollied, it is drawn from afar
To the doors of men. Mirth is indoors then
Among living creatures, increases and lasts
For as long as it lives. A long while
They have all they want—not a word against it—
But after it is gone they begin to mutter
And speak differently. A difficult matter
For a sagacious man to sound this creature.

These last examples make it obvious that the humour of folk riddles and the wit of art riddles cannot be firmly distinguished, although it is amusing that learned folklorists agree in attributing the dirty jokes to folk tradition. The Riddles have been a rather neglected department of Old English poetry, though scholars turn them over from time to time. As will be clear from the number included here, many of them, as well as conveniently illustrating the natural world of the Anglo-Saxons, have distinct poetic merit. Their pregnant brevity and enigmatic allusiveness give them a certain formal similarity to the Imagist poems of Ezra Pound which had such an influence on modern poetry. This accident may make them more accessible to us, as may the fact that they are the only body of very short poems in Old English. The most telling of them are like the simple *Swan*, the *Reed*, the *Rake*, or number 71, the *Ox*:

Small, I fed myself from four dear brothers,
Tugged at them often. Each of them gave me
To drink every day at different times
Though a small hole. I was happy in my growing up
Until I was of years to yield this task
To the dark herdsman. I went to distant places,
Trod the Welsh marches, trudged the upland
Roped beneath a beam, a ring on my neck.
I endured toil and trouble on that path,

My share of misery. Many times the iron
Sorely pricked my side. Silent was I:
To no man did I ever make complaint
Even when the pricks were painful to me.

But the most interesting riddles involve transformation, especially
those of the "I am" type. In these a material like wood, horn or
water speaks of the various forms in which it appears to men.
Number 30 is a good example.

I am fire-fretted and I flirt with Wind
And my limbs are light-freighted and I am lapped in flame
And I am storm-stacked and I strain to fly
And I am a grove leaf-bearing and a glowing ember.

From hand to friend's hand about the hall I go,
So much do lords and ladies love to kiss me.
When I hold myself high, and the whole company
Bow quiet before me, their blessedness
Shall flourish skyward beneath my fostering shade.

The last stage of wood is as the Tree: we shall meet it again in *The
Dream of the Rood*. In such riddles the riddle enables us not only
to enter into the nature of the object but to participate in its life-
process almost in a religious way.

II • VERSE WISDOM

Allied to the Riddles are the Gnomic Verses and other verse
forms involving proverbial wisdom. The Gnomic Verses, or Maxims, of the Exeter Book consist of generic laws of behaviour for
nature and society, proverbial and miscellaneous. This extract is
set out so as to emphasise the structure of the half-lines:

Frost shall freeze
            fire eat wood
Earth shall breed
            ice shall bridge

Water a shield wear.
>One shall break
Frost's fetters
>free the grain
From wonder-lock
>— One who all can.

Winter shall wane
>fair weather come again
The sun-warmed summer!
>The sound unstill,
The deep dead wave,
>is darkest longest.
Holly shall to the pyre,
>hoard be scattered
When the body's numb.
>Name is best.

A king shall win
>a queen with goods
Beakers, bracelets.
>Both must first
Be kind with gifts.
>Courage must wax
War-mood in the man,
>the woman grow up
Beloved among her people,
>be light of mood
Hold close a rune-word
>be roomy-hearted
At hoard-share and horse-giving.

>When the hall drinks
She shall always and everywhere
>before any company
Greet first
>the father of æthelings
With the first draught
>— deft to his hand she

Holds the horn
                    and when they are at home together
Know the right way
                    to run their household.

The ship must be nailed
                    the shield framed
From the light linden.
                    But how loving the welcome
Of the Frisian wife
                    when floats offshore
The keel come home again !
                    She calls him within walls,
Her own husband
                    — hull's at anchor!
Washes salt-stains
                    from his stiff shirt
Brings out clothes
                    clean and fresh
For her lord on land again.
                    Love's need is met.

                                                    (71-99)

Another translation of other Gnomic Verses is provided by the
Australian poet A. D. Hope in his essay "Poetry and Platitude":

    The Hawk shall on the glove,
The wild one, dwell, the Wolf in grove
The wretched and solitary one, the boar in the wood
Stout in the power of his tusks; the good man shall in his land
Gain glory; the javelin shall in the hand,
The spear ornamented with gold; the gem shall in the ring
Stand forth wide and high; the stream shall in waves
Mingle with the sea-flood; the mast shall be on the ship,
The sailyard remain; the sword lie on the breast,
The noble iron; the dragon shall be in the mound
Wise, proud of his treasure; the fish in the water
Bring forth its kind; the King shall in the hall
Distribute rings; the bear shall be on the heath

Old and dreadful; the waters from the hill shall
Fare flood-grey; the troops shall go together
In a glorious band; Trust shall be in the earl,
Wisdom in man; the wood upon the earth shall
Bloom with life; the mound on the earth shall
Stand forth green; God shall be in heaven,
Judge of deeds; the door shall be in the hall
The broad mouth of the building; the boss shall be on
    the shield
A firm protection for the fingers: the bird aloft shall
Sport in the air.

                       (*The Cave and the Spring*, p. 13)

The Exeter Book contains several wisdom poems, to which the editors of *The Anglo-Saxon Poetic Records* give the titles *The Gifts of Men, Precepts, Vainglory, The Fortunes of Men, The Order of the World, Soul and Body II, Resignation, Homiletic Fragment II*. Some of these might equally be called religious verse. A useful suggestive passage for how the Anglo-Saxons saw the link between creation and Creator, between wisdom and faith, opens *The Order of the World*:

Art thou willing, O man,   to exchange words
with a stranger,   a wise speaker,
  to ask a far-traveller   about Creation,
pray him to tell thee   of the natural powers,
full of life and vigour,   of all vast things made,
things that every day,   by God's deeming,
bring many marvels   to the nations of men?
O thoughtful man,   'tis a clear sign
to all those   who by their wisdom
ponder the world   in their wondering minds,
that in days long gone,   by the craft of the gleeman,
steadfast men   through their songs
could utter the truth,   say right things,
so that always asking,   remembering and telling,
other men came to know   the web of mysteries.
So let him ever ask,   —he who lives strongly,
the deep-hearted man—   of the hidden things,
write in his mind   the store of his word-hoard,

fix his thoughts on them,   ponder them well.
A high-minded thane   must not grow weary
of wisely considering   the course of the world.

(Williams, p. 176)

As Bede says of his Latin prose version of Cædmon's *Hymn*, "vers-es, however masterly, cannot be translated literally from one language into another without losing much of their beauty and dignity" (p. 251). Old English verse cannot be accurately translated into modern English prose of any elegance—its serpentine syntax, full of suspension and apposition, fails to dance in the restricted word order of modern English. Even Garmonsway's splendid prose *Beowulf* has dignity rather than beauty. Williams' literal translation above makes these lines drag. But Anglo-Saxon England was a haven for such ancient mariners as our author, for its inhabitants could not resist such invitations as that of his opening sentence.

Throughout the Middle Ages, indeed down to the time of Erasmus Darwin in the eighteenth century, verse was used to instruct, to make knowledge memorable. The Church exploited this recognised function of Old English verse for popularising scriptural history and doctrine. But the special connection between "the art of song" and "knowledge of the web of mysteries," as spelled out at length in *The Order of the World*, indicates the established role of verse in formulating this often enigmatic traditional lore. King Alfred's earnest desire for learning and wisdom, though in him it took a sharply practical form, was already deeply characteristic of English literature. Little of the wisdom literature is touched with imaginative necessity, still less with a sense of form. But it provides a context for such lines in *Beowulf* as:

But Hengest still
As he was constrained to do, stayed with Finn
A death-darkened winter in dreams of his homeland.
He was prevented from passage of the sea
In his ring-beaked boat: the boiling ocean
Fought with the wind; winter locked the seas
In his icy binding; until another year
Came at last to the dwellings, as it does still,

Continually keeping its season,
The weather of rainbows.
                              Now winter had fled
And earth's breast was fair, the exile strained
To leave these lodgings; yet it was less the voyage
That exercised his mind than the means of his vengeance,
The bringing about of the bitter conflict
That he meditated for the men of the Jutes.
So he did not decline the accustomed remedy,
When the son of Hunlaf set across his knees
That best of blades, his battle-gleaming sword;
The Giants were acquainted with the edges of that steel.

                                              (1127-45)

The behaviour of the world and of the men and women who lived in it was ruled by law and custom. Spring follows winter; blood will have blood. This predictability and inevitability are sealed into nature, and these laws are known to the wise through poetry. If limited, it is also a deeply satisfying mandate for poetry. *Swa sceal man don*, says Beowulf to Hrothgar, using the modal auxiliary verb used in all *Gnomic Verses*: "A man must act so."

FIVE : BEDE AND CÆDMON

THE Christian literature of Anglo-Saxon England has had a rather mixed reception in modern times. A serious interest in it as a whole rather than simply in its purple passages presupposes an effort to understand the desire for a kingdom which is not of this world, and a tolerance for the miraculous. Purple passages are all that can actually appear here, in black and white translation, and yet even a preliminary understanding of Anglo-Saxon culture as a whole demands acknowledgement of the set of all the early medieval thought and civilisation of the west toward Rome, and a minimal awareness of the Fathers of the Church. The Latin version of the Bible known as the Vulgate was prepared by Jerome to put the Hebrew and Greek Bible into the common tongue, for Latin was in the late fourth century not the language of learning but the vernacular of the western empire. The Vulgate and the Catholic liturgy were the basic texts of the men who wrote our manuscripts. Some writings of Ambrose, Augustine, and especially Gregory were scarcely less influential. Classical Latin was also available in libraries to a greater extent than used to be supposed. However, the most popular prose forms, at the Conversion and later, were the homily (the proper name for a sermon on the scriptural readings at mass) and the Saint's Life, a popularity which has waned. These forms only attained literary distinction late in our period in the prose of Ælfric, yet it is upon this tide that float the fragments of what we now call literature.

There was Latin literature in Britain before the Anglo-Saxons: the heresiarch Pelagius and the querulous chronicler Gildas contribute in their different ways to the early pages of Bede's *Ecclesiastical History*. Bede's older contemporary St. Aldhelm had a great reputation as writer and scholar, though modern Latinists are tempted to patronise his bewilderingly precious style (quoted on pages 42 and 43). He is one of the five Old English poets whose names are known to us, but his English verse is lost. The twelfth-century chronicler William of Malmesbury credibly reports King Alfred's stated opinion that Aldhelm was unequalled in any age in his ability to compose poetry in his native tongue (C.L. Wrenn, *A Study of Old English Literature*, p. 93). Alfred, we know, was devoted to Old English poetry, but it is possible that it was Aldhelm's brilliant facility and sophistication that so impressed the king, whose own literary virtues were of the very opposite kind. In the two intervening centuries the literacy of Wessex had been eclipsed, and in retrospect Aldhelm must have shone like a comet. William also reports a tradition of Abbot Aldhelm standing on a bridge leading to Malmesbury improvising Old English verses to the harp and successfully attracting the attention of his straying flock.

Aldhelm was the pupil of a Cilician Greek and an African Roman, and his style is both Mediterranean and British, full of multilingual plays on words in the style known as "hisperic," after a sixth-century work, the *Hisperica Famina*. Aldhelm was the star of Hadrian's school at Canterbury, and his authority was evidently recognised by his godson Aldfrith, king of Northumbria from 685 to 705. The establishment of the Canterbury school in 668 is described by Wrenn as "the most decisive happening for education, and therefore indirectly for literature, in Anglo-Saxon history" (*A Study*, p. 59). The school inaugurated the golden age whose achievements north of the Humber are, thanks to Bede, better known to us.

After Gregory himself, Theodore of Tarsus is the key figure in the development of Anglo-Saxon Christianity and letters. When he and Hadrian came to Britain, their interpreter was Benedict Biscop, a Northumbrian nobleman and a monk. Theodore made

Benedict abbot at Canterbury but he soon went north to found the monasteries first of Wearmouth (674) and then of Jarrow (681). Benedict travelled frequently to France and Italy (visiting Rome six times) to get glaziers and stonemasons to beautify these churches to the glory of God "in the Roman fashion, which he always loved" (Bede, p. 63). These acquisitions were of great benefit to local craftsmen and artists. But the chief aid to the spreading of the word were Benedict's "innumerable" books. He died in 689, says Bede, giving orders for "the most glorious and copious library which he brought from Rome, needful to the teaching of the Church, to be diligently kept whole and complete, and not marred by neglect, nor scattered abroad" (Bede, p. 63). Aldhelm showed what Saxons could do in literature, but apart from his riddles his copious Latin output does not seem to have been fruitfully imitated either in Latin or in the vernacular. Benedict Biscop's book purchases, however, put Bede in a position from which his writings could become the most widely influential in the Europe of his day. From Bede to Alcuin Northumbria produced the leading scholars of western Europe. And from a more provincial modern point of view, the *Historia Ecclesiastica Gentis Anglorum* has been continuously read for several centuries longer than any other English book.

Bede's Northumbria was not provincial: Gregory's evangelisation of the Angles was answered by a personal devotion to Rome evident in the lives of many leading men and women down to 1066. The influence of Rome was direct, widespread, and lasting. For example, among the signatories of the affirmation of the Catholic faith at the Synod of Hatfield in 680 was, Bede tells us,

> the venerable John, Arch-cantor of the church of the holy Apostle Peter and Abbot of the monastery of Saint Martin, who had recently come from Rome under instructions from Pope Agatho with the most reverend Abbot Benedict, of whom I have spoken. For when Benedict had built a monastery in Britain near the mouth of the River Wear [Monkwearmouth] in honour of the blessed Prince of the Apostles, he travelled to Rome with his colleague and partner in the work, Ceolfrid, who later succeeded him as abbot of the monastery. As he had made several earlier visits to

Rome, he was received with honour by Pope Agatho of blessed memory. From him he asked and obtained a letter of privilege, granted with his apostolic authority, which confirmed the independence of the monastery that he had founded; for he knew this to accord with the wishes of King Egfrid, with whose approval and grant he had built the monastery.

Benedict received Abbot John and conducted him to Britain, where he was to teach his monks the chant for the liturgical year as it was sung at Saint Peter's, Rome. In accordance with the Pope's instructions, Abbot John taught the cantors of the monastery the theory and practice of singing and reading aloud, and he put into writing all that was necessary for the proper observance of festivals throughout the year. This document is still preserved in this monastery, and many copies have been made for other places. John's instruction was not limited to the brethren of this monastery, for men who were proficient singers came from nearly all the monasteries of the province to hear him, and he received many invitations to teach elsewhere.

(Bede, trans. Sherley-Price, pp. 236–37)

The Gregorian chant introduced by the Cantor of St. Peter's own church in Rome is still in use today in the monasteries of the English Benedictine Congregation and their offspring in the United States.

Bede was placed by his parents under Benedict Biscop's supervision at the age of seven, became a deacon and a priest at Jarrow, and passed his life there. The *Ecclesiastical History* was the work of his later years, when he was already famous for his many commentaries on Scripture and his writings on chronology. Exegesis of the Bible was the central activity of clerical scholarship for centuries after Gregory the Great, and chronology was most important for settling the controversy over the date of Easter which long divided the British churches. Both these activities were to be useful to Bede the historian: the understanding of the true spiritual meaning of events, and the firm grasp of order and detail. On the way to the *Ecclesiastical History* Bede wrote saints' lives, including two of the most revered saint of the Anglo-

Saxons, Cuthbert of Lindisfarne (*c.*634–87), one in verse and one in prose. It says something of the difference between the worlds of Anglo-Latin and of Old English that scholars have been able to trace in the 979 verses of the *Life* of Cuthbert the influence of twenty Latin authors (including Virgil, Ovid, and Horace, as well as Augustine, Fortunatus, and Aldhelm), and that thirty-six complete MSS of the prose life survive. There are over one hundred MSS of Bede's *De Natura Rerum*, one of the five didactic works he left; others are on grammar and metre; there is also a collection of fifty homilies, and a variety of verse. At the end of his *Ecclesiastical History* Bede gives a list of the books he has written, which run to some ninety volumes. One of the last is the *History of the Abbots* of Wearmouth and Lindisfarne, from which Bolton usefully translates two passages relating to Benedict Biscop. The first expounds the ideal of monasticism with some eloquence:

> He was born of a noble family of the race of the English, but was lifted up to the merited companionship of angels forever, being of no less nobility of mind. For when he was a minister of King Oswy, and received from that giver the possession of a plot of land suitable for his degree, when he was about twenty-five years old, he disdained perishable possessions, that he might acquire eternal ones; he despised earthly warfare with its corruptible gifts, so that he might fight for the true King, and deserve to have perpetual reign in the celestial city; he left his home, his family, and his homeland for Christ and for the Gospel, that he might receive a hundredfold, and possess eternal life; he refused to serve carnal marriage, so that he might be worthy to follow the Lamb, bright with the glory of virginity, in the heavenly kingdom; he declined to engender mortal children of the flesh, being predestined by Christ to rear for Him sons in spiritual teaching to be everlasting in the heavenly life.
>
> (Bolton, *Anglo-Latin*, p. 179)

The second suggests the splendour of Wearmouth and also gives a pictorial analogy to the allegorical or "typical" tradition Bede employed in his historical as well as his exegetical works.

For also at this time he brought pictures of the Lord's history, with which he crowned round about the whole church of the blessed Mother of God, which he had built in the greater monastery; he also displayed paintings collected to show the concord in the highest sense of the Old and New Testaments, for the ornament of the monastery and church of blessed Paul the Apostle; for example, he juxtaposed in a picture Isaac carrying the faggots on which he was to be immolated, and in the next space above the Lord carrying the cross on which He was to suffer. Likewise he compared the Son of Man lifted up on the cross to the serpent lifted by Moses in the desert.

(Bolton, pp. 179–80)

I • THE *ECCLESIASTICAL HISTORY*

The *Historia Ecclesiastica Gentis Anglorum* and the Lives are the only works of Bede which have a modern readership; the exegesis and chronography which were the basis of his medieval fame have sunk below the horizon, except for medievalists. The *Ecclesiastical History*, however, is a work of great ability and of great charm. If it did not exist we might know very little of early England and of that event of much consequence, her conversion to Christianity. Historians owe a large debt to Bede, who in an age when there were few who might be called chroniclers is considered a great historian. He consulted documents whenever possible and included them often; he had a critical sense of other evidence, specifying his sources and the degree of directness of their witness. He has a sense of fact unusual in his era, and was authoritatively clear about chronology in an age which had four different days for beginning the year, and in an England which contained seven kingdoms, in each of which events were dated by the year of the reign. These professional achievements are admired by modern historians — but may be taken for granted by those who read no other medieval historians. Such readers will appreciate the transparency of his style and the clarity of his narrative, and enjoy his portraits, his stories, and his set-pieces. He has eminently the quality of fairness, a fairness grounded in

Benedictine simplicity, moderation, and scholarship, even — at times — towards erring Celts. The great but impossible Wilfrid, for instance, suffers for his immodesty only by the way his restless life is split up into separate parts of the history. There are of course biases: British pagans like Penda of Mercia are treated differently from pagans like Aethelfrith of Northumbria. Penda, who twice put an end to the Northumbrian Church, is treated with some of the horror attached to Ongentheow in *Beowulf;* but even of him Bede records that in old age he had no objection to Christianity and wished only that Christians would live up to their beliefs. Bede is consistently pained when the Welsh or the Irish are obstinate toward the authority of Peter and of reason. For Bede is orthodox as well as English; he has a high boiling-point. His tone becomes strained beyond the eirenic only twice, outside the *History,* in letters: once where he defends himself against a misconceived charge of heresy made before Wilfrid; and in his letter of 734 to Egbert, bishop of York, pointing out that it is Egbert's duty to put some disorderly monastic houses in order.

Bede's greatest bias, of course, is his desire for God. His *History* is, as its title declares, Church history, but the modern reader will be perplexed by the high incidence of miracles in this otherwise sober book, one or two directly vouched for by the author. Miracles are not to be explained. A Tibetan monk once remarked to me that in the West you do not expect miracles to happen, so they do not happen. The lives of the saints who brought the *god spel* to the Angles might be expected to be marked with signs of God's favour, and so they were. Hagiography, an essential part of the *History,* was required daily by the monastic rule for pious reading and for the Lections at Matins; and the Church had not yet appointed a Devil's Advocate to check the process of formal canonisation. Standard patterns of miracles can be recognised in the different types of saints' lives. It is notable however that in the Lives of the abbots whom Bede knew, there are no miracles. But the miraculous fits into the *Ecclesiastical History* as one element in the pattern of God's providence that was the true if mysterious pattern of history. Bede was by profession a commentator on the Bible, and the *History* is a sequel both to the history of the people of Israel and to the Acts of the Apostles. Thus Aethelfrith of Northumbria, "a very powerful and ambitious king," ruled the kingdom of the Northumbrians. He ravaged the Britons more cruelly than all other English leaders, so that he might well be compared to Saul the King of Israel, except of course that he was ignorant of true religion. He overran a greater area than any other king or ealdorman, exterminating or enslaving the inhabitants, making their lands either tributary to the English or ready for English settlement. One might fairly apply to him the words of the patriarch Jacob's blessing of his son: "Benjamin shall ravin as a wolf; in the morning he shall devour the prey, and at night he shall divide the spoil."

(Bede, I, 34, trans. Sherley-Price, p. 97)

The pagan Aethelfrith was, like Saul, a great warrior king of his people; if bloodthirsty, he was like Saul under the Old Law. His slaughter of the British monks who had come to pray for a (Christian) victory at the Battle of Chester was, writes the English monk Bede, a fulfilment of Augustine's prophecy that "the faithless Britons, who had rejected the offer of eternal salvation, would incur the punishment of temporal destruction" (Bede, II, 2, p. 107). The process of interpreting English by Israelite history is fully analogous to the parallel rows of Old and New Testament pictures in Benedict Biscop's church.

The great appeal of Bede for modern readers is the series of stories from living tradition which warm the account especially of Northumbrian history: Gregory in the market-place; Edwin's conversion and reign; Oswald at Heavenfield; Aidan's preaching on foot; the Synod of Whitby; Cuthbert's reluctance to leave Lindisfarne. Some of the most memorable of these scenes are clearly polished by loving retelling. Professional historians respect Bede because he sent Nothelm to check the Vatican archives, but perhaps, like their weaker literary brethren, they like him because he tells a good story. And from Bede as from no other writer can be gathered a picture of the physical life of Anglo-Saxon England, especially of its northern and eastern coasts.

Two of his stories must suffice: Colman on Inishboffin and Cædmon at Whitby. Bishop Colman of Lindisfarne was the leader of the losing "Scots" party at the Synod of Whitby. In IV.4 Bede relates:

Colman left Britain, taking with him all the Scots he had collected at Lindisfarne, together with about thirty English whom he had likewise trained in the monastic life. Leaving some brethren in his own church, he first visited the isle of Hii [Iona], from which he had originally been sent to preach the word to the English. He subsequently retired to a small island at some distance from the west coast of Ireland, known in the Scots tongue as Inisboufinde, meaning the Isle of the White Heifer. On his arrival, he founded a monastery, and established there the monks of both races whom he had gathered. But a dispute arose among them because in summer the Scots went off to wander on their own around places they knew instead of assisting at harvest, and then, as winter approached, came back and wanted to share whatever the English monks had gathered. Colman sought a remedy for this dispute, and after searching near and far, discovered a site suitable for a monastery on the Irish mainland, a place which the Scots call Mageo [Mayo].

(Bede, trans. Sherley-Price, p. 212)

Colman established the English monks there, leaving the Scots on the original island.

In tying up this loose end, Bede the English churchman is pleased to record the improvidence of the Gael and the pastoral skill of Colman—and especially that this English community at Mayo now flourishes. The second story is famous and has already been quoted, but must now be given in full. In the ninth century there was an "Alfredian" version of the *Ecclesiastical History* into West Saxon, which is often preferred at this point, but here C. L. Wrenn's translation from Bede's Latin is given:

In the monastery of this abbess [St. Hild] there was a certain brother specially distinguished by divine grace because he was accustomed to making poems fitting to religion and piety. This he did in such wise that, whatsoever he had learned from divine Scriptures through interpreters, this he himself after a short time would bring forth in his own tongue—that is, the language of the Angles—composed in poetic words with the greatest sweetness and moving quality.

By these poems of his the minds of many were often enkindled to the despising of the world and to the longing for the heavenly life. Yet indeed there were others after him among the people of the Angles who strove to make religious poems: but none was ever able to match him. For himself had learned the art of poesy not through men nor taught by a man: but he had received the gift of song freely by divine aid. Wherefore he could never make anything of frivolous or vain poetry, but only those verses which belong to piety, which were becoming to that religious tongue of his. In fact he had been settled in the secular way of life until he was of advanced age [*provectioris aetatis*]: and he had not at any time learned anything of poems. Hence it was that sometimes when at a party [*convivium*] when it had been decided for joyful entertainment that all in turn must recite verses to the harp's accompaniment [*cantare*, which the Alfredian translation renders *be hearpan singan*], he when he saw the harp getting near to himself would arise from the midst of the feast and go out and walk back to his house. [Here the Alfredian version adds that it was from a feeling of shame, *for scome*, that he did this.] When on a certain occasion he had done this, and leaving the house where the party was held had gone out to the cattle-pens, as their care had been assigned to him for that night, and when there he had at the normal time given his limbs to sleep, a certain man was standing by him in a dream and, greeting him and calling him by his name, said: "Cædmon, sing me something." But he in answering said: "I do not know how to sing: for it was just for this reason that I came away from the feast and departed hither, because I could not sing." Again he who was talking with him said: "Yet you can sing to me." "What," said Cædmon, "must I sing?" Then the other said: "Sing of the beginning of created things." Now when Cædmon had received this answer, immediately he began to sing verses in praise of God the creator which he had never heard, of which this is the sense [*quorum iste est sensus*]: "Now we must praise the Author of the Kingdom of Heaven, the might of the Creator and the thoughts of His mind—the deeds of the Father of glory. [We must sing] how he who is eternal

God, the Author of all marvellous things, was manifest: he who first created heaven as a roof-covering for the sons of men, and then as almighty guardian of mankind made the earth." This is the sense but not the actual order of the words [*hic est sensus, non autem ordo ipse verborum*] of what Cædmon had sung while sleeping. For poems, however excellently composed, cannot be translated word for word from one language into another without damage to elegance and dignity. Now when he had risen from his sleep, he retained in his memory everything which he had sung while sleeping. And to these verses he quickly added more in the same rhythm and metre [*in eundum modum*] in words of a poem worthy of God.

When morning had come, he went to the steward who was his chief and showed him what sort of gift he had received. He was then conducted to the Abbess and commanded to show what he had dreamed in the presence of many learned men and to recite the poem: so that by the judgment of everyone it might be tested of what kind or from whence had come what he had related. And it seemed to them all that it was a grace from heaven and granted by God. Then they expounded to him a discourse of sacred history or doctrine, and commanded him, if he could, to render this into the melody of poetry [*in modulationem carminis*]. So he, when he had finished these matters, went away: and in the morning he came back and produced it composed as had been ordered in the most excellent poetry. Wherefore the Abbess, immediately embracing the grace of God in the man, instructed him with a proposal that he should abandon the secular habit and take that of a monk. So she added him, with his goods, after receiving him into the monastery, to the company of the brethren: and she commanded that he should be taught the whole sequence of sacred Scripture. Now he, taking all that he could learn by hearing, retaining it in his mind, and turning it over like a clean beast ruminating [*quasi mundum animal ruminando*], converted it into the sweetest poetry. Indeed by the sweetness of its melody he made his teachers in their turn become his listeners. Now he sang of the creation of the world and of the origin of the human race and the whole narrative of Genesis, concerning the going out from Egypt of the Israelites and their entry into the land of promise. He sang about very many other historical parts of sacred Scripture, about the Incarnation of the Lord, His Passion, Resurrection, and Ascension into heaven, about the coming of the Holy Ghost and the teaching of the Apostles. Likewise he made many songs of the terror of Judgment to come and the horror of the punishment of hell and the sweetness of the heavenly kingdom. But furthermore he made very many other compositions concerning divine blessings and judgments, by all of which he sought to turn men's minds from delight in wickedness-es, and indeed to stir them to the love and skilful practice of good deeds. For he was a most religious man who subjected himself with humility to the disciplines of monastic rule. But against others who wished to act otherwise he was aflame with fervid zeal. Hence it was that he closed his life with a beautiful ending.

(*A Study of Old English Literature*, pp. 92–94)

II • CÆDMON

The Old English manuscript now called the Junius Book contains four poems, known as *Genesis, Exodus, Daniel,* and *Christ and Satan.* The Dutch Anglo-Saxonist Junius printed the book in Amsterdam in 1655 with a Latin title reading "The monk Cædmon's poetical paraphrase of Genesis etc." The assumption, which lasted until the twentieth century, that the poems were Cædmon's was natural, since their subjects coincide with the beginning of Bede's list of his works. But it has collapsed, as will be seen, like the idea that King Alfred had himself translated Bede's *Ecclesiastical History*; and scholars have fallen back on "Cædmonian" and "Alfredian." Only Cædmon's *Hymn* is his for certain (and the English texts are found in the margin of Latin MSS): the other poems are "school of Cædmon," the work of those "others after him among the people of the Angles who strove to make religious poems."

John Milton has a note in the Trinity MS (in which he wrote down possible subjects for epic) referring to Bede's tale of Cædmon as *perplacida historiola*, a most pleasing little story. As we have seen, the analogy between the composition of *Paradise Lost* and of Cædmon's lay of Creation extends to the end product being compared to that of a cleanly ruminative beast. Milton knew Junius and could read Old English, so the hypothesis that *Paradise Lost* owes something to the Cædmonian *Genesis* is seductive though not safe. There are striking similarities, even down to "darkness visible," the chief of which is in the dramatic conception of Satan, and in the scorn of the fallen angel's first speech in hell:

> "Is thes ænga styde ungelic swithe
> tham othrum ham the we ær cuthon,
> heah on heofonrice...."
>
> (356–58)

Literally:

> "This narrow place is very much unlike
> That other home which we knew before,
> High in heaven's Kingdom...."

What may have attracted Milton to Bede's story is the *calling* of Cædmon: the very arbitrariness of the divine intervention seizing on and then inspiring this cowherd who first taught the chosen seed. Milton boasts that Urania "dictates to me slumb'ring ... easy my unpremeditated verse." Such a process of composition implies possession by tradition, that Hebrew-based tradition of the early Church, amplifying and filling in the Bible story, which is the common basis of both Cædmon and Milton. They also both belong to the sacred tradition of inspired epic composition and utterance. Bede says Cædmon composed poems on the whole Christian cycle from Creation to Doomsday—an epic indeed, of which the Junius MS poems are only a beginning.

The Junius Book has the best intentions of the four major poetry manuscripts. It has a programme of illustration and the four poems have, compared with the other manuscripts, a logical order. But, like the others, it was copied long after its poems were composed, and the cosmic scheme breaks down in a rather disconcerting way. As we read through the manuscript, the illustrations stop and the competence of the scribes decreases. After 235 lines of *Genesis* the story begins to repeat itself in a different style, only to resume the original matter and manner at line 852. In 1875 the German scholar Eduard Sievers declared that, on the evidence of its versification and style, this interpolated passage (now known as *Genesis B*) must have been translated into Old English from Old Saxon, the language of the continental cousins of the Anglo-Saxons. What little there is of Old Saxon writing dates from the conversion of the Germans to Christianity by the West Saxon St. Boniface of Crediton in the eighth century. Sievers' hypothesis was proved to be correct nineteen years later by the discovery in the Vatican of a fragment of the Old Saxon original he had postulated. It is of the ninth century, whereas *Genesis A* is agreed to be not later than the early eighth. This is the major surprise in the manuscript, but there are several others. Each of the other poems is thought to be by a different author and it is not clear whether *Christ and Satan* is one poem or three. In general the Cædmonian poems, especially *Daniel* and *Christ and Satan*, have not until recently had the exhaustive attention that has been lavished on *Beowulf* and the Elegies.

The old view was that they were Teutonicised paraphrases of uneven literary quality, which worked best when most thoroughly assimilated to the heroic tradition, as in the conflict of loyalties in the Fall of the Angels in *Genesis B* or the Red Sea crossing of *Exodus*; but much remained unassimilated, unGermanic and moreover unBiblical. More recently a sophisticated and learned defence of these poems has gained ground, approaching them in the light of the allegorical procedures of the Church Fathers and other exegetical writers on the Bible. This allegorical approach, which at its best is historical and comparative, provides a welcome basis for understanding a powerful but now unfamiliar mode in medieval Christian poetry, and not only in the Anglo-Saxon period. Thus in *Exodus* the story of the Israelites' deliverance from Egypt proceeds, with Moses as their great war-leader and powerful descriptions of the pillars of fire and smoke, reaching a great climax of anticipation as the Egyptian host catches up with them. Then in a speech Moses tells the people how with his rod he has

parted the waters of the Red Sea, a sign of God's mercy. R.K.
Gordon's selected translation of Old English poetry reads as follows:

"... Haste is best, that ye may escape from the clutch of your
foes, now that the Lord has raised up the red waves as a rampart. The bulwarks are fairly built up to the vault of the sky,
a wondrous way through the sea."

After these words the host all rose up, the army of brave
men; the sea remained quiet. The troops raised their white
shields, the standards on the shore. The wall of waters
mounted up; upright it stood hard by the Israelites for the
space of a day; the band of men was resolute; the wall of
waves held them in safety in its firm embraces.

[A passage of about 150 lines follows of little interest. An
account of the order in which the tribes marched through
the Red Sea is begun, but is interrupted rather suddenly by a
description of Noah's flood and the story of Abraham. The
narrative is then resumed with a vivid picture of the Egyptians' overthrow.]

Panic fell on the people; the terror of the flood beset their
sad souls. The abyss threatened death. The mountainous
waters were bedewed with blood; the sea spewed forth gore;
there was uproar in the waves, the water full of weapons; a
deadly mist mounted up. The Egyptians were turned back
again; they fled in fear; they felt sudden terror; panic-strick-
en they wished to seek out their homes; less blithe was their
boasting.

(Gordon, p. 117)

Gordon's *Anglo-Saxon Poetry* was published in Everyman's
Library in 1926, and everyman might still share his opinion that
Noah and Abraham rather suddenly interrupt a passage which, in
translation at least, is of little interest. But the deliverance of Noah
from the Flood and the favour shown by God to Abraham and his
children because he had been willing to sacrifice Isaac were of

interest to the author of *Exodus* because they had the same significance as the deliverance at the Red Sea—that history shows that in adversity those who trust in the Lord are rewarded. These parallels from Genesis were not only relevant but would indeed be expected by someone who had listened to homilies in such churches as that at Monkwearmouth. Just as, in Benedict Biscop's scheme of paintings, Isaac carrying the faggots for his own sacrifice was a type of Christ carrying his Cross, so the trial of Moses recalled the previous trials of Noah, who faced death by water, and Abraham, the first patriarch of Israel. The relevance of such examples for the patriarchal kingdoms of Anglo-Saxon England must have been obvious to whoever composed *Exodus*. The tale of Constance told by Chaucer's Man of Law (see p. 98) offers merely a more polished example of such thinking.

In the light of such an approach, the introduction of Noah and Abraham as examples of justified faith no longer seems unintelligible, nor so sudden. But the modern reader might expect such *exempla* to be saved for a peroration, after the discomfiture of Pharoah's army. On the contrary, the Old English poet brings them in before his climax, when Moses stretches forth his hand over the sea. Stranger still, he leaves out his climax by having Moses *explain* that he has parted the sea with his rod. Novelists and teachers know that it is dramatically more effective to "show" rather than "tell." Why does the poet, who excels in his powerful descriptions of natural forces and the stupendous drowning of the army, miss his chance here? The solution to this must lie in a difference of priorities: the Old English poet, unlike Cecil B. De Mille, was less interested in the action than in the significance of the action. Implicitly, the action is already known to the audience.

This narrative technique is paralleled in *Beowulf*'s emphasis not upon the monster-fights so much as upon the hero's state of mind before the fight—the ethical rather than the physical trial. We see Beowulf isolated and gloomy yet resolute upon the headland; whereas the Scyldings have earlier deserted the cliff-head by the Mere. Before Wiglaf decides to join Beowulf in his trial we must hear his reasons in full, and even the history of his sword and its owners. Such delays in the action used to be seen by critics as tension-reducing digressions, but it is clear that to the audience they actually enriched the action. The maximum interest of such heroic stories is at the moments of decision—and even in secular poems these are ethical decisions. In *The Battle of Maldon*, to take a simple case, when Byrhtnoth has fallen and the retainers are left, Aelfwine speaks first:

> "Remember the speeches spoken over mead,
> Battle-vows on the bench, the boasts we vaunted,
> Heroes in hall, against the harsh war-trial!
> Now shall be proven the prowess of the man."
>
> (212–15)

Then, before advancing on the enemy, he explains his ancestry. The moment of trial or test, of this supreme interest, could be prolonged or amplified by comparison with parallel or previous cases, and this is such a regular feature of Anglo-Saxon narratives that it clearly gave satisfaction to its connoisseurs. In the stories of the Old Norse *Poetic Edda* what actually happened is of an interest so entirely secondary that it is discovered only with difficulty: we only hear what was said, and how, and even here the delight is in compression, allusion, and understatement. Something similar can be seen in the Finn episode in *Beowulf* (see p. 71).

The conventions of heroic narrative poetry, evolved for a secular purpose, were thus continued in the Biblical poems of the Cædmonian school, not only in such tried motifs as the descriptions of a people on the march or of the birds and beasts of battle, but also in the selection and order of incidents and the high proportion of speech to action. *Exodus* is not a retelling of the book of the Pentateuch so much as a rhetorical excursion upon key incidents in the story: not so much paraphrase as periphrasis. The modern reader perhaps expects from heroic poetry a story of action. There is tumultuous dramatic action in *Exodus*, but the mode is less visual than rhetorical: there is an expansion and exclamation reminiscent of Handel's oratorio *Israel in Egypt*. A few verses of chapters 12–14 of Exodus become 590 lines of Old English verse.

Allegory in its many forms is now recognised as an indispensable mode of understanding much in medieval literature. Yet it is often difficult to assess the propriety of a particular allegorical interpretation, since by its nature allegory asserts the primacy of a level of meaning which is hidden and to some extent arbitrary. Thus Solomon was an example of wisdom, but also of sensual folly, or of how wisdom can descend into folly, depending on which point the allegorist wished to make. History is still read in various ways. But some medieval allegory is so far different from any natural symbolic extension of meaning that it tends to evacuate the literal event of historical reality by insisting only on its spiritual significance. (At its extreme this means that it would not matter if a particular miracle had never actually happened, since the truth that God's power is not limited by the norms of human experience, a truth to which miracles testify, is a truth higher than the rules of empirical verifiability.) In the case of *Exodus*, allegory, the typical and figural mode of seeing the world, is a rediscovered key to the poem's purpose and unity, though perhaps at some cost to its plainer credibility.

A further difficulty of allegory is that since it is concerned with doctrine, it has nothing to say about literary qualities. The Old English *Genesis* is not a noticeably allegorical work, but it is often at its best as literature when furthest from the Bible, for example in the conflict of loyalties in Satan's attitude to his Lord on the one hand and to his own followers on the other:

> "Begin now to plan   and plot this assault!
>   If to any thane ever   in days of old
>   When we dwelt in that good kingdom   and happily
>   held our thrones
>   I dealt out princely treasure,   at no dearer time
>   Could he give me requital,   repayment for gifts,
>   If some thane would be my helper   and outward hence
>   Break through these bolted gates,   with strength
>   to wing
>   On feathered pinions   circling in the sky
>   To where new-shaped on earth   Adam and Eve
>   Abide in bliss   surrounded with abundance,
>   While we are cast out hither   to this deep hell."
>   (411–21; trans. Kennedy *Early English Christian*
>   *Poetry*, pp. 56–57)

The credible Germanic war-leader is a fine dramatic character, but he is apocryphal. The version of the Fall of Man in *Genesis B* is, however, at variance with the Biblical account (Eve is wholly deceived by Satan, who appears to her a good angel; her intention is loyal; and after the Fall the human pair immediately repent). Allegorical interpreters have succeeded in making the significance of this perfectly orthodox, but it is difficult to reconcile this account with that of the Bible. Both the Fall of the Angels and the Fall of Man are part of *Genesis B*, far more powerful than *Genesis A*, but less faithful. The Old Saxon poet of the ninth century was happier with his apocryphal demonology than with the Fall of Man in Genesis. But the tradition of the Church had hallowed the Lucifer story (now best known through the *Paradise Lost* of Milton) and the superiority of the Old Saxon to the Anglo-Saxon poet is due more to the drama inherent in what he received, which was readily imaginable in Germanic terms, than to his feeling a freedom greater than was proper before the sacred text. For whatever reason, *Genesis A* is the poem in the manuscript closest to a true paraphrase of the Biblical story. It begins piously (in Kennedy):

> It is proper and right that we praise with our lips
> And love with our hearts the Warden of heaven,
> The Lord of Hosts.

The opening phrase recalls that of the Preface to the Canon of the Mass, *dignum et justum est*: priestly and acceptable, but not comparable either with the opening of Genesis or with Satan's opening words in *Genesis B*.

Complex historical perspectives bedevil our perception of the Cædmonian poems. Much depends on one's conception of Christianity, for in comparison with the high medieval synthesis extending from the time of Dante to the end of the Gothic, and all subsequent versions and understandings, this barbarian-conversion Christianity is challengingly unfamiliar. The humane, gentle, and orthodox Bede reveals attitudes in his exegetical writings which are not easily assimilated, although no-one could be more in the centre of the stream, except perhaps Gregory the Great. But when the faith was transmitted to the Germanic barbarians, and enthusiastically accepted, it was re-expressed in a heroic vocabulary which seems at first doubly strange. Patristic doctrine, which is largely ascetic, monastic, and world-denying, was now recast in a social mould not only lay but heroic. The twin centres of the warrior culture were the battlefield and the banqueting hall, with their values of courage and generosity. But courage stands next to loyalty, then to the duty of vengeance; and the lord's generosity was not only social and convivial but involved sustained conspicuous consumption. Fighting and feasting were, in the pagan religion of the north, means not just to a glory expressed in the admiration of contemporaries and of posterity but to a living gloriousness, and a transcendence of self and of apparent human limitations. Such is the significance of the Old Norse *berserkr*, who in their war-fury went into battle naked; and of the glow that surrounds the descriptions of glee in the mead-hall. But the Church in Anglo-Saxon England spent generations trying to substitute the practice of *wergild* for vengeance; and the splendour of Bishop Wilfrid's manner of life surely did not mean that he did not preach against vainglory and the pride of life. Where there was not contradiction between heathendom and Christendom there was always at least a tension.

The incongruity resulting from this tension is more marked in poems on New Testament themes. Thus *Andreas*, an account of the acts of St. Andrew, begins:

> Hwæt! We gefrunon on fyrndagum
> twelfe under tunglum tireadige hæleth,
> theodnes thegnas....

Literally:

> Attend! We have heard in days of yore
> Of twelve under the stars, glorious heroes,
> A prince's thanes. Their might did not fail
> In warfare when banners clashed,
> After they separated, as the Lord himself
> The high king of the heavens appointed them by lot.
> Those were famous men on the earth,
> Eager chieftains, brave soldiers....

It is a shock to realise that these *frome folctogan ond fyrdhwate* are the twelve apostles. *Andreas*, like the other legendary Acts of the Apostles which flourished in the early centuries, especially in the east, concentrates on the fortitude with which the saint was prepared to face martyrdom, in this case at the hands of the man-eating Mermedonians. The courage to die for the faith, as Peter and Paul had, and as Anglo-Saxon saints like Boniface and King Edmund did, was of supreme relevance and value in conversion England. But the entirely heroic, even military, associations of the vocabulary used here seem violently inappropriate. Much of the sense of impropriety is a result of the many stages of cultural conditioning which separate the modern from the early medieval; but much of it is not, for the apostles were not a spiritual commando. The impropriety is glaring to a modern critical sense, but the Old English poet is quite unconscious: he is not daring but merely crude, with a crudity which helps him in a later storm scene. The language of praise which he inherited had an inappropriate stock of conventions.

But in *Andreas*, as in *Guthlac*, we are dealing with the extreme; as G.S. Shepherd writes:

> The conflict that advanced the kingdom of Christ in England can best be observed in the careers of such men as Guthlac, or Cuthbert, or Columba.... These were men of God in direct conflict with the magicians of the heathen: Elijahs against the prophets of Baal. On both sides the struggle was fought by psychologically and intellectually gifted men with powers of clairvoyance, of dissociation of body and mind, of prophecy and the gifts of tongues and spiritual healing. In the conversion of England the acts of the apostles were re-enacted. The ways in which the spirit moved, however fantastic they may appear to us, were real enough to the Anglo-Saxons.
>
> (*Continuations and Beginnings*, ed. E. G. Stanley, p. 7)

Shepherd also writes:

> Their zeal remains perhaps an embarrassment. In England there has never been any literacy other than Christian lit-

eracy. We are not helped in attempting a survey by being able to take two fixed bearings. At first it seems as if the whole intellectual world had been made afresh without native antecedents. A small learned class of Anglo-Saxons accomplished not, of course, a total absorption, but a massive and conscious adaptation of western and latinised Christian literacy. This is the miracle exemplified and particularised in Cædmon.

(Stanley, pp. 2–3)

The medium which Cædmon inherited and adapted was much better fitted to Old than to New Testament narratives, since it had evolved in tribal and patriarchal societies. And the baptism of Germanic motifs was accomplished with more skill: Noah sends forth a raven in *Genesis* which unscripturally feasts on the bodies of the defeated, and here the raven is a type of Satan. The themes which roused the poets of the Junius Book, apart from the continuous stress upon the faith of a leader, were cosmic and mythical rather than theological or personal: God as Creator and as Ruler of his creation; his power in controlling the forces of evil—whether diabolic or human—and of chaos, especially watery chaos, as in the Flood and the Red Sea. God's power to deliver is praised by Noah, by Moses, by Azarias, and by the three young men in the furnace. And in *Christ and Satan* we are reminded that God made the world and will end it at Doomsday, that Christ harrowed hell and has ended the imperialism of Satan. These are largely the common emphases of early Christianity: Christ is the serene Pantocrator of the Greek Church as well as the more Germanic Deliverer of *The Dream of the Rood*. He is not the suffering man of the thirteenth-century hymn of pathos, the *Stabat Mater*, nor yet the liberal wielder of ethical paradoxes, with a kind word for adulteresses and little children; still less is he like the statues in nineteenth-century Franciscan churches. The good news that the missionaries brought was knowledge of what went before and came after, a trustworthy knowledge of the pattern of the cosmos and of history, the knowledge of our deliverance from evil. Learning therefore brought an understanding of God's power, and offered the secure promise of salvation. It did not bring, as modern Christianity may seem to, a message of love without any security.

These are the themes of the Cædmonian poems, the same themes as were taught at Anglo-Saxon crosses. All the poems show God's power to save mankind. This homiletic purpose has long been recognised, as has a relationship of the poems to the liturgical readings in Holy Week. Recently it has been realised that the rhetorical style and exemplary construction, as well as the content, of the poems were also related to these readings, and the rhetorical pointing in the manuscript has been interpreted as indicating that they may indeed have had a direct use in liturgy. Before such a use for literature a merely literary criticism stands abashed.

Nevertheless a different kind of assimilation of Christian and native tradition may fitly end this chapter: not the masterpiece of Old English religious verse, *The Dream of the Rood*, which seems to inaugurate a more personal Christianity, but Bede's *Death Song*. Bede's disciple Cuthbert tells us that as the Feast of the Ascension approached in 735 Bede was still busy dictating a translation of the Gospel of St. John

into our language, for the use of the Church. And one of those who were with him said "Dear Master, there is still one chapter missing. Does it seem to you too difficult to be asked to finish it?" But he said "It is easy; take your pen, make ready, and write swiftly." And he did so. And about the ninth hour he said to me: "Run quickly and call the priests of our monastery to me once more, that I may give them little presents, such as God has given to me. Rich people in the world are careful to give gold and silver and precious things; and with much charity and joy will I give to my brothers what God has given." And speaking to each one he begged them to say Mass for him and to pray earnestly; and they willingly promised. And all mourned and wept, because he said that they should see his face no more in this world. They rejoiced when he said "It is time that I go to Him who sent me, who made me, who formed me from nothing. I have lived a long time; it is well; my loving Judge foresaw my life; the time of my dissolution is at hand; I long to be dissolved and to be with Christ." These and many other things he said with joy. The day wore on till evening, and the same boy said: "Dear Master, there is yet one sentence unwritten," and he said "Write quickly." And after a moment the boy said "Now the sentence is written." And he said "Good. In truth I can say, it is finished. Take my head in thy hands, for I would like much to sit facing the holy place where I was accustomed to pray, that, thus sitting, I may call upon my Father." And so, upon the pavement of his cell, singing "Gloria Patri, et Filio et Spiritui Sancto," he breathed the last breath from his body and thus went away to the Kingdom of Heaven.

(Williams, p. 196)

Cuthbert also wrote in a letter to the lector Cuthwine that Bede "sang the verse of St. Paul the apostle telling of the fearfulness of falling into the hands of the living God ... and in our language also, as he was learned in our songs, speaking of the terrible departure of spirits from the body." Then follows the text in this Northumbrian version:

> Fore thaem neidfaerae   naenig uuirthit
> thoncsnotturra,   than him tharf sie
> to ymbhycggannae   aer his hiniongae
> hwaet his gastae   godaes aeththae yflaes
> aefter deothdaege   doemid uueorthae.

"Before that inevitable journey no one becomes wiser in thought than he needs to be, in considering, before his departure, what will be adjudged to his soul, of good or evil, after his death-day." The poem exists in twenty-nine copies, Cædmon's *Hymn* in seventeen—Bede's name thus accounting for nearly half the surviving MSS containing Old English poetry. But the Death Song deserves to survive as an essentially Anglo-Saxon utterance. St. Paul wrote to the Hebrews: "It is a fearful thing to fall into the hands of the living God" (10.27). The cooler Anglo-Saxon understatement, in its characteristic recognition of the limits of human knowledge, is as powerful: no-one becomes wiser in thought than he needs to be.

SIX : THE POETIC ELEGIES

THE Elegies are the most compelling of Old English poems and the most popular. The poems to which scholars have given this name, all in the Exeter Book, are known as *The Wanderer*, *The Seafarer*, *The Ruin*, *The Wife's Complaint*, *The Husband's Message*, and *Wulf and Eadwacer*. Together with *Deor* and *The Dream of the Rood* these are the outstanding shorter poems; to them could be added Bede's *Death Song*, Cædmon's *Hymn*, and *Brunanburh*.

These poems called Elegies do not much resemble the pastoral elegy of the classical tradition, which in a ritual form mourns the death of a singer. Yet with the exception of *The Husband's Message*, the Old English poems all mourn death or loss, and have other themes and motifs in common, so the assimilation to elegy is convenient and the name of this group is no more inappropriate than the title of Gray's *Elegy in a Country Churchyard*. The speaker in each poem is unnamed and known neither to history nor legend. He (or she, for two of the speakers are women) is isolated, sometimes literally so; he has suffered the loss of lord and kinsmen, or spouse, and is driven by the hard conditions of exile to "give his cares utterance." In the majority of the elegies the speaker's situation is to some extent specified and a dramatic story implied, but in the two Elegies which have become most famous, *The Wanderer* and *The Seafarer*, the speaker is an exile whose soliloquy moves from his own sufferings outward to a passionate general lament for the transitoriness of life's glory. In each of the Elegies there is, then, an isolated speaker, and in *The Wanderer* and *The Seafarer* and also *The Ruin* there is a meditation upon a ruined city. The former carry this moralising gnomic strain to a Christian consolation. Consolation of a sort is found, too, in *The Wife's Complaint* and *The Husband's Message,* and in *Deor*—and this is a final similarity with classical elegy.

The impact of these poems on new readers, even via translation, is considerable. They are dramatic monologues of a power and intensity that are immediate though at times also enigmatic. Compared with other Old English poems they are dramatically expressive and emotionally direct, apparently personal, and exceptionally strong in imagery.

I • *WANDERER* AND *SEAFARER*

Though *The Seafarer* contains some of the most remarkable passages in Old English verse, the coherence of *The Wanderer* makes it a more useful introduction to the Elegies as a group. The slight punctuation of Old English verse texts does not include the use of quotation marks or their equivalent, which means that editors sometimes have to decide where speeches begin and end and how many speakers there are. Below is an entire version of *The Wanderer* that I made in 1962:

> Who liveth alone longeth for mercy,
> Maker's mercy. Though he must traverse
> Tracts of sea, sick at heart,
> — Trouble with oars ice-cold waters,
> 5 The ways of exile—Weird is set fast.
>
> Thus spoke such a "grasshopper," old griefs in his mind,
> Cold slaughters, the death of dear kinsmen:
>
> "Alone am I driven each day before daybreak
> To give my cares utterance.
> 10 None are there now among the living
> To whom I dare declare me throughly,

Tell my heart's thought. Too truly I know
It is in a man no mean virtue
That he keep close his heart's chest,
Hold his thought-hoard, think as he may.   15

No weary mind may stand against Weird
Nor may a wrecked will work new hope;
Wherefore, most often, those eager for fame
Bind the dark mood fast in their breasts.

So must I also curb my mind,   20
Cut off from country, from kind far distant,
By cares overworn, bind it in fetters;
This since, long ago, the ground's shroud
Enwrapped my gold-friend. Wretched I went thence,
Winter-wearied, over the waves' bound;   25

Dreary I sought hall of a gold-giver,
Where far or near I might find
Him who in meadhall might take heed of me,
Furnish comfort to a man friendless,
Win me with cheer.
            He knows who makes trial   30
How harsh and bitter is care for companion
To him who hath few friends to shield him.
Track ever taketh him, never the torqued gold,
Not earthly glory, but cold heart's cave.
He minds him of hall-men, of treasure-giving,   35
How in his youth his gold-friend
Gave him to feast. Fallen all this joy.

He knows this who is forced to forgo his lord's,
His friend's counsels, to lack them for long:
Oft sorrow and sleep, banded together,   40
Come to bind the lone outcast;
He thinks in his heart then that he his lord
Claspeth and kisseth, and on knee layeth
Hand and head, as he had at otherwhiles
In days now gone, when he enjoyed the gift-stool.   45

141

Awakeneth after this friendless man,
Seeth before him fallow waves,
Seabirds bathing, broading out feathers,
Snow and hail swirl, hoar-frost falling.
50   Then all the heavier his heart's wounds,
Sore for his loved lord. Sorrow freshens.

Remembered kinsmen press through his mind;
He singeth out gladly, scanneth eagerly
Men from the same hearth. They swim away.
55   Sailors' ghosts bring not many
Known songs there. Care grows fresh
In him who shall send forth too often
Over locked waves his weary spirit.

Therefore I may not think, throughout this world,
60   Why cloud cometh not on my mind
When I think over all the life of earls,
How at a stroke they have given up hall,
Mood-proud thanes. So this middle earth
Each of all days ageth and falleth."

65   Wherefore no man grows wise without he have
His share of winters. A wise man holds out;
He is not too hot-hearted, nor too hasty in speech,
Nor too weak a warrior, not wanting in fore-thought,
Nor too greedy of goods, nor too glad, nor too mild,
70   Nor ever too eager to boast, ere he knows all.

A man should forbear boastmaking
Until his fierce mind fully knows
Which way his spleen shall expend itself.

A wise man may grasp how ghastly it shall be
75   When all this world's wealth standeth waste,
Even as now, in many places, over the earth
Walls stand, wind-beaten,
Hung with hoar-frost; ruined habitations.
The wine-halls crumble; their wielders lie

Bereft of bliss, the band all fallen   80
Proud by the wall. War took off some,
Carried them on their course hence; one a bird bore
Over the high sea; one the hoar wolf
Dealt to death; one his drear-checked
Earl stretched in an earthen trench.   85

The Maker of men hath so marred this dwelling
That human laughter is not heard about it
And idle stand these old giant-works.
A man who on these walls wisely looked,
Who sounded deeply this dark life,   90
Would think back to the blood spilt here,
Weigh it in his wit. His word would be this:

"Where is that horse now? Where are those men? Where is
        the hoard-sharer?
Where is the house of the feast? Where is the hall's uproar?

Alas, bright cup! Alas, burnished fighter!   95
Alas, proud prince! How that time has passed,
Dark under night's helm, as though it never had been!

There stands in the stead of staunch thanes
A towering wall wrought with worm-shapes;
The earls are off-taken by the ash-spear's point,   100
— That thirsty weapon. Their Weird is glorious.

Storms break on the stone hillside,
The ground bound by driving sleet,
Winter's wrath. Then wanness cometh
Night's shade spreadeth, sendeth from north   105
The rough hail to harry mankind.

In the earth-realm all is crossed;
Weird's will changeth the world.
Wealth is lent us, friends are lent us,
Man is lent, kin is lent;   110
All this earth's frame shall stand empty."

143

110   So spoke the sage in his heart; he sat apart in thought.
      Good is he who keeps faith: nor should care too fast
      Be out of a man's breast before he first know the cure:
      A warrior fights on bravely. Well is it for him who seeks
115   forgiveness,
      The Heavenly Father's solace, in whom all our fastness stands.

The Wanderer is so called after the speaker mentioned in line 6: *swa cwæth eardstapa*, literally "thus spoke land-stepper" (*eardstapa* is a term also applied to the grasshopper). This speaker is the solitary mentioned in the third person in line one. He tells us he is deprived of his homeland and far from kinsmen; his lord is dead and the joys of the hall are no more. The life of men itself now seems precarious, and from line 57 onward the poem contemplates the world's decay, embodied in the image of a ruined city, and rises to the speech of exclamation beginning "Where is that horse now? Where are those men? Where is the hoard-sharer?" and ending "All this earth's frame shall stand empty." The poem frequently returns to the relationship between experience, wisdom, and speech: only one who has experienced deprivation and lived long is entitled to speak. In its conclusion the poem's wisdom directs us to our heavenly Father, where for all true stability is to be found. It will be seen that the poet has created a dramatic persona whose thoughts develop to project the view expressed at the close. The way the poem continually expands in scope is clear, wherever editors decide to begin and end speeches. Indeed, though several details and minor transitions are not perfectly apparent, there is enough evidence to say that *The Wanderer* is a work of pondered integrity and purpose, not only of intensity and eloquence. The figure of the *eardstapa* comes to seem a typical and dramatic persona rather than, as at first, a real individual; the keen realisation of exile in the opening speech—with its apparently autobiographical account of personal losses, experiences, and dreams—leads on deliberately to the more obviously composed and rhetorical meditation on the ruined city.

If a translator may be briefly autobiographical, I can explain something of the manner of my translation and at the same time suggest how *The Wanderer* now appears to me in a different light than in 1962, when the above version was made. At that time I was, as an undergraduate with no special gift for languages, studying Anglo-Saxon (as it was then called) as an obligatory part of the course leading to a B.A. in English Language and Literature at Oxford University. My admiration for Ezra Pound's version of *The Seafarer* had encouraged me to attempt verse translation of other Old English poems. Pound's version had made me sensitive to the texture of the language and of the very different versification of Old English. The exact sense of the poems was less real to me, less distinct than the feel of the language. This otherness was what I tried to render, like Pound though without his immense resource of language and rhythm, and without his absoluteness and idiosyncrasy. Hence, in part, the archaism in my version, the occasional strained effect, the abrupt rhythm, and the necessarily imperfect observance of the rules for metre and alliteration. The parts of the poem that made the greatest impact were the two speeches (lines 8–63 and 92–110): the first the testament of personal experience, the second the fruit of that experience applied to the world as a whole; both are deeply felt and overwhelmingly pessimistic. The five lines at the beginning, the moralising bridge passage in the middle, and the five lines at the end made a less profound impression, and I found the Christian conclusion less than wholly convincing. Though more coherent than *The Seafarer*, *The Wanderer* was in a few places a little obscure, and its dramatic effectiveness was more apparent than its completeness as a resolved work of art, compared with *Beowulf*, *Maldon* or *Deor*—not to mention the formal perfection of the products of a later literary culture such as, say, Gray's *Elegy*. The language and the culture are now more fully available to me — more securely and extensively, if locally less intensively — and the genre of *The Wanderer* seems clearer, its artistic and moral strategy more defined, and its movement from the dramatic to the ruminative more natural.

In translating the selection published as *The Earliest English Poems*, I left *The Seafarer* to the end, wanting to avoid any unconscious reminiscence of Pound's version. I had decided to dispense with overt archaisms such as the -eth form, to observe Old English metre as far as possible, and not to let a phrase impair the cohesiveness or drive of a sentence. *The Seafarer* is a more dramatic and less reflective poem for the most part, and apparently much more personal and autobiographical than *The Wanderer*—more "modern." But its last 21 lines are unmistakably a homily, ending, "Thanks be to the Holy One therefore, the Prince of Glory, the everlasting Lord, that He has raised us up forever. Amen." This conclusion seemed unassimilable to some editors in the nineteenth century, when these elegies were given their present Romantic titles. The Victorians attributed the conclusion to an interpolator or a monastic editor. This figure of the monkish interpolator was a great convenience to a number of those who sought in Old English a pagan past, of whom Ezra Pound was one of the last. He wrote in a "Philological note" to his *Seafarer* that he was deliberately translating a word meaning "angels" (line 78) as "Angles" and omitting the reference to the devil two lines earlier, as well as "the dignified but platitudinous address to the Deity" at the end.

Pound's *Seafarer* is a bravura realisation of the effect of reading the original on a poetic sensibility with great sensitivity to rhythm and language and a mind coloured by American attitudes of a hundred years ago to the early English past. Pound was also an adherent of the Analytic approach to editing early texts, and had the confidence of genius. Analysis (the distinguishing by an editor of the exact limits, and sometimes the provenance, of the various contributions to a text presumed to be composite, by means of linguistic and stylistic criteria) has long been completely out of fashion. Scholars are not so sure that a Christian twist which may at first seem incongruous may not have been intentional; nor that what appears to be discordant with modern Christianity may not simply be the Christianity of the time. Nevertheless Pound's *Seafarer* is much the most intense impression of an Old English poem available to those who have none of the language; it is also a poem about the existential situation of the modern artist, and at times becomes almost personal.

The original *Seafarer* is a more extreme and bewildering poem than *The Wanderer*. It opens on a painfully autobiographical note which is also a deliberate claim to authenticity:

> The tale I frame shall be found to tally:
> The history is of myself.

The Seafarer's sufferings are realised in harsh physical imagery that suggests keen emotional loss — the loss of lord and companions, as in *The Wanderer*, but also a spiritual dissatisfaction and anxiety expressing itself in a scorn of men's social life on land and, in reaction, a thirst for the ardours of the sea journey.

> The thriving of the treeland, the town's briskness,
> A lightness over the leas, life gathering,
> Everything urges the eagerly mooded
> Man to venture on the voyage he thinks of,
> The faring over flood, the far bourn.
> And the cuckoo calls him in his care-laden voice,
> Scout of summer, sings of new griefs
> That shall make breast-hoard bitter.
>   Blithe heart cannot know,
> Through its happiness, what hardships they suffer
> Who drive the foam-furrow furthest from land.
> Spirit breaks from the body's chest
> To the sea's acres; over earth's breadth
> And whale's range roams the mind now,
> Homes to the breast hungry and thirsty.
>
> Cuckoo's dirge drags out my heart,
> Whets will to the whale's beat
> Across wastes of water: far warmer to me
> Are the Lord's kindnesses than this life of death
> Lent us on land.
>
>   (46–66)

The struggle expressed in the paradoxical attitudes to happy land-life and to the sea, and in the ominous image of the cuckoo, culminates here in an experience of ecstatic yearning which is resolved in a preference for the joys of heaven. From this point onwards a contempt for this world can be seen to unite the rest of the poem. The old heroic determination to achieve a kind of personal immortality by fame, familiar from *Beowulf*, is given a Christian reinterpretation:

.I do not believe
Earthly estate is everlasting:
Three things always threaten a man's peace
And one before the end shall overthrow his mind;
Either illness or age or the edge of vengeance
Shall draw out the breath from the doom-shadowed.
Wherefore, for earl whosoever, it is afterword,
The praise of livers-on, that, lasting, is best:
Won in the world before wayfaring,
Forged, framed here, in the face of enmity,
In the Devil's spite: deeds, achievements.
That after-speakers should respect the name
And after them angels have honour toward it
For always and ever. From those everlasting joys
The daring shall not die.

(66–80)

Likewise a lament for the passing of the great heroes of old, as found in *Widsith*— "there are no gold-givers like the gone masters / Who between them framed the first deeds in the world" — modulates into a lament for old age - "Once life is going, this gristle slackens" — and eventually into Christian criticism of the futility of lavish heathen burial practices:

A man may bury his brother with the dead
And strew his grave with the golden things
He would have him take, treasures of all kinds,
But gold hoarded when he here lived
Cannot allay the anger of God
Towards a soul sin-freighted.

(97–102)

This kind of open preaching is no longer one of the legs upon which literature stands. Yet the modern reader can still respond to the craving for stability expressed toward the end of the poem. Once the consolations of the heroic life had been seen not to be sufficient, what was there to put in its place? There was something.

Great is the terrible power of God, before which the earth shall turn aside; He established the firm foundations, the expanse of the earth, the heavens above. Foolish is the man who does not fear his Lord; death shall come upon him unprepared. Blessed is the man who lives in trust; grace shall come to him from the heavens. The Lord shall confirm that spirit in him, for he believes in His might. A man should manage a headstrong spirit and keep it in its place, and be true to men, fair in his dealings. He should treat every man with measure, restrain enmity towards friend and foe. He may not wish his cherished friend to be given over to the fire nor to be burnt on the pyre, yet Doom is stronger and God is mightier than any man's conception. Let us think where it is that we may find a home and then consider how we may come thither, and then indeed we may strive so that we may be able to enter into that everlasting blessedness where all life is in the Lord's love, the bliss of heaven. Thanks be to the Holy One therefore, the Prince of Glory, the ever-lasting Lord, that He has raised us up forever. Amen.

(103–24)

This conclusion is fully assimilated into Anglo-Saxon terms: "Doom is stronger and God is mightier than any man's conception." The anguish of the Psalmist and his fainting for the Lord's courts found a natural home in the Anglo-Saxon heart; even the Roman Christian emphasis on Father, home, and duty seems congenial to an old idea of the English temperament. The central ethical stress—"A man should manage a headstrong spirit and keep it in its place"—grows out of the unappeased extremes experienced earlier in the poem.

The Wanderer and *The Seafarer* are often dated later than *Beowulf*, which gives a very elastic period for their composition, but may be right in so far as they seem to belong to a stage subsequent to the communal and social world of the heroic poems. The destiny or salvation of the individual is faced in non-social terms. The joys of hall, of lordship and thaneship, companionship and friendship, are seen as transitory. The generalising, gnomic, and proverbial strain in Old English poetry is given the difficult task of offering norms for the unknown and the metaphysical.

The persona of the exile who speaks each poem is detribalised, alienated, lordless. This outlaw figure fascinated the poets, perhaps because they were to some extent outsiders, like the speaker of *Widsith*, or Deor himself, who has lost his position. The hero himself is lonely at the moment of trial. There are testing non-social moments in *Beowulf*—for the slave as he steals the cup, for Wiglaf as he penetrates the mound, for Beowulf himself, and for the monsters. But in *Beowulf* the theme of the Elegies is more clearly anticipated in the "Lay of the Last Survivor," in the lament of Hrethel, and in the prophecies of Wiglaf and the Messenger, for passages which deal with the end of heroic society. All these occur toward the end of the Old English epic, which is also an elegy. First, the "Lay":

> "There's no joy from harp-play,
> Glee-wood's gladness, no good hawk
> Swings through hall now, no swift horse
> Tramps at the threshold. Terrible slaughter
> Has carried into darkness many kindreds of mankind."
> (2263–67)

The Lament for Hrethel:

> He sorrows to see among his son's dwellings
> The wasted wine-hall, the wind's home now,
> Bereft of all joy. The riders are sleeping,
> The heroes in the grave. The harp does not sound,
> There is no laughter in the yard as there used to be of old.
> He goes then to his couch, keens the lament
> For his one son alone there; too large now seem to him
> His houses and fields.
> (2455–62)

Wiglaf's Prophecy:

> "Now there shall cease for your race the receiving of treasure,
> The bestowal of swords, all satisfaction of ownership,
> All comfort of home. Your kinsmen every one
> Shall become wanderers without land-rights

As soon as athelings over the world
Shall hear the report of how you fled,
A deed of ill fame. Death is better
For any earl than an existence of disgrace."

(2864–91)

The Messenger's Prophecy:

> "No fellow shall wear
> An arm-ring in his memory; no maiden's neck
> Shall be enhanced in beauty by the bearing of these rings.
> Bereft of gold rather, and in wretchedness of mind
> She shall tread continually the tracks of exile
> Now that the leader of armies has laid aside his mirth,
> His sport and glad laughter. Many spears shall therefore
> Feel cold in the mornings to the clasping fingers
> And the hands that raise them. Nor shall the harper's melody
> Arouse them for battle; and yet the black raven,
> Quick on the marked men, shall have much to speak of
> When he tells the eagle of his takings at the feast
> Where he and the wolf bared the bodies of the slain."

(3015–27)

In all these passages the feeling is one of lament, specifically poetic, for loss, as in the Welsh lament for the hall of Cynddylan. The poet's harp is prominent in all but the third, the sentence of banishment pronounced on the disloyal thanes. There is a knot of common elements—feasting, laughter, horses, armour—the mention of any of which evoked intensely the whole theme, so central as never to be commonplace, of the hall as locus of the heroic life itself. The elegiac final prophecy of the dispersal, almost the orphaning, of the entire Geat people, and of the birds and beasts of prey feasting where men had feasted, seems to lead on naturally to the situation envisaged at the end of *The Wanderer* or in *The Ruin*: the ruined hall, and ultimately an earth uninhabited by men. *Beowulf* is a narrative, however, whereas the Elegies are meditative set pieces cast in a dramatic form: most of them—not *The Wife's Complaint*, *The Husband's Message*, nor *Wulf and Eadwacer*—address with conscious thought one of the problems which the story of *Beowulf* embodies. What is the way for the man for whom transitory human society is not enough?

The Church offered an alternative society — the communion of saints — and a more hopeful ethos to the individual isolated by this sense of life as fleeting: a loving Father's changelessness. The early Church's imminent expectation of the end of the world was preserved by its Fathers and institutionalised by the monastic life for the whole of the Middle Ages. This vision offered a radical critique of the heroic ideal of the joys of the hall, and its future projection in a heathen Valhalla. Yet the bliss of heaven, with the angels praising the Lord of Hosts, was not, with its implicit image of a court, absolutely unlike Valhalla. This overlap between apparent opposites is one of the factors that lend both power and a common denominator to most of the poems called Elegies. The absent lord is replaced by the longed-for Lord, the ruined hall by the heavenly court. Unwilling exile — in *The Seafarer* — modulates into chosen ascesis.

The heroic vocabulary of these two poems is not, then, incompatible with a spiritual meaning. And the spiritual meaning could also be quite surprisingly literal. Here is the entry for the year 891 in the Parker MS of the *Anglo-Saxon Chronicle*:

> In this year the host went east; and king Arnulf fought against the mounted host, before the ships came, with the East Franks and the Saxons and the Bavarians, and put it to flight. And three Irishmen came to king Alfred in a boat without any oars, from Ireland, whence they had stolen away because they wished for the love of God to be on pilgrimage, they cared not where. The boat in which they set out was made of two and a half hides, and they had taken with them provisions for a week and after a week they came to land in Cornwall, and soon went to king Alfred. Thus were they named: Dubhslaine and Macbeathadh and Maelinmhain. And Suibhne, the best teacher among the Scots (from Ireland), died.
>
> (Garmonsway, p. 82)

The similar story of St. Brendan and his companions abandoning themselves in a coracle to the mercy of wind and Atlantic wave is not as fantastic as a modern sceptic might at first think. Only the most absolute faith in God's providence could have allowed the monks to build their retreats, as they constantly did, on islands: not only such relatively favoured spots as Iona but on barren Atlantic rocks like Skellig Michael. The impulse to sail round the world, cross the Antarctic, or climb Everest alone still prevails in more secular form. But scores of Celtic hermits carried the traditions of the hermits of the Egyptian desert into Britain and western Europe, seeking wildernesses and desert places, and finding them. This naked spiritual journey to God sometimes involved an asceticism which description may make incredible or excessive but was genuine; such extremes were certainly excluded from the regular organised life of the Order of St. Benedict. But both the Celtic and the Italian traditions were well known in Anglo-Saxon England in learned and simple forms. The Mercian warrior prince St. Guthlac cast out the devils that inhabited the island of Crowland in the fens only after terrible ordeals. Concrete histori-cal evidence is not at all scarce, then, that in this age many took quite literally and physically the command to leave everything and seek first the Kingdom of heaven, the homeland of the soul from which, in this world, we are exiles. Several Anglo-Saxon kings gave up their thrones and went to Rome to die. The same belief in the transience of this world and the permanence only of heav-enly joys is expressed eloquently toward the end of the medieval period by that worldly court poet Chaucer, as the conclusion of his *Troilus and Criseyde*, in his *Retractions*, and in his most popular poem, *Truth*:

> Know thy contree, look up, thank God of all;
> Hold the heye wey, and lat thy gost thee lede;
> And trouthe thee shal delivere, it is no drede.

(Acknowledge thy native land—look up, thank God for everything: stick to the high road and let your spirit lead you; and have no fear, Truth shall preserve you.)

This cheerfully sophisticated integration of so firmly non-secu-lar a view into the body of society itself was not achieved in the less stable conditions of the earlier middle ages. But their literary culture, being monastic, was based firmly upon the idea of life as a pilgrimage through this world. The word pilgrim comes from Latin *peregrinus*, and Alfred's three Irish hermits were *peregrini pro amore Dei*, wanderers for the love of God. The image of life as an insecure voyage through a troubled sea was more apt and compelling to the earlier Middle Ages than the allegorically more convenient figure—equally Biblical—of life as a land journey, used by John Bunyan in *Pilgrim's Progress*.

Scholars have recently found many Biblical, liturgical and homiletic passages which offer contexts for the final images of *The Wanderer* and *The Seafarer*. The heroic stoicism and Germanic gloom recognised by earlier scholars, and Celtic parallels, have given way to a tendency among commentators to relocate the poems in a Christian, Mediterranean, and allegorical tradition of exegesis. Thus the ruined city in *The Wanderer* is the City of this World, and the "far folk-land flood-beyond" of *The Seafarer* is heaven. The evidence is impressive, but, like all discussion of sources and analogies and all allegorisation, not wholly conclusive. Certain it is that both poems express new ideals in an old medium and an old vocabulary, and that the conversion to new ends lends a power that is not without turbidity. *The Seafarer*, initially more dramatic and confusing, is the more radical and eventually perhaps the more integrated of the two, since the spiritual ideal of its end transcends and replaces the secular plight in which it began. *The Wanderer* is more reasonable and easier to follow, but the transformation it enacts between heroic and spiritual values is less complete. What is the tone of this lament?

"Where is that horse now? Where are those men? Where is the
        hoard-sharer?
Where is the house of the feast? Where is the hall's uproar?"

(92–93)

Surely this is the accent of sorrow and loss, of painful deprivation, not of medicinal consolation. The incompleteness of this consolation, however, may make *The Wanderer* a more acceptable poem today.

II • OTHER ELEGIES

The pair of poems just discussed has always held pride of place among the Elegies, for a variety of reasons. Old English is a language which has had to be studied: in some ways it is much more of a "dead language" than Latin, which has been in continual use since the founding of Rome, though latterly the language of the Catholic Church rather than of international learning. Lost in the later Middle Ages, Old English was reinvestigated in the sixteenth century but remained the interest of a circle of (chiefly clerical) antiquarians until the nineteenth, when it benefitted by the general revival of things medieval. It finally achieved enough prominence to merit in 1855 a parody, in Lewis Carroll's *Jabberwocky*. At about this same time, it was incorporated into the courses leading to a degree in English Language and Literature at Oxford and University College, London—and other places, not including Cambridge. Among the motives for its inclusion in such courses was the thought that "scientific" philological study, combined with an historical approach, made the new and apparently soft subject of English into a hard discipline comparable with that of the classical languages. This approach to the study of English persists in continental universities. (At Cambridge, English Literature proved its toughness by the rigour of its critical practice.) Introduced under such unliterary auspices, there was little desire to offer the kind of "Old English without tears" courses which have developed as Old English has been partially disestablished. Consequently the texts chosen for Old English Readers, supremely *Sweet's Anglo-Saxon Reader*, which served this market for over a hundred years—had a preponderance of extracts with a recognisable historical content or context, and an ethos of (masculine) heroism: *Maldon*, and parts of the *Chronicle* and *Beowulf*. In Sweet's *Reader* the only Elegies were the pair already considered, which offer the pedagogical advantage that they can be compared and contrasted. They are of similar length, and share the same mood, theme and even thematic development, and are suitable for undergraduate study in being reasonably free from textual and editorial problems. Above all, their genuine similarity seems to suggest for them almost a common cultural origin or referential context of the sort that is lacking for most Old English verse. A certain kind of scholarly mind finds the absence of an identifiable context frustrating, and the attempt to fill the positivistic vacuum with Germanic, Celtic, and Latin literary sources or historical situations has been unremitting.

For the other Elegies—*The Ruin, The Wife's Complaint* (or *Lament*), *The Husband's Message* and *Wulf and Eadwacer*—no such context appears and it is perhaps this which long excluded them from Old English Readers, and unfortunately from popular currency, though everyone who reads a translation of *The Ruin* seems to respond to it. These Elegies can be considered equal to *The Wanderer* and *The Seafarer* in poetic interest, though all are handicapped by some minor incompleteness or obscurity. *The Ruin* is ruinous in its text, and the same poker or brand on the back of the Exeter Book has also seriously damaged *The Husband's Message*, which besides ends with a runic signature. *The Wife's Complaint* and *Wulf and Eadwacer* both grow out of dramatic marital situations which are not unambiguously clear in their outlines. Likewise scholars cannot decide whether the husband and wife of the titles are related and, if so, how. But the emotional and dramatic impact of these four poems is not usually complicated by the possibility of symbolic or allegorical interpretation which envelops *Wanderer* and *Seafarer*.

The Wife's Complaint begins in a way now familiar: the testimony of an exile:

I have wrought these words together out of a wryed existence,
The heart's tally, telling off
The griefs I have undergone from girlhood upwards,
Old and new, and now more than ever;
For I have never not had some new sorrow,
Some fresh affliction to fight against.
The first was my lord's leaving his people here:
Crossed crests. To what country I knew not,
Wondered where, awoke unhappy.
I left, fared any road, friendless, an outcast,
Sought any service to staunch the lack of him.

(1–11)

A difference of accent is confirmed, however, when it turns out
that the theme of the poem is not so much exile as estrangement
and banishment caused by intrigue:

> Then his kinsmen ganged, began to think
> Thoughts they did not speak, of splitting the wedlock;
> So — estranged, alienated — we lived each
> Alone, a long way apart; how I longed for him!
>
> In his harshness he had me brought here;
> And in these parts there were few friendly minded,
> Worth trusting.
>   Trouble in the heart now:
> I saw the bitterness, the bound mind
> Of my matched man, mourning-browed,
> Mirk in his mood, murder in his thoughts.
>
>   (12–21)

The husband has banished the wife to exile in an underground
cave where the misery of her life is conveyed very powerfully:

> Our lips had smiled to swear hourly
> That nothing should split us — save dying —
> Nothing else. All that has changed:
> It is now as if it never had been,
> Our friendship. I feel in the wind
> That the man dearest to me detests me.
> I was banished to this knoll knotted by woods
> To live in a den dug beneath an oak.
> Old is this earthen room; it eats at my heart.
>
> I see the thorns thrive up there in thick coverts
> On the banks that baulk these black hollows:
> Not a gay dwelling. Here the grief bred
> By lordlack preys on me. Some lovers in this world
> Live dear to each other, lie warm together
> At day's beginning; I go by myself
> About these earth caves under the oak tree.

Here I must sit the summer day through,
Here weep out the woes of exile,
The hardships heaped upon me. My heart shall never
Suddenly sail into slack water,
All the longings of a lifetime answered.

(22–41)

The woman now curses the man responsible for turning her "friend" against her:

May grief and bitterness blast the mind
Of that young man ! May his mind ache
Behind his smiling face! May a flock of sorrows
Choke his chest! He would change his tune
If he lived alone in a land of exile
Far from his folk.
                        Where my friend is stranded
Frost crusts the cracked cliff-face
Grey waves grind the shingle.
The mind cannot bear in such a bleak place
Very much grief.
                        He remembers too often
Less grim surroundings. Sorrow follows
This too long wait for one who is estranged.

(42–53)

The tendency to gnomic generalisation indulged at the end may seem one of the few common elements connecting this poem with the rest of the Old English poetic corpus. However, the poem employs several commonplaces: the desolate landscape of the husband's isolation is paralleled in *The Wanderer's* vision of the end of the world; the deliberate breaking-up of a marriage or marriage-alliance by jealous kinsmen comes twice into *Beowulf*; the use of a female voice to express mourning for past happiness is well known in medieval Latin poetry as well as from *Beowulf's* own funeral; even the connection of the base of an oak tree with despair is a medieval commonplace, occurring twice in Chaucer. More generally characteristic of Anglo-Saxon is the oppressive emotional tension and reproach entailed in the fatal influence of mistaken decisions in the past upon a hopeless present stoically endured, a situation and feeling broodingly imprinted in a bleak landscape. But there remains a special quality in *The Wife's Complaint* which it is tempting to call personal, despite all these traditional and universalising features, a quality that would remain if the story behind the poem were ever to be conclusively identified or even if a patristic source were to be found for it, which seems unlikely. It reads coherently as a direct, personal and literal complaint, of a sort which would have interested Thomas Hardy.

Wulf and Eadwacer is another exception to the masculine tradition of war-comradeship in Old English poetry, and is also a "realistic" and bitter poem, though the story in this case would seem to have been polished by retelling, if not to the extent found in *Waldere* or *Finnsburh*. The strophic pattern of the 19-line poem, with its refrain, is reminiscent of *Deor*, but the situation is more like that of a ballad than of an heroic poem. Henry Bradley identified it succinctly in 1888, declaring that

> the poem is a fragment of a dramatic soliloquy. The speaker, it should be premised, is shown by the grammar to be a woman, Wulf is her lover and an outlaw, and Eadwacer (I suspect, though it is not certain) is her tyrant husband.

Wulf and Eadwacer

The men of my tribe would treat him as game:
If he comes to the camp they will kill him outright.

Our fate is forked.

Wulf is on one island, I on another.
Mine is a fastness: the fens girdle it
And it is defended by the fiercest men.
If he comes to the camp they will kill him for sure .

Our fate is forked.

It was rainy weather, and I wept by the hearth,
Thinking of my Wulf's far wanderings;
One of the captains caught me in his arms.
It gladdened me then; but it grieved me too.

Wulf, my Wulf, it was wanting you
That made me sick, your seldom coming,
The hollowness at heart; not the hunger I spoke of.

Do you hear, Eadwacer? Our whelp
           Wulf shall take to the wood.
What was never bound is broken easily,
           Our song together.

The dramatic technique of *Finnsburh* and the enigmatic implication of *Deor* converted expressively to secular ends. The survival
of this passionate fragment extends our ideas of the range of Old
English poetry in directions which suggest concern with varieties
of affection and of human material well beyond what Walter
Bagehot refers to as the lettuces of the monastery garden. The
garden of Exeter's monastic cathedral, as we have seen, also contained onions.

The theme of these last three Elegies is the separation of man
and woman, not of man and lord, the exile is not heroic, and the
longing is not metaphysical. Happily *The Husband's Message* offers
yet another corrective to received ideas of Anglo-Saxon elegy. It
is a chivalric, courtly, and unpessimistic poem. The message of the
title is spoken by the staff upon which the sender's words are
carved. The idea of an object speaking—prosopopoeia, as it is
called in classical rhetoric—is familiar from the riddles. The
poem ends with a runic oath carved on the staff:

So I set together S and R twinned,
E A, W, D. The oath is named
Whereby he undertakes until the end of his life
To keep the covenants of companionship
That, long ago, you delighted to repeat.

                                       (49–53)

Probably we are to think of the whole poem not only as spoken by the staff but also as carved upon it. Runes were the old form of Germanic writing, an alphabet of straight-sided characters, some of which had heathen associations, designed to be cut originally into wood, as here. *Run* means "secret" in Old English, and the runes survive chiefly in inscriptions, often with some magic power, upon such things as swords. *The Dream of the Rood*, in which the Cross speaks, is carved in runic letters upon the Ruthwell Cross. The word *write* originally meant "to cut, carve, inscribe," and the Reed Pen riddle (see p. 102) lays heavy stress on the private nature of communication between writer and reader which such cryptographic writing, especially runic writing, preserved. This secret riddling quality is something never entirely absent from the compositional style of Old English poetry, whether in its poetic periphrases, its understatements, its formulaic variation (especially on names) or its love of twists, ellipses, and obliqueness—all of which provoke wonder.

"Now shall I unseal myself to yourself alone" begins the staff bearing the message, dramatically enough. The text following, in which it gives its own history, is damaged, but the message itself is *en clair*:

> *Hwæt!*
>   The carver of this token entreats a lady
> Clad in clear stones to call to mind
> And hold in her wit words pledged
> Often between the two in earlier days:
> Then he would hand you through hall and yard
> Lord of his lands, and you might live together,
> Forget your love. A feud drove him
> From his war-proud people.
>   That prince, glad now,
> Gave me this word for you: when you shall hear
> In the copse at the cliff's edge the cuckoo pitch
> His melancholy cry, come over sea.
>
> You will have listened long: leave then with no notice
> Let no man alive delay your going:
> Into the boat and out to sea,

Seagull's range; southward from here
Over the paths in the foam you shall find your man,
Make landfall where your lord is waiting.

(14–30)

The rest of the poem tells how the lord has now prospered and is surrounded by friends. It is courtly and complimentary, like the speeches at Heorot. The diplomatic care with which the lady is reminded of her oath might conceivably imply some doubt or difficulty about her obeying the cuckoo's call, in which case we may have the obverse of the situation in *The Wife's Complaint* or even of that in *Wulf and Eadwacer*. All is speculative in such archaeological reconstruction. It is worth remembering that "the Sutton Hoo Lyre" now on show in the British Museum was for decades exhibited as "the Sutton Hoo harp"—quite a different instrument. These two love Elegies can be fitted together to make a story with a happy ending or an unhappy one, but it seems more scrupulous to leave the happiness of the invitation in *The Husband's Message* to stand.

The exception proves the rule: the Elegies are fiercely sorrowful poems, linked together by theme and mood and their speakers' situations. Much of their eloquence comes from the concentrated emotional energy released by their knotted formulas. The formulas of exile, endurance, separation, desolation, and longing are turned loose, with great evocative power.

The authors of the last three elegies followed the advice of W. H. Auden, in "In Memory of W. B. Yeats," to

Sing of human unsuccess
In a rapture of distress;

In the deserts of the heart
Let the healing fountain start....

Their elegiac eloquence is more refreshing than some scholars' detailed reconstructions of the meaning of *The Wanderer* and *The Seafarer*. Some readers will be pleased as well as surprised to find Anglo-Saxon poems which do not bring the consolation of philosophy.

The Alfred Jewel

SEVEN : ALFRED AND OLD ENGLISH PROSE

OLD English verse is an ancestral art: the poems are older than the oldest manuscripts in which they are preserved, but the art is centuries older than its committal to written form. The old heroic verse especially, though possessed in its artfulness, seems almost a natural and organic thing, so sure is it of itself and of its place at the table of Anglo-Saxon life. The origins of verse as an oral art go back to Teutonic beginnings before the Christian era. Its compositional technique and actual versification seem to decline from *Beowulf* onwards, partly because its transfer to a written mode was a shock to its reproductive process, and partly because the old patterns of accidence and syntax, on which it relied, were breaking down.

Prose had been used for law codes, but, in contrast with verse, the use of prose for a range of tasks stems from a decision of Alfred, king of Wessex from 871 to 899. The worthy citizen in Molière's play *Le Bourgeois Gentilhomme* was astonished to discover that he had been speaking prose all his life. But though the Angles and Saxons had been speaking Old English for centuries, there is little evidence that this speech was cultivated for compositions of an unmetrical form, unlike Old Irish for instance, whose heroic saga is always in prose. Absence of evidence here is not conclusive, and there is a significant exception in the story of Cynewulf and

Cyneheard inserted in the *Anglo-Saxon Chronicle* for the year 757. Thousands of sermons, for example, must have been preached in Old English in the seventh century and some may have reached written form, but none survives. Writing was then a clerical monopoly, and its language was Latin; such Englishmen as Bede and Alcuin could write very good Latin prose and cultivated Latin verse. Their Latin and their learning were internationally admired, and the Northumbrian English, who had learned Latin from the Irish and Italians in the seventh century, were the teachers of the Germans and the Franks in the eighth. But by the later ninth century Northumbria was internally divided, and then overrun by the Vikings. The Mercia of King Offa (d. 796) was a place of order and surely of some civilisation, but its writings have not survived. The Viking raids of the ninth century destroyed all the kingdoms of England except Wessex, and when in 871 Alfred came to the throne, he testified that Anglo-Latin was virtually dead.

Alfred therefore arranged for "the books most needful for all men to know" to be translated from Latin into English, and these included Bede's *Ecclesiastical History*. It was as a part of the same programme that the *Anglo-Saxon Chronicle* began in Wessex at this time. Alfred's purposes in starting up the process which eventually came to be known as English literature were, in the proper sense of the word, political, and practical rather than artistic. Nor does the prose of his reign have anything aesthetic or humanistic about it. It is rude and rudimentary; Alfred's own prose is at times laborious, and never crisp, as the *Chronicle* can be; it is nevertheless purposeful and effective, and contains two considerable passages which are deeply memorable with a kind of moral splendour.

Historically, prose writing often arises to meet needs which are political: prose is a tool of civilisation, poetry a more natural expression of culture. Prose before Alfred had been used principally to enshrine Germanic customary laws, as under Ethelbert of Kent and Ine of Wessex. Indeed Alfred used Ine's laws, together with those of Moses, as a source of his own. But Latin was used for charters and wills until the ninth century and for royal writs until much later; the scribes were ecclesiastics. If it seems strange that no early Old English sermons survive, we have to recall that even the translation of St. John's Gospel which Bede, the patron saint of all Anglo-Saxon scribes, was dictating at his death, has perished. Apart from a small amount of legal writing, and the exceptional mini-saga of Cynewulf and Cyneheard already referred to, the only English from before Alfred appears in the glosses inserted between the lines of the Latin texts of the Psalms and Canticles; this does not deserve to be called prose.

Effectively, then, King Alfred of Wessex was the father as well as the patron of English prose, for from his school come the first six books translated from Latin to English, and the first original work in English, the *Anglo-Saxon Chronicle*. Alfred, who could not read before he was twelve and began to learn Latin only at the age of thirty-five, not only proposed and organised this programme of translation but played the major part in it himself. Alfred announces his programme and his reasons for it in his Preface to the *Pastoral Care*.

The *Pastoral Care*, a handbook for bishops and so for Christian pastors generally, was written by Gregory the Great when he became pope in 591; it is known as the *Regulae Pastoralis Liber* or *Cura Pastoralis*. Alfred, as will be seen, wanted an educated clergy as the first step in national renewal, and he sends the copy of his translation, which the Preface introduces, to Wærferth, bishop of Worcester, who had already translated for Alfred St. Gregory's *Dialogues*. Qualified judges of the two translations say that it is clear that Wærferth was a better Latinist than Alfred and his learned helpers. But Alfred's late translations became more accurate as well as more fluent.

The Preface has long been recognised as a document of exceptional interest. It is preserved in a manuscript of Alfred's time (Hatton 20 in the Bodleian Library in Oxford) which is headed *"Theos boc sceal to Wiogora ceastre,"* "This book is to go to Worcester." The readings of this text can be checked against another manuscript of the time now existing only in a transcription by Junius. The linguistic and historical uniqueness of the Preface is obvious, but it is a testimony of much wider human interest, revealing very clearly Alfred's personal analysis of the condition of England and, with an attractive candour, the workings of his purposeful mind as he proposes remedies. The Preface begins like a royal writ with a third-person formula familiar from official correspondence in antiquity and from Biblical epistles, but changes into the first person, and then into the first person plural. Alfred's "we" is not the royal plural but speaks for the community of the English, the Angelcynn, with a feeling of kinship. It is at this moment in the history of Anglo-Saxon England and of Old English literature that, for the first time, we meet someone.

King Alfred sends greetings to Bishop Wærferth with his loving and friendly words, and would declare to you that it has very often come to my mind what wise men there were formerly throughout the English people, both in sacred and in secular orders; and how there were happy times then throughout England; and how the kings who had rule over the people in those days were obedient to God and his messengers, and both maintained their peace and their morality and their authority at home, and also enlarged their territory abroad; and how they prospered both in warfare and in wisdom; and also how zealous the sacred orders were both about teaching and about learning and all the services which they had to perform for God; and how men from abroad came here to this land in search of knowledge and instruction, and how we should now have to get them from abroad, if we were to have them. So complete was its decay among the English people that there were very few this side of the Humber who could comprehend their services in English, or even translate a letter from Latin into English; and I imagine that there were not many beyond the Humber. There were so few of them that I cannot even remember a single one south of the Thames when I succeeded to the kingdom. Thanks be to Almighty God that now we have any supply of teachers. And therefore I command you to do, as I believe you wish, that you disengage yourself as often as you can from the affairs of this world, so that you can apply the wisdom which God has given you wherever you are able to apply it. Think what punishments then came upon us in this world when we neither loved [this wisdom] ourselves nor permitted it to other men — we loved only to be called Christians, and very few [of us] loved the virtues.

When I remembered all this, then I also remembered how, before it was all ravaged and burnt, I had seen how the churches throughout all England stood filled with treasures and books, and there was also a great multitude of God's servants — they had very little benefit from those books, because they could not understand anything of them, since they were not written in their own language. As if they had said: "Our forefathers who formerly held these places loved knowledge, and through it they acquired wealth and left it to us. One can see their footprints here still, but we cannot follow after them and therefore we have now lost both the wealth and the knowledge because we would not bend our mind to that course." When I remembered all this, then I wondered greatly at those good wise men who formerly existed throughout the English people and had fully studied all those books, that they did not wish to translate any part of them into their own language. But then I immediately answered myself and said: "They did not imagine that men should ever become so careless and learning so decayed; they refrained from it by intention and hoped that there would be the greater knowledge in this land the more languages we knew."

Then I remembered how the law was first found in the Hebrew language, and afterwards, when the Greeks learned it, they translated it all into their own language, and all the other books as well. And afterwards in the same way the Romans, when they had learned them, they translated them all into their own language through learned interpreters. And all other Christian nations also translated some part of them into their own language. Therefore it seems better to me, if it seems so to you, that we also should translate certain books which are most necessary for all men to know, into the language that we can all understand, and also arrange it, as with God's help we very easily can if we have peace, so that all the youth of free men now among the English people, who have the means to be able to devote themselves to it, may be set to study for as long as they are of no other use, until the time they are able to read English writing well; afterwards one may teach further in the Latin language those whom one wishes to teach further and wishes to promote to holy orders.

Then when I remembered how the knowledge of Latin had previously decayed throughout the English people, and yet many could read English writing, I began amidst other various and manifold cares of this kingdom to translate into English the book which is called *Pastoralis* in Latin and "Shepherd's Book" in English, sometimes word for word, sometimes in a paraphrase, as I learned it from my archbishop Plegmund, and my bishop Asser, and my priest Grimbold and my priest John. When I had learned it, I translated it into English as I understood it and as I could interpret it most intelligibly; and I will send one to every bishopric in my kingdom; and in each there will be a book-marker worth fifty mancuses. And in the name of God I command that no one remove the book-marker from the book, nor the book from the minster; it is uncertain how long there may be such learned bishops, as now, thanks be to God, there are almost everywhere; therefore I desire that they should always lie at that place, unless the bishop want to have it with him, or it be anywhere on loan, or anyone be copying it.

(Swanton, *Anglo-Saxon Prose*, pp. 30–32)

In more secure periods, literature is quite distinct from the educational base which permits it; we do not attribute Shakespeare's achievements to the excellent teaching at Stratford grammar school. Alfred's Preface, itself of small artistic ambition, is however an embodiment as well as the foundation of what is considered in this volume. Without his wisdom and provision the educational successes of Archbishop Dunstan and the Benedictines of the reign of Alfred's great grandson Edgar would not have been possible; and without the Benedictine Renewal there would today be no manuscripts. Alfred, we are told by his biographer Asser, loved the old poetry and knew much by heart. The vital relation of this poetry and its values to his own heroic life and the spirit of his people would be something Alfred took for granted. What no one could take for granted at Alfred's accession was the survival of his kingdom. Having ensured that, Alfred set out to rebuild that Latin Christian culture which made the survival of Angelcynn worthwhile, and to educate the free-born laity. It is clear from the Preface that "wisdom" and national independence were not separate in Alfred's mind. Wisdom and learning go hand in hand with prosperity in war and peace. At Bede's time (see p. 35) and the blessed time when Alcuin was summoned from York to be the master of Charlemagne's school, Angelcynn was prosperous; now the Danes had overrun most of the country and we had to import scholars if we were to have any learning at all. The learning and wisdom Alfred speaks of are not those sought in a modern liberal university but are a specifically Christian learning and an ethical wisdom—wise conduct, such as preserves communities and kingdoms.

Alfred's imported helpers—Mercian, Welsh, Frankish, and Old Saxon—succeeded in translating the books, but there is no direct evidence that the schools he set up were an immediate success. The monastic ideal was almost dead: John the Old Saxon, mentioned in the last paragraph of the Preface, was nearly murdered by the monks at Athelney. Yet it was in the remnants of Alfred's old school at Glastonbury that Dunstan was educated. The *Chronicle*, begun at the capital, Winchester, was distributed to several monastic centres and kept up. It faltered during the glorious reign of Alfred's grandson, Athelstan, but revived under Edgar. It is hard to resist the conclusion ardently leapt at by Alfred's admirers in the nineteenth century: *unus homo nobis ... restituit rem*—one man, alone, restored to us our whole state. The practical part of this restoration, the defeat of the Danes, preceded the ideal part, as we shall see. But it is clear that the success of the Treaty of Wedmore was built upon Christian ideals, the validity of which Guthrum had been forced to recognise.

Alfred's achievements are undeniable. His character is known to us from Asser and the *Chronicle*; but it can also be observed in his own writing. The steady advance of his thinking through the Preface is impressive: the chain of argument, expressed in the heavy connectives which couple the clauses, is forged by a palpable personal strenuousness. And Alfred's sense of responsibility is an educated one. The notion of transmission of culture he employs is common but profound: the notion of *translatio studii*, whereby wisdom and political authority were transplanted from Israel and Greece to Rome and so to the west. It was still valid in the renaissance of the twelfth century, where, a French author wrote, *chevalerie et clergie* came from Rome to France. It was expressed also at that time in the myth made popular by Geoffrey of Monmouth, of Brutus the Trojan, grandson of Aeneas, as founder of Britain; and made a late appearance in literature in Bishop Berkeley's "Westward the course of empire takes its way." If Alfred's prose style is virile rather than graceful, his care makes his language attractive: "Therefore it seems to me better, if it seems so to you also," he says to Waerferth, "that we too should translate into the language which we all can understand those special books which be most needful for all men to know." It is not fanciful to read back into that courteous phrase of consultation at the outset of this sentence some of the largeness which informs the proposal at the end of the sentence to make all the sons of freemen in Angelcynn able to read English. Alfred's unbookishness shows in the picture of the cleric who can see the spoor left in the inky track of his literate precessors but cannot follow the scent. He was himself famous as an indefatigable huntsman.

The most telling phrases of all in the Preface, however, are "Then, when I had thought about all this, I even thought also how I had seen ..." and "if we have the peace (*stilnesse*)." Alfred was a thoughtful man, but his reign had afforded him more things to think about than time to think. This bent is reflected in later popular tradition of him as the wisest of kings, an English Solomon. This is also the point of the legend of Alfred burning the cakes: the disguised fugitive in the swineherd's hut forgot to turn the cakes he was supposed to be watching, for he had larger things to think about.

I • *THE ANGLO-SAXON CHRONICLE*

Before turning to Alfred's translations it is proper to look at the *Chronicle*, which was probably in hand by this time, and its account of his reign. The *Anglo-Saxon Chronicle* exists in seven manuscripts; the seven versions are basically the same until the year 891 but diverge considerably in entries for reigns subsequent to Alfred's, partly as a reflection of the history of the part of the country where each version was kept up. The *Chronicle* developed originally inside the framework of the Easter Tables, the calendar used by the Church to calculate the date of Easter in future years. Years were identified for the purposes of memory as the year of the eclipse, of the flood, or of the death or accession of a king, and such events were noted against such years. These simple annals do not make a chronicle, still less a history, but the decision was taken in Alfred's reign to turn the annals into a more adequate record. The Parker Chronicle, the manuscript of the *Chronicle* kept at Winchester (so called after Elizabeth's Archbishop Parker — "Nosy Parker" — who published it) is closest to the first manuscript. The Parker Chronicle begins with a sketchy history of the world, based on the summary at the end of Bede's *Ecclesiastical History* and also on some unidentified universal history, and incorporates the genealogy of the West Saxon kings (going back to Adam by way of Woden and some kings mentioned in *Beowulf*) and an account of the Saxon conquest. But it comes to life with the accession of Egbert of Wessex and its account of his grandson Alfred's wars against the Danes.

The *Anglo-Saxon Chronicle* is the only vernacular history, apart from Irish annals, from Europe in the dark ages, and it is on a large scale, the Peterborough version of the *Chronicle* ending only in 1154. It is very selective, of course, being initially entirely West Saxon, neglecting early Northumbria (for which we have Bede) and eighth-century Mercia, of which we know too little. We learn surprisingly little of Alfred's all-conquering grandson Athelstan. It is local, miscellaneous, and inconsistent. But it is the prime source of information for several reigns, and invaluable history. It is also evidence that England was a country worth living in, and is, for many stretches, very well written in its laconic way, especially when compared with the rhetorical and factually unreliable Latin hagiography of the time. Before *Beowulf* was widely accepted at its proper artistic value — that is, before Tolkien's British Academy lecture of 1936 — the *Chronicle* was regarded, in the words of F. P. Magoun, quoted by Garmonsway (p. xv), as "the most important work written in English before the Norman Conquest," even from a literary point of view.

The episode of Cynewulf and Cyneheard which appears in the Parker Chronicle for the year 755 is the chief item of interest to literary history previous to Alfred's reign. It is a uniquely early piece of popular saga-telling in English, of the sort that surfaced otherwise in Latin and in a different dress, and deserves inclusion here for its vividness and economy. The sequence of events is unfortunately obscured toward the end by the use of "they" rather than the proper names which for modern readers are themselves sufficiently difficult. This use of pronouns indicates oral origin.

755 [757]. In this year Cynewulf and the councillors of Wessex deprived Sigeberht of his kingdom for unlawful actions, with the exception of Hampshire; and this he kept until he slew the ealdorman who remained faithful to him longer than the rest. And Cynewulf then drove him away into the Weald, and he lived there until a herdsman stabbed him at the stream at Privett, thereby avenging the ealdorman Cumbra. And that Cynewulf frequently fought great battles against the Welsh; and after ruling thirty-one years he wished to expel a prince called Cyneheard; and that Cyneheard was the brother of that Sigeberht. And then he learnt that the king was visiting a mistress at *Merantun*, with but a small retinue; he surprised him there, and surrounded the bower before the men who were with the king became aware of him. And then the king perceived this, and he went to the door and then gallantly defended himself until he caught sight of the prince, and then rushed out on him and severely wounded him; and they all set on the king until they had slain him. And then from the woman's cries the king's thanes became aware of the disturbance, and whoever then was ready and quickest ran thither; and the prince offered each of them money and life, and none of them would accept it, but they went on fighting continuously until they all lay slain, except one Welsh hostage, and he was badly wounded. When in the morning the king's thanes who had been left behind heard that the king was slain, they rode thither, and his ealdorman Osric and Wigfrith his thane and the men whom he had left behind, and found the prince in the fortified place where the king lay slain, and they had closed the gates upon themselves, and then they went thereto. And then he offered them their own choice of money and land if they would grant him the kingdom,

and they told them that kinsmen of theirs were with them who would not desert them [or *kinsmen of theirs were with him who would not desert him*]; and then they replied that no kinsman was dearer to them than their lord, and they never would follow his slayer; and then they offered to let their kinsmen depart unharmed. And they replied that the same had been offered to their comrades who had been with the king; then they said that they themselves did not care for this "any more than your comrades who were slain with the king." And they went on fighting around the gates until they forced their way in and slew the prince and the men who were with him, all except one who was the ealdorman's godson, and he spared his life, although he was wounded many times.

And that Cynewulf reigned thirty-one years, and his body lies at Winchester, and that of the prince at Axminster; and their direct paternal ancestry goes back to Cerdic.

(Garmonsway, pp. 46–48)

The sense of personal loyalty to a lord, stronger even than the bond to a kinsman as is testified by the behaviour of both sides in this fight, and by the loyalty of the hostage, is a continuing theme in Anglo-Saxon life, as we shall see in *Maldon*. The sanctity of obligation, whether by oath, word, blood-tie or simply of law, seems particularly strong in Germanic societies. While "Cynewulf and Cyneheard" is an exception in its form, its content is classically Germanic, combining defence of a narrow place with a clash of loyalties, as in *Finnsburgh* and *Waldere*. Some of the same motives are to be found in the story of Alfred's success against the Danes.

After Offa's death the power in England was gradually wrested from Mercia to Wessex by its formidable king Egbert, and West-Saxon predominance was maintained by Egbert's son Aethelwulf, father of Alfred. But the marauding attacks of the Danes on the coasts of eastern and southern England became more severe throughout these two reigns, culminating in 855 when the Danes, or "the heathen army," overwintered in the Isle of Sheppey in Kent. Although Wessex always resisted, the entries beginning in 865 show how fast things were sliding.

865 In this year the heathen army encamped on Thanet and made peace with the people of Kent. And the people of Kent promised them money for that peace. And under cover of that peace and promise of money the army stole away inland by night and ravaged all eastern Kent.

866 In this year Ethelbert's brother Ethelred succeeded to the kingdom of the West Saxons. And the same year a great heathen army came into England and took up winter quarters in East Anglia; and there they were supplied with horses, and the East Angles made peace with them.

867 In this year the army went from East Anglia to Northumbria, across the Humber estuary to the city of York. And there was great civil strife going on in that people, and they had deposed their king Osbert and taken a king with no hereditary right, Ælla. And not until late in the year did they unite sufficiently to proceed to fight the raiding army; and nevertheless they collected a large army and attacked the enemy in York, and broke into the city; and some of them got inside, and an immense slaughter was made of the Northumbrians, some inside and some outside, and both kings were killed, and the survivors made peace with the enemy.

(Whitelock, Douglas and Tucker, The Anglo-Saxon Chronicle, p. 45)

By the year 871 only Wessex and Mercia were left of the Old English kingdoms and only two of Aethelwulf's five sons were left alive. Alfred, the youngest, was twenty-three.

871 In this year the army came into Wessex to Reading, and three days later two Danish earls rode farther inland. Then Ealdorman Æthelwulf encountered them at Englefield, and fought against them there and had the victory, and one of them, whose name was Sidroc, was killed there. Then four days later King Ethelred and his brother Alfred led a great army to Reading and fought against the army; and a great slaughter was made on both sides and Ealdorman Æthelwulf

was killed, and the Danes had possession of the battle-field.

And four days later King Ethelred and his brother Alfred fought against the whole army at Ashdown; and the Danes were in two divisions: in the one were the heathen kings Bagsecg and Healfdene, and in the other were the earls. And then King Ethelred fought against the kings' troop, and King Bagsecg was slain there; and Ethelred's brother Alfred fought against the earls' troop, and there were slain Earl Sidroc the Old, and Earl Sidroc the Younger and Earl Osbearn, Earl Fræna, and Earl Harold; and both enemy armies were put to flight and many thousands were killed, and they continued fighting until night.

And a fortnight later King Ethelred and his brother Alfred fought against the army at Basing, and there the Danes had the victory. And two months later, King Ethelred and his brother Alfred fought against the army at *Meretun*, and they were in two divisions, and they put both to flight and were victorious far on into the day; and there was a great slaughter on both sides; and the Danes had possession of the battle-field. And Bishop Heahmund was killed there and many important men. And after this battle a great summer army came to Reading. And afterwards, after Easter, King Ethelred died, and he had reigned five years, and his body is buried at Wimborne minster.

Then his brother Alfred, the son of Æthelwulf, succeeded to the kingdom of the West Saxons. And a month later King Alfred fought with a small force against the whole army at Wilton and put it to flight far on into the day; and the Danes had possession of the battle-field. And during that year nine general engagements were fought against the Danish army in the kingdom south of the Thames, besides the expeditions which the king's brother Alfred and [single] ealdormen and king's thegns often rode on, which were not counted. And that year nine (Danish) earls were killed and one king. And the West Saxons made peace with the army that year.

872 In this year the army went from Reading to London, and took up winter quarters there; and then the Mercians made peace with the army.

(Whitelock *et al.*, pp. 46–47)

Asser has a fuller account of the Battle of Ashdown, at which, he says, Alfred led the Christian forces "like a wild boar." By 874 Mercia had fallen, and in 878 the Danish army made a surprise invasion into deepest Wessex and, as had never happened before, in midwinter.

878 In this year in midwinter after twelfth night the enemy army came stealthily to Chippenham, and occupied the land of the West Saxons and settled there, and drove a great part of the people across the sea, and conquered most of the others; and the people submitted to them, except King Alfred. He journeyed in difficulties through the woods and fen fastnesses with a small force.

And the same winter the brother of Ivar and Healfdene was in the kingdom of the West Saxons [in Devon], with 23 ships. And he was killed there and 840 men of his army with him. And there was captured the banner which they called "Raven."

And afterwards at Easter, King Alfred with a small force made a stronghold at Athelney, and he and the section of the people of Somerset which was nearest to it proceeded to fight from that stronghold against the enemy. Then in the seventh week after Easter he rode to "Egbert's stone" east of Selwood, and there came to meet him all the people of Somerset and of Wiltshire and of that part of Hampshire which was on this side of the sea, and they rejoiced to see him. And then after one night he went from that encampment to Iley, and after another night to Edington, and there fought against the whole army and put it to flight, and pursued it as far as the fortress, and stayed there a fortnight. And then the enemy gave him preliminary hostages and great oaths that they would leave his kingdom, and promised also that their king should receive baptism, and they kept their promise. Three weeks later King Guthrum with 30 of the men who were the most important in the army came [to him] at Aller, which is near Athelney, and the king stood sponsor to him at his baptism there; and the unbinding of the chrism took place at Wedmore. And he was twelve days with the king, and he honoured him and his companions greatly with gifts.

(Whitelock et al., pp. 49–50)

The terms of Wedmore were observed: the Danish army withdrew to East Anglia and settled there. This was the recognition of the division of England between Saxons in the south and west and Scandinavians in the parts of the north and east eventually known as the Danelaw. From Wedmore stemmed the acceptance of the king of Wessex as king of England, a status formally granted to Alfred's successors by the inhabitants of the Danelaw. We owe much to Alfred: if it had not been for the depredations of the Danes, literature in English might not have been necessary; if it had not been for Alfred's resistance, England might have become an enlarged version of Yorkshire.

The county of Somerset is so called after the *Sumorsaetan*, literally the summer-dwellers: the marshes around Athelney and Glastonbury afforded grazing only in the summer when they dried out. In the winter of 878 they would have been inaccessible to foreigners. As was well known to the annalist, the situation of Alfred was exactly that of many heroes of legend, and he presumably was well able to consider it in the ways the authors of *Maldon* or *Brunanburh* did those battles. But the account remains resolutely factual: only in the placing of two key phrases at the end of sentences might one detect a 'heroic' ordering: *buton tham cynynge Ælfrede* (except King Alfred) and *ond his gefægene wærun* (and they rejoiced to see him). These are in the tradition of the understated final comments in *Beowulf* such as the epitaph on Scyld Shefing: *thæt was god cyning*.

Accidental or not, this creates an epic effect. It is also notable that the entry for 878 has a symmetry: the Danes attack stealthily after Twelfth Night, and in the end, after Guthrum's baptism, are feasted for twelve days. Alfred's godson was to observe the terms of the treaty.

The *Chronicle* has many later passages of the highest interest, even in Alfred's reign, which ends with another onslaught by a Viking army, which had been starved out of the Frankish empire; this campaign is reported in much detail, which suggests that the *Chronicle* was a going concern in the 890s. But the extracts above will have to suffice as samples. Not much can be gleaned about the style of such practical and unpretentious prose from reading samples in translation, but it should be apparent at least that this plain efficiency owes little to encomiastic Latin compositions, and may be called native.

One of the happiest accidents of Anglo-Saxon archaeology was the discovery in 1693, four miles from Athelney, of the Alfred Jewel. This very beautiful jewel, in gold, rock crystal and enamel (see p. 161) shows a man holding two sceptres, and reads + ÆLFRED MEC HEHT GEWYRCAN (Alfred ordered me to be made). Alfred concludes his epistle to Wærferth with a mention of an *æstel*, usually translated "bookmarker," one of which is to accompany every copy of the *Cura Pastoralis*. The *æstel* is of great monetary value, and there is the tempting possibility that Alfred may have sent one to John the Old Saxon, one of his helpers with the translation, who became abbot of Athelney, and that the Alfred Jewel is John's *æstel*. The date and style of the jewel are right, and the socket at its base could have held a quill with which to point the words while reading. In any case the survival in this spot of this exquisite eye-shaped jewel, speaking to us of its maker Alfred, seems providential, an emblem of the survival of Alfred's kingdom. "Athelney" means "noble island."

II • BOOKS MOST NEEDFUL

The peace following Wedmore was only relative: Alfred set about organising proper national defences by building both ships and a system of fortified *burghs*. But, with what *stilnesse* he had, he pursued his project of translating the most needful books. After Gregory's *Dialogues* (done by Wærferth of Worcester) and *Pastoral*

Care, Alfred translated or had translated (*heht gewyrcan*) four other books: Bede's *Ecclesiastical History*, Orosius' *Histories*, Boethius' *Consolation* and Augustine's *Soliloquies*. It was once received that Alfred, though basing his translation, as he says, on the explanations of his scholarly helpers, had translated all of these himself. Even sceptics accept that Alfred's part in the two latter books was great, and he is credited with the addition of a few pages on northern geography to the text of Orosius. His hand is not obvious in the West-Saxon translation of Bede.

The choosing of the books most needful for all men to know is not a task that falls to many writers. It is a measure of how unfamiliar Alfred's mental context now is that only two of the surviving works mean anything today to the educated general reader—those of Bede and of Boethius—and only scholars read these. As Fathers of the western Church, Gregory and Augustine are well known, though Augustine's *Soliloquia* are not much read.

The condition of England, however, as presented in the Preface to the *Pastoral Care*, dictated certain priorities: Augustine's *Confessions*, for example, would not have had for Alfred the exceptional interest among his works that their personal psychology lends them for the modern reader. Alfred's programme began with Gregory's *Dialogues*, a set of miracle-crammed saints' lives translated for him by Wærferth. Here Alfred was resuscitating what remained of the clerical tradition, which was in so serious a decline. Wærferth was a Mercian and wrote in the Mercian variety of Anglian, not in West Saxon. Mercian dialect is also evident in two lesser works of Alfred's reign, the *Life of St. Chad* and the *Martyrology*, and it seems that there was an unpublicised Mercian foundation to the West-Saxon literary achievement. Mercia's century had passed, but West Mercia clearly preserved some latinity at least, and the hagiographic tradition central to the world-view and morale of the Anglo-Saxon clergy. The fact that Worcester, Wærferth's see, was never sacked by the Danes must have helped in this survival. There was a poetic continuity also, and the proximity to Wales of the diocese of the people of the Hwicce may be connected with a Celtic strain in the Anglian Elegies. Worcester was to be the centre of a continuing Anglo-Saxon tradition after the Conquest, and the area contributed much to literature in Middle English—*Piers Plowman*, for example.

If Gregory's *Dialogues* were of comfort to the hard-pressed West Saxons, the *Pastoral Care* was directly edifying to the clergy. England's fundamental debt to Gregory still loomed large after three centuries. From spiritual heroism and pastoral provision, Alfred next turned to history in Bede and Orosius. The West-Saxon version of Bede is shorter by one quarter than the Latin of the *Ecclesiastical History*. Bede's scholarly interests are not emulated: the English version omits papal documents and the details of the controversy over Easter. Rather than history, England needed the national story in memorable form, and the translation gave the popular and pious elements a lively strength. If its style is uneven it is also at times poetic: "he translates, for instance, the bald *paruissimo spatio* of the conversion-of-Edwin sparrow into *an eagan bryhtm* 'the twinkling of an eye'" (Stanley B. Greenfield, *A Critical History of Old English Literature*, p. 32). Alfred's translator also contributes a West-Saxon version of Cædmon's *Hymn*. Some scholars are patriotic enough to prefer the English version to the Latin of the *Church History*; and some of its passages have more sap.

Orosius, an Iberian disciple of Augustine of Hippo, wrote his *Universal History* (431) at Augustine's request, to show the falsity of the pagan view that the decline and fall of Rome were due to the rise of Christianity; for which reason it is also known as the *Historiae aduersum paganos*. Orosius offered Alfred a supplement to Bede: a universal (that is, Mediterranean) account of the period from the Creation to the Fall of Rome, for which he was used as an authority throughout the Middle Ages.

Gregory's taste for wonder-working is not ours, but he was an apostolic teacher who changed the world for the better, and his theology remains of interest. Orosius was a propagandist and an encyclopædist, kinds of writing which quickly become obsolete. Alfred left out about three-quarters of Orosius' text, and translated the remainder freely, adding many details. The accounts of the voyages of the Norwegian Ohthere and the Englishman Wulfstan, which he inserts into the sketchy northern part of Orosius' geographical introduction, are outstanding. They were used by the Elizabethan Hakluyt in compiling his *Voyages*. Alfred's purpose generally was not propagandistic (that battle had been won) but practical, to provide a compendium of knowledge useful to his people. The second-hand encyclopædia disappears when we arrive at this sentence: "Ohthere told his lord, King Alfred, that he lived farthest to the north of all the Norwegians." There follows an account of Ohthere's voyage to the White Sea, and of the Lapps, Perms and Finns, then a most specific description of the goods which made up Ohthere's wealth, all in this direct style, ending with a geography of southern Scandinavia, given from a coasting mariner's point of view, and ending:

> And from Sciringesheal [on Oslofjord], he said that he sailed in five days to the trading town which they call Hedeby [Old Schleswig]; this stands between the Wends and the Saxons and the Angles, and belongs to the Danes. When he sailed there from Sciringesheal, then Denmark was to the port and open sea to the starboard for three days; and then for two days before he came to Hedeby there lay to his starboard: Jutland, and Zealand and many islands. The Angles dwelt in those lands before they came here to this country. And for those two days there lay to his port those islands which belong to Denmark.
>
> (Swanton, p. 35)

The penultimate sentence, for which Alfred seems entirely responsible, is a reminder that these were now the lands of England's enemies. The text carries on:

> Wulfstan said that he had travelled from Hedeby and that he was in Truso [northern Poland] within seven days and nights, since the ship was running under sail all the way. Wend-land was on his starboard, and to his port was Langeland and Laaland and Falster and Skane; and all these lands belong to Denmark. And then to our port was the land of the Burgundians [the island of Bornholm], and they have their own king.

Wulfstan continues, in what is now a first-person narrative, to describe his voyage along the southern shore of the Baltic to the mouth of the Vistula, and has much of interest to report, for example the strange Estonian custom of refrigerating the bodies of their dead. Such ethnography and geography would require footnotes if quoted more extensively, but the freshness of these accounts is evident. Their narrative drive and factual detail seem word-for-word as told to Alfred, but owe something to the king's grasp and clarity. Orosius himself does not seem to have quickened Alfred, as Boethius and Augustine were to; in general, Alfred cut Orosius heavily without adding very much.

Each of Alfred's versions is freer and better than the last. His Latin and his English improved, and as he entered into Boethius and Augustine he felt the stimulus and confidence to change and to add much. The ideal of translation in the Middle Ages — and much later — was not a literal accuracy, except with the Bible, and even there Jerome had taught that sometimes one had to translate sense for sense rather than word for word. (St. Jerome's Latin edition-cum-translation of the Hebrew and Greek Bible, the Vulgate, lies behind much of the theory as well as the content of medieval literature.) Alfred used this commonplace distinction of Jerome's prominently at the end of the Preface to the *Pastoral Care*, and it occurs again in the Proem to his Boethius. But the freedom he employs goes much further than *sensum exprimere de sensu*: he cuts ruthlessly and adds liberally, so that his version of Augustine's *Soliloquies* eventually departs wholly from his original. Alfred did not have the modern academic and often somewhat mechanical notion that the translation should be the faithful slave of a text: he was translating an author for what gave the author his authority, namely his wisdom. Translation, if the word implies mechanical replication, is a misleading term for Alfred's works. His Boethius begins:

> King Alfred was the interpreter of this book, and translated it from Book Latin into English, as it now stands. Sometimes he set down word for word, sometimes sense for sense, rendering it as clearly and intelligibly as he could, despite the many and various worldly cares which beset him both in mind and body.

These words may have been penned by someone who had read Asser's *Life of Alfred*, which continually stresses the physical afflictions which beset the king. Nevertheless they can be taken as accurately representing Alfred's aims as a translator, to transmit and interpret his author rather than produce a complete running gloss on his text. It has been one of the strengths of English literature, as of the English language, that it has not been afraid to import from abroad, using methods of translation more active than those approved of in school examinations.

Wisdom was Alfred's quarry in the *Preface*, and few were held wiser in the Middle Ages than Boethius. Boethius' *Consolation of Philosophy* was translated by Chaucer and Queen Elizabeth I among later English writers, and more frequently translated into European languages in the Middle Ages than any book except the Bible. Dante placed Boethius next to Bede in Paradise and called him *l'anima santa*. In 1883 the Church recognised the local cult of him as a saint in Pavia. Boethius was a Roman statesman of noble family: his father had been consul, he was consul himself, and in the year 522, when he was forty-three, his two sons were both consul. Boethius had translated much of Aristotle into Latin, and some Plato; he had written on mathematics and music as well as philosophy, and like some latter-day Cicero exemplified the full range of classical culture and the virtues of the Roman senator to a rare degree.

But suddenly, by some revulsion now obscure, the Emperor Theodoric, a Goth and an Arian, threw his most trusted adviser into prison for treason; Alfred says that Boethius was secretly trying to protect the rights of the Catholic Church in the western empire. It was in prison in Pavia that Boethius wrote his *De Consolatione Philosophiae*. In 524 Theodoric had him tortured to death. The violent change from the highest office in the empire to an abject and unjust humiliation was a copybook example of the later medieval idea of tragedy.

Boethius' *Consolation* is a vindication of divine justice and providence in spite of all painful appearance and experience to the contrary. It takes the characteristic medieval form of a dialogue between the downcast author and a figure who appears to him, in this case Philosophy personified as a noble lady. Eventually Philosophy persuades Boethius of the rightness of her case: she explains the operations of Fortune and shows that true felicity is to be found in the supreme Good. Her arguments are based on reason and natural law rather than on Christian revelation, and, although Boethius was a Catholic, the work seems to be addressed to the educated pagan rather than the Christian. It was however treasured by Christians as a persuasive and impressive work of theodicy (vindication of divine justice), learned and eloquent and moreover fully orthodox especially on the difficult reconciliation of divine foreknowledge and human free will, on which he is easier to follow than St. Augustine. Chaucer still regarded Boethius as the great authority on this question. For the Middle Ages the *Consolation* was the embodiment of classical philosophy, Platonic, Aristotelian, and Stoic, not theoretical but fortifying in its ethical wisdom. The *Consolation* still reads as the work of a noble mind, and some of the Metres (which alternate with prose throughout) are fine indeed. Boethius seems in retrospect an inevitable choice; a wise statesman who suffered great trials, physical and mental, his example must have meant a lot to Alfred.

Alfred adapted and added much to the text, following commentators and also drawing on his own experience. It must be admitted that as literature his version does not live up to the original. Alfred reduces the five books with their thirty-nine Metres into forty-two prose chapters. One of the best of the Metres is a treatment of the myth of Orpheus and Eurydice. The nature of his audience meant that Alfred had to paraphrase the story, which he does in an engaging if naive way, and this has been admired; but he adds that this lying fable teaches that a man must be resolute in turning his back on his old sins (Eurydice) if he is to seek the light. The moral allegory of Boethius has this sense, but with an austere tact and concision; Alfred spells it out painfully. The outrage is not just to modern romantic feelings for Eurydice, or the equation of woman and sin, which may come from a commentator on Boethius. There is a loss of quality such that for a moment the Enlightenment scorn for the Middle Ages as entirely dark becomes intelligible. But in literature aesthetic concerns are the flower of which the remote root is mere literacy. Boethius, with Cassiodorus, was one of the last active Roman contributors to the classical tradition; Alfred wrote in an England where clerics could not read Latin, laymen could not read, and English had hardly been written. The fact of his writing is itself of great significance (it was an accomplishment that eluded Charlemagne), and he shows himself well aware that he lacked both learning and art.

We know from another manuscript of Boethius that Alfred went back and turned his prose Metres into verse.

On the whole the interest of Alfred's Boethius now lies not in the translation but in what he added. A notable addition, not suggested by a commentator, is his reflection that he has found it true that a king needs men of prayer, men of war, and men of work if he is to carry out his duties:

> For every good gift and every power soon grows old and is heard of no more if wisdom be not in them. Without wisdom no faculty can be fully brought out: for whatever is done unwisely can never be accounted as skill. To be brief, I may say that it has ever been my desire to live honourably while I was alive, and after my death to leave to them that should come after me my memory in good works.
>
> (Wrenn, p. 220)

The first of these three sentences might have been lifted from a prose version of Hrothgar's homily to Beowulf; the third is a commonplace that might form part of a dying speech by Beowulf. The second, however, is not a traditional Germanic generalisation but has the stamp of Alfred's character on it.

Alfred, it seems clear, identified with Boethius. Unsaddled with our historical and critical awareness, he generously baptises Boethius' Platonic conceptions: Lady Philosophy becomes Wisdom, and the Good becomes God. "Where now are the bones of Fabricius?" asks Boethius. Alfred adds: "What now are the bones of the famous and wise goldsmith Weland?" This was a good and perhaps a necessary supplementary question for the inhabitants of Wessex, who knew about Wayland's Smithy on the Berkshire Downs, but may well never have heard of Fabricius, an incorruptible Roman general of the third century BC. Where are they now, is a question so frequently asked in the Old English Elegies and in the Latin of the period that scholars speak of the *ubi sunt* formula. It was not a formula for Alfred, however, who has a further point to make, and a rather different one: "I call him wise," he continues about Weland, "for the skilful man can never lose his skill, nor can he more easily be deprived of it than the sun may be moved from its place." Alfred believed strongly that wisdom was something that could be learned and, moreover, would not be diminished by death but increased in eternity. Boethius might not have disagreed, but it was not the point he was making here. It is curious to think that Boethius might, like the modern reader, have suspected that Wayland, being legendary, had no bones, while the Anglo-Saxon acceptance of him as historical might have been shared by Theodoric, who appears with him in *Deor*. (In *Deor* Wayland is a captive and Theodoric is a tyrant.) One consequence of the revival of learning (of which Alfred was the first English proponent) was that classical culture replaced Germanic tradition. The Renaissance finished the job that the Norman Conquest began, of depriving Old English literature of its heritage, so that Saxon things, now that they too have been revived, challenge our usual sense of cultural congruities and continuities.

These academic refinements would not have bothered Alfred, who in his version of Orpheus and Eurydice gives three heads to Charon rather than to Cerberus. He had made the wisdom of this precious book available to his people, had found a kindred spirit, and had been able to pass on some of his own experience. The value of experience, a value prized in Old English poetry from the beginning, is a constant theme in Alfred. From his writing, which began in a struggle for the mastery of the very elements of language, emerges a voice of experience which is at once that of a whole culture and yet identifiably personal.

The last of his books is his most personal, and is indeed a farewell to books. Alfred's version of the *Soliloquia* of St. Augustine adds to his original a new third book, and amplifies the second book considerably; at the end of books I and II the manuscript designates the work as "the Blooms of Alfred," by which title the *Soliloquies* are sometimes known today. The "blooms" are the flowers picked by an anthologist who had ranged far afield into Gregory and Jerome as well as other works of Augustine. Augustine of Hippo (354–430) was the most powerful thinker among the Fathers of the western Church, and the most eloquent writer. The *Soliloquia* were uncompleted at his death: they concern the immortality of the soul and take the form of a dialogue between himself and Reason. Alfred's new third book draws on Augustine's *Of Seeing God*, a work which Reason recommends to

Augustine himself. Alfred's third book casts Augustine's treatise into dialogue form, and gives Reason the last word: "Therefore it seems to me that that man is very foolish and very much to be pitied who will not increase his intellect while he is in this world, and also wish and desire that he may come to the eternal life, where nothing is hidden from us." The wisdom, therefore, which Alfred has sought in this life shall profit a man hereafter.... Alfred's thinking and his capacities as a student of others' books and as a writer have developed far since the *Pastoral Care*. Not only can he now draw on the range of patristic writing, he shows initiative in recasting his materials into a form which suits his own purposes and yet respects literary decorum, and he is able to end his life's work in the C major keynote: wisdom has metaphysical value and increases our happiness in eternity.

The additions Alfred makes to the *Soliloquies* are all interesting, and often noble. It is however possible only to quote his Preface to the work, a Preface less well known than that to the *Pastoral Care* but even more splendid. This is Michael Swanton's translation of it:

> Then I gathered for myself staves and posts and tie-beams, and handles for each of the tools I knew how to use, and building-timbers and beams and as much as I could carry of the most beautiful woods for each of the structures I knew how to build. I did not come home with a single load without wishing to bring home the whole forest with me, if I could have carried it all away; in every tree I saw something that I needed at home. Wherefore I advise each of those who is able, and has many waggons, to direct himself to the same forest where I cut these posts; let him fetch more there for himself, and load his waggons with fair branches so that he can weave many a neat wall and construct many an excellent building, and build a fair town, and dwell therein in joy and ease both winter and summer, as I have not done so far. But he who taught me, to whom the forest was pleasing, may bring it about that I dwell in greater ease both in this transitory wayside habitation while I am in this world, and also in that eternal home which he has promised us through St. Augustine and St. Gregory and St. Jerome, and

through many other holy fathers; so I also believe that for the merits of them all, he will both make this road easier than it was hitherto, and also enlighten the eyes of my mind so that I can find out the straight road to the eternal home and to the eternal glory and to the eternal rest which is promised to us through those holy fathers. So be it.

It is no wonder, though, that one should labour for such material, both in the carrying and in the building; but every man, after he has built a cottage on land leased by his lord, with his help, likes to rest in it sometimes, and go hunting and fowling and fishing, and from that lease to provide for himself in every way, both on sea and on land, until the time when, through his lord's favour, he should merit chartered land and a perpetual inheritance. So may the rich benefactor, who rules both these transitory habitations and those eternal homes bring it about. May he who created both and rules both grant that I may be fit for each: both to be useful here and especially to attain thither.

Augustine, Bishop of Carthage, made two books about his own meditations, those books are called Soliloquia, that is, concerning the deliberation and doubts of his mind—how his reason answered his mind when his mind was uncertain about anything, or it wished to know anything that it could not clearly understand before.

(Swanton, pp. 37–38)

Scholars always quote: "and dwell therein in joy and ease both winter and summer, as I have not done so far," which is certainly revealing. But far more remarkable is the management of the whole metaphor of the forest of wisdom and learning, and of building a habitation for the soul, which the king of eternity may confirm by charter as a perpetual inheritance (an analogy with Anglo-Saxon "book-land"). This is expressed in a way not simply concrete, direct and practical—those Anglo-Saxon virtues in which Anglo-Saxons delight—but with a sustained intellectual strength and metaphysical confidence not unworthy of Augustine or of Dante, though more homely. Both Prefaces, at the beginning and end of Alfred's literary career, show an architectural strength, but the second suggests that his quest for wisdom was not in vain and that his reputation for it was justified.

Of other books attributed to Alfred, the prose psalms in the *Paris Psalter* are probably his; in the whole of the Anglo-Saxon period the Psalter would probably have followed the Gospels as "books most needful for all men to know." The first extant translation of the Gospels is *The West-Saxon Gospels* of the early eleventh century; other versions, like Bede's St. John, have not survived. Continuous Old English glosses were written between the Latin lines of the *Lindisfarne Gospels* and the *Rushworth Gospels* in the late tenth century. The *Vespasian Psalter* was glossed in early ninth-century Mercia. But Alfred's prose psalms seem to be the first surviving version from the Psalter. The many passages of the Bible read at mass or sung in services throughout the year must have been in some sense translated to the people ever since the conversion. Quite apart from Alfred's Psalms, the Old Testament translations of Aelfric, and the *West Saxon Gospels*, it is, therefore, unhistorical or reprehensibly absent-minded to regard the fourteenth-century Wycliffe as the first English translator of the Bible.

EIGHT : VERSE OF THE CHRISTIAN

ESTABLISHMENT

THE Cædmonian poems of the Junius Book reviewed in chapter 5 were versions of Bible narratives. The greater part of the later verse in the three other main manuscripts may also be called religious, though it is less directly concerned with the *god spel*, being composed after the Christian establishment; Cynewulf, the author of some of these poems, lived in the earlier ninth century. Of the later poems, only *Judith* (in the *Beowulf* manuscript) is directly based on a story from the Bible. The Bible *via* the liturgy could also be said to have inspired the complex three-part sequence known as *Christ* which begins the Exeter Book; and *The Dream of the Rood* in the Vercelli Book is a version of the Crucifixion. The bulk of the remaining religious verse, however, is based on matter which has now largely fallen out of conscious Christian tradition, some of which — miracles and relics — has been in disrepute since the humanists of the Renaissance turned a rational eye upon it. Lives of the saints make up the greater part of this literature: *Andreas* is a life, or rather an account of the "acts," of St. Andrew the apostle; and is followed in the Exeter Book by *The Fates of the Apostles*. The New Testament Acts of the Apostles had been early supplemented by accounts, often no doubt imaginary, of the extraordinary doings and deaths of apostles and disciples other than Peter, James, John, and Paul. The heroic resistance made by faithful early Christians to persecution and torture, their deaths, and the attendant miracles, are the staple of these apocryphal tales; and such glorious and grisly manifestations mark *Juliana* (the life of a fourth-century virgin martyr) and the two poems on the Anglo-Saxon saint Guthlac just as much as *Andreas*. Andrew converts the cannibals of Mermedonia; Juliana defies the tortures of the pagan to whom she had been betrothed; Guthlac routs the devils inhabiting his hermitage at Crowland. The wonders worked by God to glorify his faithful equally mark the ordeals of each of these three saints, and miracles similarly break out at the decisive points of *Elene*, the story of how St. Helena, mother of the emperor Constantine who in 312 had triumphed through the Cross, came to find the True Cross in Jerusalem. Helena's story grew up in the fourth century during the establishment of Christianity in the empire—a century in which saints were more often confessors than martyrs. The triumph of Christianity was celebrated by, among others, Lactantius, who wrote on Constantine's vision of the Cross. He is also credited with an allegorical poem on the Phoenix, a version of which forms the most polished specimen of old English religious verse. In the same tradition of supernatural natural history is the *Physiologus* of the Exeter Book: the whale is a symbol of the devil, the panther of Christ, just as the life-cycle of the phoenix is a figure of Christ's resurrection. The *Phoenix* is, like its original, the product of a much more securely integrated and sophisticated Christian culture than the naively demon-bashing *Juliana*. Among a group of smaller poems, *Soul and Body*, *Doomsday*, and *Judgement Day* are very like later medieval sermons in their subject matter, though touched with lyrical or dramatic force. Other pious verse overlaps with the large category of moral and wisdom literature, such as *Solomon and Saturn*.

Old English religious verse is, then, very various in kind, in content, and in quality: none of it, apart from *The Dream of the Rood*, has achieved any popularity in translation. Even among Anglo-Saxonists, who have strong digestions, some of it has not been tackled with enthusiasm. In extended form, which is how it often comes, it seems matter uninviting to the modern eye. *Andreas* has 1722 lines, *Elene* 1321, and although they are respectively perhaps the most spirited and the most accomplished of these poems, each contains much that is incredible or puzzling to the modern layperson. The extremities of *Guthlac* and *Juliana* are harder to take; indeed, the modern reader may not be without at least an initial sympathy for the pagan to whom Juliana had been promised. Juliana might have brought out the Gibbon even in a modern believer such as Evelyn Waugh—who wrote a remarkable book about St. Helena, as well as two other works of hagiography in his *Edmund Campion* and *Ronald Knox*. Waugh's life of the Blessed Edmund Campion, the Jesuit who suffered under Elizabeth, has something of the old élan of hagiography; his unmiraculous *Knox* is much flatter; *Helena*, significantly, is a historical romance not without humour. Waugh provides a useful comparison to the old hagiographers, for he was a convinced believer, in a way which has become rare among educated Anglo-Saxons, in the literal truth of the Incarnation and Resurrection, the actuality of miracles, and the relevance of relics. The different styles of his lives can be related to the amount that was unknown about each subject: Waugh had known Ronald Knox, and his *Life* of Edmund Campion is well documented; but Helena, though some particulars are known to history, was for the novelist an appealingly shadowy figure. The modern British authority Attwater remarks:

> St. Helen's name is particularly connected with the finding, buried close to the hillock of Calvary, of the cross on which the Saviour suffered. Such a discovery was certainly claimed about this time, but the earliest writers do not mention St. Helen as having anything to do with it: she may, indeed, have been dead before it happened, but since the end of the fourth century it is with this discovery that St. Helen is always associated. Whether the wood that was found was in fact that of the true cross is another and different question, and one that is now impossible of solution.
>
> (Donald Attwater, *Penguin Dictionary of Saints*, p. 166)

For Bede, who wrote on the Holy Places, or for Alfred, who was presented with a fragment of the True Cross by Pope Marinus, the original disappearance of the Cross might have been the only "question" (the solution to which was that the ashamed Jews had hidden it). Why should St. Helena not have had its location revealed to her? To the audience of *Elene*, unconcerned with critical-historical theories of the origin and growth of cultus and legend, the Cross was the central fact of history, and an actively powerful presence. "In 633, at Heavenfield," as Swanton points out, "Oswald of Northumbria had re-enacted the original Constantinian story, erecting a great wooden cross and praying for the assistance of God before engaging in battle, the wood of this cross being subsequently believed to work miracles" (M. Swanton, ed., *The Dream of the Rood*, p. 45). Divine participation in a natural order not distinguished from a supernatural order was common experience; nor did such faith necessarily involve simple credulousness. Gregory the Great, the godfather of this kind of literature in England, in the homily that lies behind Cynewulf's *Christ II*, states that the miracles of apostolic times did not happen in his own day, and commends the doubt of doubting Thomas: "for it was through his doubt that he came to touch the marks of the wounds, and cut out from our breast the wound of doubt" (Shippey, p. 160). As Christ had said to Thomas (John 20.29): "Blessed are they that have not seen and yet have believed."

Convenience, rather than a categorical difference, is the reason for the separate treatments given here to Cædmonian and Cynewulfian poetry, for although the later poems are, with the splendid exception of *Judith*, not biblical narratives, they inhabit the same cultural continuum as the former. Although Cynewulfian poetry can in places be pietistic and superstitious, and although it derives from apocryphal sources, it is no more "secondary" than the Cædmonian versions of the Old Testament, which, far from being an evangelical sowing of the simple word, rework the material to emphasise certain themes. Primitive Christianity should not be looked for in Old English literature, which was the product of an educated clergy, though the lives of many of the clergy were simple and holy enough, in emulation of those whom they honoured. Compared with the rhetorical competence of Cynewulf, who is clearly familiar with Latin composition, Cædmon's afflatus is more heroically Germanic; yet the Cædmonian poems too are informed by a well-knit Christian culture and body of doctrine defined by the Latin Fathers of the

Church. The understanding of the Bible worked out by the Fathers was, naturally, indistinguishable from the Bible itself, and had been permanently embodied in the liturgy. The Bible came not as an isolated text to be interpreted but as the bearer of a series of events teaching powerful lessons, the chief of which was the good news that faith brings salvation. This is also the lesson of the lives of saints and the witness of the martyrs, just as Oswald's victory at Heavenfield was a repetition of the Emperor Constantine's victory of the Cross at the Milvian Bridge. All such Christian narratives, biblical or otherwise, are allegorical in the simplest sense that the story teaches a lesson, the lesson that God glorifies his faithful. The deeds of the saints are a continuation of the acts of the apostles — and of the acts of the Jewish patriarchs.

The Reformation of the sixteenth century enforced a distinction between the Bible and tradition, and between the canon and the apocryphal books. But the Christian tradition of most reformed churches still contains much that is not to be found in the canonical scriptures, except by violent recourse to implication: especially in what concerns Satan and hell. In the early Middle Ages the most popular apocryphal episode was the Harrowing of Hell — Christ's release of the prophets and patriarchs from hell during the three days of his death, as recorded in the apocryphal Gospel of Nicodemus. This finds a reflection in the clause of the Creed, "he descended into hell." The Protestant Milton excludes the Harrowing from *Paradise Lost*, probably as a Catholic accretion, compensating for it by the picture of Christ triumphant in the war in heaven. But the story of *Paradise Lost* is substantially a rationalised spelling out of the story common to the Middle Ages, visible on the church wall and dramatised in the cycles of mystery plays, and implicit also in the early liturgy — and in Old English religious poetry. Some early Christian tradition which we now might call apocryphal was received as a part of the deposit of faith, and was institutionalised by the extension and establishment of the Church, particularly in the propagation of the faith in the Church's liturgical year and the growth of local martyrologies and calendars of saints' days. At its dedication a new church had an immediate material need for a saint's relic and another for a life of its patron saint; lives multiplied and legends arose, usually from a kernel of fact or tradition, which local cults often embroidered in the conviction that their patron saint would not have fallen short of the great exemplars of holy life and death.

I • SAINTS' LIVES: *ANDREAS*

The patronage of a saint was a valued thing. St. Andrew, for example, was the first of Christ's disciples. Gregory the Great was a monk of St. Andrew's monastery on the Coelian hill in Rome, and so was the man he chose as apostle of the Angles, Augustine. Numbers of churches were dedicated to Andrew in England. The poem *Andreas* is extant in the Vercelli Book in the cathedral of St. Andrew at Vercelli, a station on the English pilgrimage route to Rome, where Andrew's brother Peter had suffered death. St. Andrew's cathedral was founded at Vercelli in the early thirteenth century by Cardinal Guala on his return from a visit as Papal Legate to England, where he had held the benefice of St. Andrew's, Chesterton, Cambridgeshire. It is easy to see how an earlier cleric attached to a church dedicated to St. Andrew in England, such as Wilfrid's abbey at Hexham, might have wished to turn into English verse the Latin *Acts of Andrew and Matthew in the Lands of the Cannibals*. Two prose versions of these Acts also survive in Old English, both much simpler than the verse *Andreas*. (No extant Latin version is the exact source of *Andreas*, but the Latin versions we have are simpler than the third-century Greek original; in the sixth century Gregory of Tours produced a work-manlike series of versions of saints' lives pruned of the excesses of their oriental originals.) Hearing the life, the local congregation would now feel closer to the apostle, their friend and advocate at heaven's court; they also had a more concrete link, through the saint whose relic was sealed in their altar. Popular medieval Christianity, like popular Latin Christianity today, had a literal unembarrassed material grasp on the Incarnation and its consequences which should not be misunderstood as mere externality. There are signs that a non-partisan modern scholarship has finally recovered from the disdainful recoil of the Enlightenment from popular religion, and begun to approach the cult of the saints with a more sympathetic understanding, not as pagan survival or idolatry, but as authentic Christian worship. This recovery is of much psychological, cultural, and Christian interest, but of course does little to rescue the average saint's life — with its blood, demons, and visions — for literature, strange though much post-modernist literature has become.

Andreas is an account of the apostle's sea-borne mission to the land of the cannibals, where he delivers Matthew from prison and miraculously endures the tortures that, prompted by the devil, the cannibals impose on him. Angelic and divine powers first drown some of the cannibals, then restore them to life; they become Christians, and weepingly wave Andrew goodbye as he sails back to Achaia. This fervent and sensational tale is redeemed from the two-dimensionality of a cartoon by an occasional inner gravity, especially in Andrew's moments of doubt, as before obeying the divine command and setting out for Mermedonia. The dramatic action of the poem is narrated with much zest and a thundery descriptive energy. At moments it has a spiritual and physical tension, like a sacred canvas of the Catholic Reformation of the late sixteenth century, such as some by Tintoretto or El Greco. The story is more literally intended than the above account may suggest; the starving cannibals suffer agonies when they discover that Matthew, whom they had been saving for their next meal, has been spirited out of prison; less realistically, they torture Andrew for days rather than eating him. There are subtler moments, as where Andrew tells the master of his ship (who is Christ in disguise) that he will not weary his understanding further by telling him more of Christ's miracles. Most of the interest in *Andreas* accrues in the long account of the sea-voyage and the testing conversations that the unrecognised Lord holds with Andrew, full of echoes of the post-Resurrection appearances in the New Testament. These powerful motifs ring bells that otherwise remain obstinately silent. The violent trials of strength in Mermedonia are unbelievable and unattractive. But they cannot merely be dismissed by any who take seriously the Acts of the Apostles itself— or, for example, the mission and death of St. Boniface of Crediton. This remarkable fisher of men spent nearly half his long life in successful missionary journeys among the heathen tribes of Southern Germany; he was finally hacked to pieces by some Frisians at Dokkum, where he had been reading a book in his tent. The ethos of his life, which ended in 754 or 755, and of the lives and letters of other eighth-century Anglo-Saxon missionaries to the Germans, suggests an audience for *Andreas*. The Acts of the Apostles is itself full of cures, raisings from the dead, deliverances from prison, mass conversions, escapes from ordeals, and worstings of devils. And missionary activity in the eighth century actually exhibited a faith and purposefulness not far short of that shown by Andreas in this work of fiction.

Andreas is the Greek form of the first apostle's name, and the extravagant romance of his story is also Greek. This folk-tale fantasy is compounded by a second strangeness, for the style of the poem, in marked contrast to its content, is northern, Germanic, epic, and martial. It begins thus, in C.W. Kennedy's version:

> Lo! we have heard of twelve mighty heroes
> Honoured under heaven in days of old,
> Thanes of God. Their glory failed not
> In the clash of banners, the brunt of war,
> After they were scattered and spread abroad
> As their lots were cast by the Lord of heaven.
> Famous those heroes, foremost on earth,
> Brave-hearted leaders and bold in strife
> When hand and buckler defended the helm
> On the plain of war, on the field of fate.
>
> One was Matthew....
>
> (Kennedy, p. 122)

This blast on the aurochs' horn may remind us that Christ gave the apostles, not sweetness and light, but powers. However, spiritual combat in *Andreas* is presented in terms so heroic and physical that it scarcely seems spiritual, though the sea-voyage may have some allegorical intention. The inherited thought-forms of Germanic battle-poetry so condition the tale that the most prominent topic in early discussions of *Andreas* was the poem's debt to *Beowulf*. There are striking verbal similarities, and, besides such common themes as the struggle between good and evil and the folk-tale wonders, there is cannibalism. Some of the verbal echoes are so very close that it was generally thought that the author of *Andreas* was paying tribute to the master of *Beowulf*. But after the oral formulaic work of Parry and Lord outlined in chapter 3, the hypothesis of direct influence no longer seems necessary: coincidences, however striking, are to be expected in poems from the same repertory.

The emphasis formerly laid on possible debts to *Beowulf* begged the question of the nature and quality of *Andreas* itself; nor can the poem be rescued by the critics' repeated praise for the realism of its description of Andrew's sea-voyage to Mermedonia: "Halyards were humming," as Kennedy has it in his version. Both the epic formulas and the salt spray are merely incidental features of the heroic poetry of the north: the critical issue is what to make of the strange tension between a story whose reason for existence is religious, and a narrative version of it which constantly reminds us of secular values and a different tradition. The incongruity can be neither denied nor avoided. Readers of *Andreas* today are likely to be medieval specialists, who may find it impressive, intriguing, quaint, and repulsive by turns. Only if they are Christians will the poem's entertainment value be secondary; Christian readers will have something in common with the original audiences, though probably not enough. They are likely to react as northern European protestants do to those Italian cathedrals which seem to have been faced with Neapolitan ice-cream, or to Bernini's statue of a sensually swooning St. Teresa receiving the stigmata, that is, with a cultural shock: for them such a medium has associations which make it most inappropriate for conveying this message. Dr. Johnson felt the same about *Lycidas*. He disliked Milton's use of the pastoral convention and of classical mythology, but added: "This poem has yet a grosser fault. With these trifling fictions are mingled the most awful and sacred truths, such as ought never to be polluted with such irreverent combinations." Syncretic Renaissance artists, however, knew what they were doing in "mingling" Christianity and paganism: they relied on a Christian transcendence.

But in *Andreas* the synthesis is incomplete, and the transposition into heroic terms is quite unconscious. Of recent critics of *Andreas*, only T.A. Shippey seems to have faced up to this incongruous clash of form and content honestly and with understanding. The saint's-life tradition is already in a somewhat debased form in the source story of *Andreas*, borrowing its horror from sailors' tales of the barbarous Scythians (Mermedonia perhaps gets its name from Achilles' Myrmidons). Shippey makes a good case for the epic style dignifying the thin oriental story, especially making more solemn the apostle's relationship with his Lord, and bringing out the crucial moments of inner resolve in deciding crises. Christian faith can be validly rendered by thanelike loyalty, as in *The Dream of the Rood*. And the heroic purpose of Andreas himself, expressed in the poem's speeches rather than its action, is artistically and ethically more significant than the conversion of the cannibals. It is nevertheless possible to prefer the simple prose version of Andreas' "acts" given in one of the Blickling Homilies; though the verse *Andreas* has moments of rich metaphoric life, it can seem, in comparison with the artless prose, incoherent. There is certainly a paradox in a noble style dignifying ignoble matter, especially when the noble style is secular and the ignoble matter supposed to convey "the most awful and sacred truths."

Andreas is an example, like the late *Judith*, of the Germanic style absorbing its Christian matter. The verse associated with the name of Cynewulf is by comparison more thoroughly Christian in its style and ideas as well as in its matter. The name of Cynewulf appears in runic disguise toward the end of four poems: *Elene* and *The Fates of the Apostles* in the Vercelli Book, and *Juliana* and *Christ II* in the Exeter Book. Most of the rest of the Christian verse in these manuscripts was at one time thought to be Cynewulf's also, but, just as it has become clear that Cædmon did not compose the Junius Book, scholars have restricted Cynewulf to the four "signed" poems. The name is hidden in a runic acrostic, unmistakable in Old English, if untranslatable in modern English. Cynewulf's intention was not primarily to claim authorship of the poems, nor fame, but to ask that his readers should pray for him by name. The self-consciousness about writing exhibited in such a "signature" contrasts with the anonymity of an oral *scop*. *Beowulf* is truly an anonymous poem, the product of a culture rather than an author. However, Cynewulf's poems, in their more sophisticated and conventional way, are virtually anonymous, as the end of his *Elene* shows.

II • *ELENE*

Elene is principally a narrative of the finding of the cross, the festival of which (the "Invention") is May 3 in the Catholic Church. After telling the story the poet continues:

> May hell's door be closed
> And the entrance to heaven,   the angels' realm
> And eternal bliss,   be open for ever,
> And his lot appointed   with the Lady Mary
> For every man   who keepeth in mind
> The most hallowed feast,   under heaven, of the Cross
> Which the Great Lord of all   clasped with His arms. *Finit.*
>
> > (1229-35; Kennedy, p. 212)

The author then gives an account of himself, in verses distinguished from the narrative by leonine rhymes. Kennedy translates:

> Thus, old and death-bound   through this doomed flesh,
> I have wondrously gathered   and woven this lay.
> At times I have pondered   and patterned my thought
> In the anxious night-watches.   I knew not the truth
> Concerning the Rood   till with radiant power
> Wisdom made wider   the thoughts of my mind.
> Soiled by past deeds   and shackled with sin
> I was vexed with sorrows,   bitterly bound,
> Burdened with cares,   till the King of might
> Through His radiant grace   granted me knowledge
> To comfort old age,   a glorious gift;
> Instilled it in mind,   made steadfast its light,
> Made it more ample,   unfastened the flesh,
> Unlocked the spirit,   gave the gift of song
> Which I've used in the world   with gladness and glee.
> Full oft I took thought   of the Tree of glory,
> Not once alone,   ere I learned the truth
> Of the radiant Cross   as I read it in books,
> In the fullness of time   to set forth in writing
> The tale of that Standard.
>
> > (1236-57)

This appealing self-portrait may all be true: Cynewulf's age, his nocturnal meditations upon the Cross, and his late discovery, guided by grace, of the true story of the Cross. But they are also very much what was expected of the pious scribe of that day; they reappear, much concentrated, in *The Dream of the Rood*.

Cynewulf continues with the passage including his name. Kennedy's version translates the runes by italicised words, placing the letter which begins the Old English runic words in the margin.

Until then was strife,

C	The *hero* perishing haunted with care,
	Though he shared in the mead-hall many a treasure
Y	And appled gold. He bewailed his *woe*;
N	A *death-bound* soul he suffered sorrow,
E	Secret fear, while his *horse* before him
	Measured the mile-paths, proudly prancing,
W	Decked with jewels. *Joy* has fled,
	Mirth with the years. Youth has vanished
U	And olden pride. *Our* portion was once
	The splendour of youth; now the days of our years
	After time appointed have passed away.
L	Life's joy has waned as the *waters* flow,
	The hurrying floods. For all under heaven
F	*Wealth* is transient. The treasures of earth
	Wane 'neath the clouds most like to the wind
	When it rises loud in the hearing of men,
	Ranging the heavens, faring in fury,
	And then all suddenly is barred in silence,
	In its narrow prison strictly constrained.

(1257-76)

The interest of this passage is not in the technical problems of the runic signature but in the successful Christianisation of the common Germanic picture of the heroic life, familiar from *Beowulf* and the Elegies. Here the final inadequacy of the consolations of that life is spelt out rather than cloudily implied. Yet the unavailing and transitory nature of the good and attractive things of the noble life is given some of the pathos of experience:

Cynewulf's name is woven through it, and its wisdom is not unearned. The message is conventional enough, but it is properly grounded in an Anglo-Saxon vocabulary in the images of the flood and the wind.

With a skilful transition Cynewulf looks forward now to the end of the world:

> So all this world   shall vanish away
> And on all she brought forth   the fire shall seize
> When the Lord Himself   with legions of angels
> Shall come to Judgement.   A just doom
> Shall each man hear   from the mouth of his Judge.
> He shall pay the penalty   for all vain words....
>
> (1276-81)

The Judgement (the original sense of "Doom") is pursued for another forty lines; the souls of the "soothfast" pass lightly through the flames; the "sinful" are purified in them; "accursed transgressors" burn forever—they do not come again into the mind of God. Doomsday was a subject to which the Old English poets turned often; Cynewulf brings it in, together with his signature, to the end of all four of his poems.

That the Cross is the token, almost the agent, of our salvation is to be understood behind the final passage of *Elene*, on the bliss of heaven. The Christianity of the dark ages is distinguished from that of more enlightened times by the intensity of its belief in the joys of heaven. Cynewulf's happily orthodox doctrine of purgatory and hell, and his integration of his humble self into the picture, are characteristic of his thorough absorption of an established Christian understanding. He writes well about Christian doctrines, truths, and mysteries, and about the divine plan revealed in cosmology and history; this sense of design shows up in his own compositions, which have a subtle sense of parallel and paradox. The stories he has to tell are improved by him as narratives but also in their balance and theological significance. Unfortunately his raw material has some ineradicably naive elements. Thus the action of St. Elene is principally that of a victorious campaign by the empress over stubborn Judaism, a victory won by superior power, spiritual and temporal. The struggle between Helena and

Judas Cyriacus is presented in a series of steps, at each of which the Jewish cover-up of their failure to recognise the Messiah and their concealment of the Cross yields to Christian truth; the eventual appearance of the True Cross is an outward and visible sign of a spiritual victory. Cynewulf orchestrates the themes well, showing the priority of ethos over action which seems a fundamental Anglo-Saxon trait, so that the miracle confirms the moral victory, rather than seeming to force it—as sometimes happens, as a result of divine nepotism and string-pulling, in the *Iliad*. Even so, Judas has to endure a week without food at the bottom of a dry well before he cracks and takes Helena to Calvary.

The story comes from the fifth-century *Acta* of Judas Cyriacus, which Cynewulf follows while blending in much from other sources, patristic on the one hand, and Anglo-Saxon on the other. The doctrine of the former improves the speeches and theology; the latter strengthens the poem's drama and morality. The story springs from Constantine's vision of the Cross, which in the poem brings him victory over a barbarian host on the Danube; after the victory his enquiries lead him to send his mother Helena to find the Cross in Jerusalem. The battle on the Danube and Helena's sea-voyage are successfully given epic treatment.

Then Helena addresses the wise men of the Jews:

> Well have I learned through the secret words of the prophets in God's scriptures, that in days past ye were dear to the King of heaven, loved by the Lord and daring in deeds. Lo! in your folly ye fiercely flung away all wisdom, when ye reviled Him who purposed to deliver you from damnation, from fiery torment, from bondage, by His glorious might. Ye spat with filth on the face of Him who by His precious spittle restored the light of your eyes....'
>
> (Gordon, p. 216)

One thousand of their wisest are summoned to answer an enquiry the empress wishes to make. She asks them how it was that they did not hearken to the words of their own prophets. In a third meeting, 500 experts in the law explain that they are unaware of their offence. One of these, Judas (not the same person as the betrayer of Jesus) tells the Jews that the empress must be seeking the Cross of which his grandfather had spoken to his father. This Judas is represented as the brother of Stephen the first martyr (chronology is absent from such legends) and recounts Stephen's martyrdom at the hands of Saul. At this point in the story the reader realises with relief that its theme is not simply the physical recovery of the Cross but the psychology of conversion, of which Saul/Paul is the great model. Judas is represented sympathetically, like the Old Testament Jews in the Cædmonian *Genesis* and *Exodus*. The Jewish rejection of the Messiah is cause for sorrow, not for contempt, and the loyalty of Judas to his people's tradition is cause for respect.

The Jews now make Judas their representative and he is left alone with the queen. How is it, Helena asks Judas, that you know all about the Trojan war and yet have forgotten these more recent events at home? Judas stoutly stalls, and, in an incident modelled on Peter's denial of Christ, finally denies all knowledge of Calvary. The truth, however, must prevail, and after a week at the bottom of his well, Judas chooses heaven. The Cross is found by a sweet vapour arising from the ground; it is distinguished from its two fellows by bringing back to life one recently dead when it is raised over the corpse. At this climactic moment the Devil appears in person, but is routed by Judas: "Know thou the more clearly that in folly thou didst forsake the brightest radiance and the love of God...." (Gordon, p. 228). Judas is converted, takes the name Cyriacus, and is made bishop of Jerusalem. Helena makes the nails of the Cross into a bit for the bridle of Constantine's horse—a sign that it was by the Cross that he had conquered. Cyriacus remains, a bishop healing his people; Helena sails back to Rome. The feast of the Invention of the Cross is established. *Finit*—then Cynewulf's epilogue.

The story is in its own terms a good one, and its more naive elements are treated without sensationalism; there is no Jew-baiting. Indeed, it is clear from the epilogue that the theme of conversion from the Old Law of sin and the flesh—of nature and pagan honour—to the New Law of love is one that Cynewulf applies to himself finally: he too has had to suffer to find the Cross, implying that we must if we are to do the same. This final application is gently done, without emotional blackmail. Customarily the battle and sea-voyage are praised in *Elene*, and the dialectic (like the legend) dispraised. But Helena is not a ruthless imperatrix, nor is Judas a convenient stool-pigeon. The speeches exchanged are of much interest. The process of his conversion (he is the hero of the tale) is not unlike the coming to the light of Boethius under pressure from Lady Philosophy: it persuades because it is painful as well as reasonable.

Elene is then a civilised poem compared to *Andreas*, and not only because the Jews are not cannibals. We may smile at Cynewulf's chronology, and wonder at the process whereby the words of Zacharias (14.20)—"In that day that which is upon the bridle of the horse shall be holy unto the Lord"—should be fulfilled in this way. But the moral sobriety accorded to the difficulty of *metanoia*, the true change of heart involved in conversion, wins respect. *Elene* is one of the most successful of Old English religious poems, a work of considered art.

III • *CHRIST*

Christ II is Cynewulf's other success: based not upon a story but upon a homily, it is a very different kind of poem. *Christ*, "the first, the longest, and in some ways the most impressive poem of the Exeter Book," as Shippey calls it, is a three-part poem (or three poems arranged as a triptych) on Christ's Coming, his Ascension, and his Second Coming. They have more recently been referred to as the *Advent Lyrics*, *Ascension*, and *Doomsday*, and form a thematic unity, though a single authorship is not plausible. *Christ I* is based on twelve antiphons used by the Church in the liturgy of Advent, expressing the longing of the faithful for the coming of the saviour. It is a lyrical and elevated sequence, itself suitable for liturgical use, though more elaborated than the invocatory prayers from which it grew. It is instinct with the understanding of the messianic prophecies of the Old Testament which gave rise to the Advent liturgy, and to one familiar with that tradition, preserved in some Christmas carols, its programme is not at all obscure. It begins:

> Thou art the wall-stone   the workers rejected
> Of old from the work.   It befits Thee well

That Thou shouldst be Head   of the glorious hall
Locking together   the lengthy walls,
The flint unbroken, in a firm embrace,
That ever on earth   the eyes of all
May look with wonder   on the Lord of glory.
With cunning skill   display Thy craft
Triumphant, Righteous;   and quickly raise
Wall against wall.   The work hath need
That the Craftsman come,   the King Himself;
That He then rebuild   what now is broken,
The house under its roof.   He wrought the body
The limbs, of clay;   now the Lord of life
Must rescue from devils   the droves of the wretched,
The damned from their terrors   as He oft hath done.

(1–16; Kennedy, p. 85)

This is theology turned into drama, building on the drama of the liturgy, and naturalised into English conceptions without loss of precision: the building which "the Craftsman, the King Himself" is invited to repair is not just the temple, the Church, and the fabric of mankind, but also an English hall.

The naturalisation of such a theological symbol into modern and local terms has been a constant requirement of a developing Church; by contrast, modern efforts to do this, in English at least, lose both in theological richness and in precision. The doctrine of the Church as the mystical body of Christ is finely implicit throughout these lines.

The petitions to Mary, to the Trinity, and to the Redeemer in several aspects are fervent and dramatically effective: "Bring us salvation, weary slaves of pain," cry the patriarchs tormented in hell. These prayer-poems also have a firm intellectual control; there is none of the incongruity into which enthusiasm often took Old English poets when domesticating the metaphysical or the remote. This is true even of the unexpected seventh section, *Eala ioseph min* ("O my Joseph"), in which Mary asks why Joseph rejects her. He replies with delicacy and pathos:

I suddenly am
deeply disturbed, despoiled of honor,

for I have for you heard many words,
many great sorrows and hurtful speeches,
much harm, and to me they speak insult,
many hostile words. Tears I must
shed, sad in mind. God easily may
relieve the inner pain of my heart,
comfort the wretched one. O young girl,
Mary the virgin!'

(trans. J.J. Campbell; Greenfield, p. 127)

Their dramatic dialogue ends with "I am His temple" and "Prophecy had to be/In Himself truly fulfilled." No source has been found for this vivid anticipation of the later medieval mystery plays. *Christ III* (or *Doomsday*) is also dramatic but more diffuse and unequal than the *Advent Lyrics*. All three parts of *Christ* show a co-ordinated theological understanding of the world and its history which is impressive even to the secular mind. Thus Mary is the temple of fallen humanity which needs to be restored by the coming of the Craftsman who is also the cornerstone: theological interconnections and correspondences give *Christ* a fullness of meaning not found outside *The Dream of the Rood* in Old English religious verse. The completeness comes from the community of purpose between these poets and the Church — it is poetry of the Church.

Cynewulf's *Christ II* (or *Ascension*) lacks some of the lyricism of *I*, and some of the dramatic energy of *III*, but it is a consistently exalted work, integrated around the theological programme of its source, Gregory the Great's 29th Homily on the Gospels. Cynewulf supplements this from Bede's hymn *On the Lord's Ascension*. Both hymn and homily are conveniently translated in Allan and Calder's *Sources and Analogues of Old English Poetry*, a volume which stands as a comprehensive correction to any idea that the religious poets simply translated or versified what had inspired them. A churchman like Cynewulf would not have had to turn to written authorities to mug up the theology of the Ascension: it would be present to him through the liturgy as much as through reading. Without an imaginative awareness of the Church's liturgical year, in which the Christian cosmology and the theological mysteries are relived in a perpetual cycle of public meditation and prayer, the phenomenon of the total absorption of the central Christian traditions in a theologically advanced and subtle form—in an already poetic form—by a representative and unexceptional mind such as that of Cynewulf, remains unaccountable. His *Ascension*, which is addressed to an eminent (unknown) patron, begins:

> By the spirit of wisdom,   Illustrious One,
> With meditation   and discerning mind,
> Strive now earnestly   to understand,
> To comprehend,   how it came to pass
> When the Saviour was born   in purest birth
> (Who had sought a shelter   in Mary's womb
> The Flower of virgins,   the Fairest of maids)
> That angels came not   clothed in white
> When the Lord was born,   a Babe in Bethlehem.
> Angels were seen there   who sang to the shepherds
> Songs of great gladness: that the Son of God
> Was born upon earth   in Bethlehem.
> But the Scriptures tell not   in that glorious time
> That they came arrayed   in robes of white,
> As they later did   when the Mighty Lord,
> The Prince of splendour,   summoned His thanes,
> The well-loved band,   to Bethany.
>
> (*Christ*, 440-56; Kennedy, p. 983)

Gregory's homily starts from the question, Why, since the angels who were present at the Ascension wore white garments of joy, did not the angels who announced the Nativity also do so? This problem, which has not detained modern commentators on the Bible, seems more intelligible after the impatience for the Nativity of the *Advent Lyrics*. Gregory's answer is that the Nativity, although joyful, represented a humiliation of divinity whereas the Ascension, which saddened the disciples, was an exaltation of humanity. This magnificently oblique opening up of the meaning of the Ascension of Christ bursts with the paradoxes which delighted the scholastics down to their last literary manifestation in the metaphysical divines of the seventeenth century. The more practical Cynewulf is interested in the results for humanity of the

Ascension: although sorrowful, the apostles were sent out by their Lord to evangelise the world—a hard task, but one which gave purpose to Cynewulf, as to Gregory and Bede before him:

> "Go now through all   the regions of earth
> Over wide-running ways.   Make known to the nations,
> Preach and publish,   radiant faith;
> Baptizing the people,   turn them to heaven.
> Destroy their idols,   break and abolish;
> Snuff out enmity,   sow seeds of peace
> In the minds of men   with abundant might;
> And I will be with you   and bring you blessing
> And steadfast strength,   wherever you may be."
> Then suddenly in air   came a rush of sound
> A host of heaven's angels,   a beauteous, bright band,
> Messengers of glory,   in gathering throngs.
> Our King rose up   through the temple's roof,
> Where the gazing throng   of His chosen thanes
> Remained on earth   in their place of meeting.
> They saw their Lord   ascend on high,
> Their God from the ground.   Their souls were sad,
> Their spirits burning   within their breasts;
> They mourned in heart   that they might no longer
> See their Beloved   beneath the sky.
> Then sang their songs   the heavenly angels,
> Adored the Prince,   and praised life's Lord,
> Rejoiced in the light   that shone from the Saviour.
>
> (480–502; Kennedy, p. 99)

There is much more of the joy of the angels at the return of the triumphant Lord, cross-cut with the sorrow of the Lord's earthly thanes. "Why remain ye waiting, ye men of Galilee?" demand the white-clad pair of angels, enlarging zestfully on the triumphs of the Harrowing of Hell (see p. 283) and the Second Coming. The pain of the apostles' mourning seems almost intensified by these angelic ecstasies at the entry of the Lord into heaven. This is now described: "Clothed in white came angels to meet him."

The sustained contrast between the joy of those who understand and the sorrow of those who do not is the polarity off which the whole of *Christ* works. The author of the *Ascension* explains:

> Lo! now we have heard   how the Healing Saviour
> Through His hither-coming   has granted us grace,
> Has freed and defended   the folk under heaven,
> God's Mighty Son,   that everyman
> In his days on earth   by his deeds may choose:
> The shame of hell   or the splendour of heaven,
> The shining light   or the loathsome night,
> The rush of glory   or the gloom of darkness,
> Rapture with God   or riot with fiends,
> Glory with angels   or anguish with devils,
> Or life or death,   as he may find dearer
> While body and spirit   abide in this world.
> Glory to the Trinity   and eternal thanks!
>   (585-98; Kennedy, pp. 101-2)

The joy of salvation is the joy of choice: the light of grace allows men to choose the light (this is the meaning of the white garments) and to escape the darkness. Hence the vigour with which Christ ascends in the poem, springing up to heaven with Germanic energy but also with the clarity of Byzantine theology, expressed in the mosaics of Ravenna. The sense of liberation is palpable, but so is the centrality of the Trinity. The rest of the poem is more relaxed and benign, a canticle of praise and thanks — to the Father for the created universe:

> He assigns us food   and bounty of substance,
> Wealth in wide lands,   and kindly weather
> Under sheltering skies.   The sun and moon,
> Candles of heaven,   most stately of stars,
> Shine unto all men   throughout the earth ...;
>   (603-07; Kennedy, p. 102)

Thanks also to the Son (who in a remarkable development of a figure in Job is surnamed a Bird) for redeeming us from the curse of Adam; and to the Spirit for his gifts (a favourite Anglo-Saxon theme), which include wisdom and song:

He sends to one
Wisdom of speech   in word and thought,
Excellent insight;   he may sing and say
All things well   who has wisdom's power
Locked in his heart.   Loud before men
One stirs with fingers   the sounding harp,
Strikes sweetly the glee-wood.

(663–69; Kennedy, p. 104)

Gratitude for the gifts of the Creation and for the six "leaps" of Christ prophesied in the Song of Songs (another fine lyrical development) conclude however with the necessity to avoid sin and to fear the Second Coming (the seventh "leap"):

The Judgement is near;   we shall know reward
According as we have won it   by our works
During days of life   dwelling on earth.
The Scriptures tell us   how the Treasure of might,
God's Glorious Son,   in the beginning
Stooped to the world,   to the womb of the Virgin,
Holy from heaven.   Verily I await,
And also dread,   a sterner doom
When the King of angels   shall come again,
I who obeyed not well   what my Saviour bade me
In the Books.

(783–93; Kennedy, p. 107)

Cynewulf again weaves his name into his vision of Doomsday, a powerfully realised Apocalypse. This last is the book of the Bible least comfortable to the modern western cleric who, as Alexander Pope says, "never mentions hell to ears polite," still less the Harrowing thereof. Nor is mass angelic ecstasy any longer a compelling recruiting image. Yet the *Ascension* remains the clearest and most coherent verse example of the Anglo-Saxon theological understanding of the universe, man's place in it, and the joy which the doctrine of salvation brought. It is a positive vision, in which the Devil is kept in his place: well in view, waiting, nasty, but dazzled by the prevailing light. There is no more impressive large-scale exposition of orthodoxy in the Old English canon, and it

214

helps to put into perspective, for example, the Christianity that there is in *Beowulf*. The conclusion of the poem, however, is what will allow most modern readers to take it on board: Cynewulf is strongly aware of human dimness and weakness.

> Dire is our need   ere that day of terror
> That we think of the soul's beauty   in this barren time.
> Now is it most like   as if on ocean
> Across cold water   we sail in our keels,
> Over the wide sea   in our ocean steeds,
> Faring on in our flood-wood.   Fearful the stream,
> The tumult of waters,   whereon we toss
> In this feeble world.   Fierce are the surges
> On the ocean lanes.   Hard was our life
> Before we made harbour   o'er the foaming seas.
> Then help was vouchsafed us   when God's Spirit-Son
> Guided us to the harbour of salvation   and granted us grace
> That we may understand   over the ship's side
> Where to moor our sea-steeds,   our ocean-stallions,
> Fast at anchor.   Let us fix our hope
> Upon that haven   which the Lord of heaven,
> In holiness on high,   has opened by His Ascension.
>
> (847-66; Kennedy, p. 109)

The idea of heaven as a haven at the end of life's voyage was still there in the English language for G.M. Hopkins, who has a poem with the title "Heaven-Haven." Cynewulf was not a great poet, but an accomplished composer of verse on great themes, an artist with a clear theological understanding and, like George Herbert, a genuine religious nature. He is entirely conventional, civilised, modest, sincere, and skilful: a tribute to the health of the conventions of the early ninth century.

Doomsday, the subject which calls forth Cynewulf's desire to inscribe his name in the Book, and the subject of *Christ III* and two other poems (*Judgement Day I* and *II*), features largely in our impressions of the medieval view of the world, perhaps because there are so many grisly depictions of damnation, in paint or in words. Also, since few readers of this book will believe literally in either boiling oil or harps, the harps seem insipid, and the boiling oil, grinning demons, and toasting forks are more memorable, if only as a nightmare. On the evidence of Old English literature, Doomsday was indeed never far away from the Church's thoughts. But the bliss of heaven seems in these texts at least as real and intensely imagined as the pains of hell, and gets much more space. Fifteenth-century Italian frescoes are not a good guide to Anglo-Saxon attitudes; still less are the luridly detailed fantasies of hellish tortures by Hieronymus Bosch, the Netherlandish painter who died in 1520.

Even when fear of damnation is the theme, damnation is presented with the tremendous generality of the twelfth-century *Dies irae* sequence (later included in the Requiem Mass), rather than with the morbid individual terror of the Gothic decadence or even the disciplined particularity of Dante. Early Christians expected the Second Coming rather shortly; as generations went by, it seemed less imminent, but toward the year 1000 there grew up popularly a literalist interpretation of the millennium mentioned in Apocalypse 20, after which Satan will be released from his prison. But there is not much mark of this in Old English verse. In general the chief emphasis of the religious writings is upon salvation—not so much upon the opportunity offered by redemptive grace, as a simple relief that a choice was available: "Doom" did not mean Fate (a pagan view) but Judgement, and Christ as Judge takes account of human choice. The heroic literature of the past had had an ethical focus on heroic choice, and also emphasised wisdom. Christianity made this choice a lifetime's business, and the reaction of the Old English religious poets was often one of joy and of longing; fear is not so prominent, and fatalism (sometimes supposed the chief characteristic of the Anglo-Saxons) quite absent.

IV • *THE DREAM OF THE ROOD*

The instrument of this opportunity was the Cross, and it is fitting, if unchronological, to end this chapter with *The Dream of the Rood*, a poem which itself ends with the same updraught of exultation at Christ's triumph that marked Cynewulf's *Ascension*:

The Son was victorious on that expedition [the Harrowing of Hell], mighty and triumphant, when He came, the Almighty Sovereign, with a multitude, a host of spirits, into God's Kingdom, to the bliss of the angels and all of the saints who had previously dwelt in glory, when their Ruler came, Almighty God, into His own kingdom.

(Alexander, *The Earliest English Poems*, p. 91)

The Dream of the Rood is the Victorian title given to a 156-line poem found in the late tenth-century Vercelli Book. But 15 of these lines appear, carved in runic script on a high stone cross which stands at Ruthwell, Dumfriesshire, near the north shore of the Solway, beyond the western end of England's border with Scotland. The Ruthwell Cross, which is covered with Biblical scenes sculpted in deep relief, is a product of Northumbria's golden age, and was erected and carved before the death of Bede in 735. At the Reformation, the Ruthwell Cross was destroyed by order of the Scottish Kirk as an idolatrous monument, but the fragments left by this act of iconoclasm were put together again and re-erected by the minister of Ruthwell early in the nineteenth century. Although much detail had been lost in the destructive zeal of the Reformation, it is clear that the runic text of the poem was originally about fifty lines long. The manuscript text of the poem is in standard late West Saxon with Anglian traces, whereas the runic text transliterates into early Northumbrian. (The runes were deciphered in 1840 by Kemble, before he knew of the publication of the Vercelli Book.) The Ruthwell Cross and the Vercelli Book are more than 1000 miles apart: tantalising evidence of how complex the life-history of an Old English poem could be. Two lines from the poem are also found on an early eleventh-century reliquary encasing a fragment of the True Cross now in Brussels. It is likely that a version of the poem was composed before the Ruthwell Cross was carved; that it reached the south, perhaps receiving new popularity at the time when Alfred was presented with a fragment of the True Cross by Pope Marinus in 885; and that it survived to be copied into the Vercelli Book a century later. Thus the original poem was composed three centuries before its appearance in the form it has in the Vercelli text, which is probably an expanded version of the original.

It is also probable that the fragment of the True Cross at Brussels is the one Marinus gave Alfred. It is curious that what some would regard as the finest Anglo-Saxon monument and the best Old English poem — which in its Ruthwell form may also be extremely early — are not now to be found in England.

The Ruthwell Cross, one face of which can be seen on page 33, stood for almost a thousand years at Ruthwell, initially in the open air. But in 1642 it was dismantled and defaced by order of the General Assembly of the Kirk. So far from being an idol, the Rood at Ruthwell was a sign: its whole surface was animated with panels in high relief, each surrounded by a text. It is necessary to describe the Ruthwell Cross with some fullness. The faces of the cross-shaft each show six scenes, mostly from the New Testament. Page 33 shows the south face, at the bottom of which (recessed below ground level and not in the photograph) is a Crucifixion (systematically defaced). Above this are the Annunciation; the healing of the man born blind; Mary Magdalen wiping with her hair the feet of a Saviour who blesses with one hand and in the other holds a book; the Visitation; and an archer shooting a bird, the meaning of which is disputed. The small crosspiece replaced between the archer and the bird is modern, though the evangelists on the north face are original. The north (and principal) face has in the centre of the shaft a Christ in Judgement, corresponding to the forgiving Saviour on the south face. In general, the south face shows the scheme of Incarnation and Salvation: the north face shows scenes of temptation overcome in the desert and the recognition of the Saviour by the animal kingdom. Around each panel is a Latin text in Roman lettering, except that the Visitation has the Latin text in runes. All the scenes have as a theme the acknowledgement by his Creation of Christ as Saviour. Both the figures themselves and the iconographic scheme have close parallels only in Byzantine art, which is hardly surprising, as Swanton points out, in a province of the Church guided by Theodore of Tarsus, archbishop from 668 to 690. Some gold medallions from Adana, near Tarsus itself, show similar New Testament scenes. But the closest parallels are from Ravenna, particularly a sixth-century ivory throne there (probably made in Alexandria), which has several similar panels in a similar scheme. The Ravenna throne also has the motif which fills the narrower sides of the Ruthwell Cross—the so-called "inhabited vine scroll"—around the panels of which are cut in runic script the passages from *The Dream of the Rood*. The birds and animals which inhabit the vine-scroll and peck at its grapes symbolise the dependence of the faithful upon the saving merits of the blood of the True Vine of John 15:1-7. The birds and beasts in this Tree of Life are wild, like those in the desert scenes on the north face. The Ruthwell Cross is a preaching cross, erected in a missionary area on the edge of a "wilderness," and all its scenes are recognition or conversion scenes. The clearly visible Magdalen panel shows Mary wiping Christ's feet with a great tress of her hair, having washed them with her tears: her bowed figure represents the convert.

The inscriptions on the Ruthwell Cross are part of its original conception: the Latin titles, *tituli*, identify or interpret the panels they border. The relation of the Old English to the vine-scroll is less obvious. However, the poem is a vision of the Cross, in which the Cross speaks: Christ's discourse at the Last Supper ("I am the true vine") had been conflated with other texts, especially Psalm 104:16-17: "The trees of the Lord are full of sap; the cedars of Lebanon, which he hath planted; where the birds make their nests." This lends a rich significance to the Tree of Life affording shelter, and the True Vine giving immortal sustenance: the saving blood of Christ available to mankind through the Eucharist. This eucharistic sense accounts for the popularity of the inhabited vine-scroll as a motif on rood-screens in the later Middle Ages—for example, that at the Priory at Little Malvern.

Roods, and the screens they stood on between nave and chancel, have largely been removed from churches in Britain, but earlier British Christianity took a very full part in the cult of the cross. There is ample evidence, not only of the cult of the cross from Constantine onward, but of the popularity of standing stone crosses at this time; Swanton reports in his edition, to which the present discussion is indebted, that the remains of some 1,500 of them survive—most of them in Northumbria. The battle of Heavenfield re-enacting the Constantinian miracle took place in 633. Cuthbert (who died in 687) set up many preaching crosses. And Coelfrid of Wearmouth and Jarrow was in Rome in 701 when the miraculous finding of a relic of the True Cross by Pope

Sergius I (matching the relics at Constantinople) was cause for celebration. Coelfrid's return may have given rise to the fervour which led to crosses such as that at Ruthwell and its neighbour at Bewcastle (thirty miles east) being erected during the reign of the learned King Aldfrith (685-704). The cult of the Cross propagated by contagion. Venantius Fortunatus had welcomed the entry in 569 of a relic of the cross into Poitiers by composing the greatest of the hymns in its honour: *Vexilla regis prodeunt*, "The standards of the king go forth"; and *Pange, lingua*: "Sing, my tongue." The standards of the king went forth in large numbers, and many tongues sang its glories.

The monumental stone crosses of Northumbria are, George Henderson suggests in *Early Medieval*, reincarnations of Oswald's wooden cross at Heavenfield, which was not far from "the wall with which the Romans formerly enclosed the island from sea to sea," according to Bede. Bewcastle and Ruthwell are both just north of Hadrian's Wall, and the standards of the king carried by the Angles were indeed advancing, north and west. By 731 the Northumbrians had to put a bishop into the originally Celtic area of Whithorn.

There are a great many Celtic crosses of later date in Ireland and Scotland, and such free-standing crosses are found only in the British Isles. They are in a style characteristic of these islands, and therefore called insular: a fusion of Celtic, Scandinavian, and Mediterranean motifs and techniques. It seems that these "Scotic" crosses derive not one from the other but both from the east, where the cult began. The Celtic crosses are often covered with interlace, whereas human figures in monumental relief and with inscriptions are only found on the Northumbrian examples; the model for the sculptural technique is Roman, though the iconography is eastern. Indeed, some letters in the Latin inscriptions, such as B for V, are Byzantine. It has recently been argued by Eamonn O'Carragain that the Ruthwell cross is not Celtic but entirely Roman in its artistic affinities.

It is some relief to insular pride, then, that no direct antecedent has been found for the poem quoted on the flanks of the Rood, a poem perhaps as great as the hymns of Venantius Fortunatus and more dramatic if less perfect.

Hwæt!
A dream came to me
      at deep midnight
When humankind
      kept their beds
— the dream of dreams!
      I shall declare it.

It seemed I saw the Tree itself
Borne on the air, light wound about it,
— a beam of brightest wood, a beacon clad
In overlapping gold, glancing gems
Fair at its foot, and five stones
Set in a crux flashed from the crosstree.

Around angels of God
      all gazed upon it,
Since first fashioning fair.
      It was not a felon's gallows,
For holy ghosts beheld it there,
And men on mould, and the whole Making shone for it
— *signum* of victory !
      Stained and marred,
Stricken with shame, I saw the glory-tree
Shine out gaily, sheathed in yellow
Decorous gold; and gemstones made
For their Maker's Tree a right mail-coat.
             (1-17; Alexander, p. 106)

The radiant vision of the Cross high in the heavens is at first not unlike Constantine's, but the dreamer's sense of sin dramatises his relation to the Cross, for it was human sin which made the Crucifixion necessary. The Cross is a sign of human shame and of divine glory simultaneously:

Yet through the masking gold I might perceive
What terrible sufferings were once sustained thereon:
It bled from the right side.
      Ruth in the heart.

Afraid I saw that unstill brightness
Change raiment and colour
      —again clad in gold
Or again slicked with sweat,
      spangled with spilling blood.

Yet lying there a long while I beheld,
sorrowing, the Healer's Tree
Till it seemed that I heard how it broke silence,
Best of wood, and began to speak:

                    (18–27)

The Cross not only suffers, as Christ did in his human nature, but now speaks, as so many Anglo-Saxon things do in the Riddles.

"Over that long remove my mind ranges
Back to the holt where I was hewn down;
From my own stem I was struck away,
      dragged off by strong enemies,
Wrought into a roadside scaffold.
      They made me a hoist for wrongdoers.

The soldiers on their shoulders bore me,
      until on a hill-top they set me up;
Many enemies made me fast there.
      Then I saw, marching toward me,
Mankind's brave King;
      He came to climb upon me.

I dared not break or bend aside
Against God's will, though the ground itself
Shook at my feet. Fast I stood,
Who falling could have felled them all.

Almighty God ungirded Him,
      eager to mount the gallows,
Unafraid in the sight of many:
      He would set free mankind.
I shook when His arms embraced me

but I durst not bow to ground,
Stoop to Earth's surface.
Stand fast I must.

I was reared up, a rood.
I raised the great King,
Liege lord of the heavens,
dared not lean from the true.
They drove me through with dark nails:
On me are the deep wounds manifest,

Wide-mouthed hate-dents.
I durst not harm any of them.
How they mocked at us both!
I was all moist with blood
Sprung from the Man's side
after He sent forth His soul.

Wry weirds a-many I underwent
Up on that hill-top; saw the Lord of Hosts
Stretched out stark. Darkness shrouded
The King's corse. Clouds wrapped
Its clear shining. A shade went out
Wan under cloud-pall. All creation wept,
Keened the King's death. Christ was on the Cross."

(28-57)

The stout thane obeys his heroic Lord and endures all for his sake:
by virtue of the Incarnation, Creation is dignified, and, in the last
two lines quoted above (which appear in the Ruthwell inscriptions), the Cross suffers in the name of all created nature.

But there quickly came from far
Earls to the One there. All that I beheld;
Had grown weak with grief,
yet with glad will bent then
Meek to those men's hands,
yielded Almighty God.

They lifted him down from the leaden pain,
    left me, the commanders,
Standing in a sweat of blood.
    I was all wounded with shafts.

They straightened out His strained limbs,
    stood at His body's head,
Looked down on the Lord of Heaven
    —for a while He lay there resting
Set to contrive Him a tomb
    in the sight of the Tree of Death,
Carved it of bright stone,
    laid in it the Bringer of victory,
Spent from the great struggle.
    They began to speak the grief-song,
Sad in the sinking light,
    then thought to set out homeward;
Their hearts were sick to death,
    their most high Prince
They left to rest there with scant retinue.

Yet we three, weeping, a good while
Stood in that place after the song had gone up
From the captains' throats. Cold grew the corse,
Fair soul-house.
                    They felled us all.
We crashed to ground, cruel Weird,
And they delved for us a deep pit.

The Lord's men learnt of it,
His friends found me ...
It was they who girt me with gold and silver ...

                                            (58-77)

Just as the Rood co-operated with its Lord during his great struggle, it could afterwards bend to allow the apostolic "commanders"
to take down the corpse. The Rood has brought us up to the
time when it was found (the Invention of the Cross), and at this
point (half-way through the Vercelli text) its story becomes more

like a sermon. It shares in the glory of the Ascension and tells the dreamer that it was chosen to be exalted above all trees just as Mary was exalted above all womankind. It bids the dreamer to tell mankind about the tree of glory on which God suffered death as a man, and warns him of the Second Coming and Doomsday:

> Nor can anyone there be unconcerned about the word that the Ruler shall utter. He shall ask before the multitude, Where is the man who is willing to taste bitter death for the Lord's name's sake? — as He had formerly done on the tree. But they shall then be afraid, and few shall think what they shall begin to answer to Christ. Yet no one there shall need to be afraid who has borne in his bosom the best of signs. But every soul on earth who intends to dwell with the Lord shall come to the Kingdom through the Rood.
>
> (110-21)

The dreamer speaks the remainder of the poem: "Then prayed I to the tree with cheerful heart and high zeal, alone as I was and with small retinue." This last phrase has already been applied to the dead Christ in line 70. As it is an understatement meaning "with no retinue at all," its repetition diminishes its effect here; yet it also suggests that the humiliation and isolation which befell Christ, and his Cross, now affect the dreamer (and his reader: we too are to repent). He wishes now to seek

> that tree of victory ... : my hope of protection is all bent on the rood. I have not many powerful friends on earth. On the contrary they have departed hence out of the world's joys, have sought out the king of glory and live now in the heavens with the Almighty Father, dwelling in glory; and every day I look for the time when the Lord's rood, which once I gazed on here on earth, shall fetch me forth from this fleeting life and then shall bring me where there is great rejoicing, happiness in the heavens, where the Lord's people is seated at the feast, where there is bliss everlasting; and then He shall appoint me to a place where after I may dwell in glory, and fully share in joy among the blest.
>
> (127-44)

The poem ends with the hope that the Redeemer will be the dreamer's friend: he who gave mankind hope and led the virtuous out of hell to the bliss of heaven.

Scholars used to find the second half of the poem, after the Invention, stylistically different, more diffuse, and inferior; this part of the poem is here rendered in prose. In view of the purposes and procedures of the time, however, such a devotional application of the vision is to be expected; if it is an addition, it is coherent with the theology of the vision though more commonplace in conception. The bewildering paradoxes of the Crucifixion dramatised in the first half are not better treated in later English verse, even in John Donne's "Good Friday, 1613: Riding Westward" or the climax to David Jones' *The Anathemata* (1954). Of the two poets, it is Jones who measures up better, if less brilliantly than Donne. Jones, a fine artist, made an inscription based upon the text of *The Dream of the Rood*. His poem comes closer to the Old English poem's spirit. Of the two modern poems, Jones' *Anathemata* has the greater sympathy with the creature, of wood or flesh, and the greater confidence in the Victor: the young hero who ungirded himself, who, in the words of the Rood, "came to climb upon me." The quickly changing aspect of the Cross in this dream vision, from blood to gold, from the sweating instrument of torture to the key of heaven, together with the loyal endurance of created nature, is given piercing expression: partly by means of the violent contrasts native to the structure and tradition of Old English verse, partly through a daring extension of the anthropomorphic tradition of the Riddles. Mankind are called "reordberend," the voice-bearers, in line 3. But here the instrument of salvation is endowed with the human gift of speech, as the serpent had been in Eden.

As with *Beowulf*, the form fits and expresses the content perfectly, though the Crucifixion story, if familiar, is uniquely difficult. The poet's success fully exploits the familiarity and avoids the difficulty by his sustained series of allusions to what we know too well, allusions made from a standpoint unfamiliar but liberating and appropriate. Nothing else in Old English religious verse has the theological tact and the intense artistic economy of the opening of *The Dream of the Rood*. Its fineness can be matched in Herbert, Vaughan or Hopkins, and its passion in Langland. But what in the whole of later tradition has such strength? Both the poem and the Rood from which it speaks deserve a better posterity than the Norman Conquest and the Reformers for long allowed them. Only recently has the unique richness of this poetic monument — one of the greatest of all English artistic achievements — begun to be recognised.

NINE : THE BENEDICTINE REVIVAL

THE reign of Edgar (959–76) and the Benedictine Revival which it inaugurated usher in the third clearly defined period in the literary history of Anglo-Saxon England: the age of a fully-fledged literary prose and of the poetry manuscripts which survive, and of a few notable late poems: *The Phoenix, Judith, Brunanburh*, and *The Battle of Maldon*. *Brunanburh* is to be found in the *Anglo-Saxon Chronicle* for the year 937, celebrating a comprehensive victory of Wessex over all its enemies; but the *Chronicle* itself attains the richness and interest of its first Alfredian entries only at a later period, toward the end of the tenth century, whereafter it continues on and off in local versions until after the Conquest—in the Peterborough continuation until 1154. This monastic age is also the age of good stone churches, of the Winchester School of manuscripts, and of a general flowering of the decorative arts. Dunstan, Archbishop of Canterbury 960–88, was himself a skilled metalworker, as was his pupil and ally Aethelwold of Winchester; Dunstan represents himself in the manuscript illumination shown on page 228, and it was in Aethelwold's Winchester that the illumination was produced. In its profusion of manuscripts, the Wessex of Dunstan, Aethelwold and Aelfric is much more completely represented today than the early Northumbria of Bede. The artistic achievement of the Northum-

St Dunstan at the feet of Christ

brian golden age was more striking: a signally mature and intense fusion of very diverse traditions, Germanic, Celtic, Roman, and Byzantine. The precocious richness of the Anglian century or so which produced the Sutton Hoo treasure, Bede, the Lindisfarne Gospels, the Ruthwell Cross—and, possibly, *Beowulf* itself— outshines that of the West-Saxon century before 1066, which has left a greater harvest of things in themselves less absolutely remarkable. But this latter age offers a spectrum of civilisation in which we can recognise many of the cultural elements which were to come together, transformed, in the renaissance of the twelfth century.

The English Benedictine Revival, though partly of native origin, owed much to the Benedictine Reform on the continent. This began with the version of the Rule worked out by Benedict of Aniane in the ninth century and was most conspicuously practised at the Burgundian monastery of Cluny, founded in 910, and other houses such as those at Ghent, where Dunstan spent one of his periods of exile, and at Fleury-sur-Loire, where Oswald studied. Here the learning and art of the Carolingian renaissance flourished again. But English clerical culture matured in an age of secular decline. The reign of Ethelred II (978–1016), in which the poetry collections were made and there was a spread of vernacular literacy, was also the age of Danegeld, disunity, and declining effectiveness, which led to the rule first of Danish and at last of Norman kings. In the false light of retrospect it seems that the heroic resistance of Alfred and the political and then artistic achievement of his successors only made England all the more tempting a prize for her less civilised neighbours. William took over a thriving concern, as his inventory in Doomsday Book shows.

Our image of the Norman Conquest is presented through a triumph of English art known as the Bayeux Tapestry. This justly famous artefact is not a true tapestry but a linen strip 230 feet long which is embroidered in a cartoon-like series of narrative pictures of great vigour and clarity, preserved at Bayeux in Normandy. English embroidery, later known as *opus anglicanum*, was appreciated throughout western Europe, as were English jewellery, metalwork, and carving. Especially prized were the illuminations of the manuscripts of the Winchester school founded by Aethelwold.

Edgar's New Minster Charter

Aethelwold's Benedictional: Entry into Jerusalem

These manuscript paintings illustrated texts copied in a clear script which is still used as a model by calligraphers. Most of this art and craft was a result of the Benedictine Revival, as were the enlarged stone churches, the style of communal singing known as the Gregorian chant—and the ceremony used for the anointing of King Edgar at Bath in 973, which became the basis of the English coronation service, and later the British. It can be said that, with the possible exception of some verse and some embroidery, nearly everything of artistic and cultural merit from the late West-Saxon period was created directly or indirectly by the reformed Benedictines. The richness of line and colour of these naturalistic pictures within their abundantly decorated frames shows that the monks made the best use of the material world to show forth its spiritual significance. These Benedictines were not only patrons but artists themselves, from the abbot Eadfrith who copied the Lindisfarne Gospels in about 698 to Dunstan, who worked in gold, designed ecclesiastical vestments, and was a notable manuscript artist (see pages 230 and 231).

This state of affairs, a contrast both with the austerity of the later Cistercians and with the craft shops to be found at some modern monasteries, was not a restrictive monopoly. Without the Benedictine Revival there would have been little art in late Anglo-Saxon England. The proliferation of royal land-grants for monastic foundations rebounded on the Church in the reaction of the lay landowners which followed the death of Edgar. But in Alphege, the Archbishop of Canterbury martyred by Vikings in 1012, and Wulfstan, archbishop of York in the early eleventh century, the English had leaders better than their king. Wulfstan was a statesman, and the authority of his voice in the *Sermo Lupi ad Anglos* (Word of Wulf to the English) came from popular assent as much as from the Church.

The literary achievement of this Benedictine Renaissance, as it is also called, could be summed up as the restoration of learning. Apart from the making of the poetry manuscripts, without which there would now be no Old English literature to speak of, there was the creation of a proper vernacular prose for a civilised range of purposes. The best-known of this prose is homiletic, especially that of Aelfric and Wulfstan. Just as oratory was the central current of Greek and Roman democracy, homilies and sermons were the medium through which the Church communicated with the faithful, a rather larger proportion of the people, perhaps, than was included in the classical democracies. Fortunate parish priests could rely on the cycles of sermons and saints' lives prepared by Aelfric for most of the feasts in the Church's year: the circulation and effect of his civil, gentle and clear prose must have been considerable, as was the political impact of Wulfstan's *Sermo*. Wulfstan sometimes used Aelfric as the basis for his own homilies — church writers habitually collaborated — but he also was the author of legal codes for the reigns of three kings, and of the remarkable *Institutes of Polity*; and other writings, liturgical and biographical. It was in monasteries, too, that the *Chronicle* was kept up. So the range of late Old English prose includes not only translations of the Bible, sermons, and saints' lives, but the lives of kings, the writing of chronicles, legal and political thought, and the scientific books of Byrhtferth of Ramsey; even, in the delightful *Apollonius of Tyre*, a romance. There are sundry clerical, medical, and general works extant from this period — collections of proverbs, recipes, and cures — which round out the impression of a society where vernacular prose had begun to do many of the things we expect it to do today. English prose had not previously had this range of functions, and would not assume them again after 1066 for three centuries, and even then French lingered in the law, and Latin remained the language of learning. There seems to have been little feeling in the year 1000 that a subject was so learned that it could not be treated in English; Anglo-Latin in this period is dominated by clerical biography. By this criterion, England was then an articulate and confident society, though its self-confidence came from an acceptance that while Latin would not do for communicating with the laity, the laity had to be catered for.

The minor figure of Byrhtferth of Ramsey is associated with more than one genre of writing, and in this as in other respects is representative of Anglo-Saxon scholarship at this date. His distinction rests in his *Manual* for computing the calendar, a scientific work of some note written in English alternating with Latin, and in commentaries on Bede's scientific books; astronomy had a direct bearing on the Church's calendar. Byrhtferth wrote a Latin life of St. Oswald, the founder of Ramsey abbey, and studied under the scholar Abbo, who paid a teaching visit to the new abbey at Ramsey between 985 and 987. Abbo came from Fleury-sur-Loire, which by then had surpassed Cluny as a centre of the Benedictine Reform (it also boasted St. Benedict's remains). Abbo wrote a Latin *Passio* or account of the martyrdom of St. Edmund, king and martyr, which Aelfric translated; Abbo's source was St. Dunstan, whose life was also written by Byrhtferth. Dunstan, Aethelwold, and Oswald, abbots of Glastonbury, Abingdon, and Ramsey, later elevated to the premier sees of Canterbury, Winchester, and York, were the triumvirate who led the monastic revival: their names come up continually in Edgar's reign. Aelfric and Wulfstan were Byrhtferth's greater contemporaries, and like him beneficiaries of the educational policy of the previous generation of reformers. Some idea of the level of learning and style of Byrhtferth may be gained from his preface to his *Manual*. The translation is that of S. J. Crawford in the Early English Text Society edition:

"I command to depart from me the mermaids, who are called sirens, and also the Castalian nymphs, that is to say the mountain elves, who dwelt on mount Helicon; and I will that Phoebus depart from me, whom Latona, the mother of the sun and Apollo and Diana, bore in Delos, as ancient triflers have declared; and I trust that the glorious cherubin will come to me, and with his golden tongs bring to my tongue from off the heavenly altar a spark of the burning coal and touch the nerves (*recte* sinews) of my dumb mouth, that I may thereby have the power by sagacious study to translate this Paschal cycle into English in a scholarly fashion."

(Garmonsway, p. xix)

This is not the place for a history of the Revival, though it has been said that Dunstan dreamed, Aethelwold acted and Oswold organised. Apart from Aethelwold's chasing of the married canons out of the Old Minster at Winchester, the movement was truly a revival rather than a reform. When Aelfric was born, in about 955, there were not many monks nor any true monasteries left. With royal support, the three bishops founded and built new minsters rather than purging old ones. Some idea of the lives the new monks lived can be gleaned from the *Regularis Concordia* or Common Observance of the Rule, drawn up at Winchester. The monks rose at 1.30 a.m. in summer, having retired at 8.15 p.m.; in winter they rose at 2.30 a.m. and retired at 6.30 p.m. There was one meal a day in winter, two in summer. Most of the hours in this long day were spent in celebrating the liturgy in the minster, though two hours in the morning went on work of a manual, craft or literary sort. Aelfric must have spent more than two hours a day in producing his encyclopaedic programme of readings. But his *Colloquy* shows that if he lived laborious days, those days did not lack delights.

I • AELFRIC'S *COLLOQUY*

The *Colloquy* is a conversation in Latin between a master and his pupils, and has proved popular with historians and others for reasons which become obvious on reading. It is composed by Aelfric as an aid to the teaching of Latin, in sequel to his Latin *Grammar* and *Glossary*, while he was master of oblates at the monastic house of Cernel (now Cerne Abbas in Dorset) in the 990s. The Latin text has interlinear glosses in late West-Saxon, which are unlikely to be by Aelfric. The colloquy was a common teaching device in medieval monastic schools, which were attended not only by child oblates studying to become monks but sometimes by the sons of local lay society. Aelfric takes the part of the *magister*, and the pupils take the parts of different adult occupations in society. So engaging and vivid are their replies that several historians have imagined that Aelfric was teaching real (Latin-speaking) ploughmen, huntsmen, and fishermen (Aelfric's *Colloquy*, ed. G.N. Garmonsway, p. 14). The point of the exercise, however, is that the boys should have learned their replies in advance of the lesson, using the *Grammar* and *Glossary* to do so; not unlike the drills of modern language courses. Extensive quotation seems justified in view of the gain in colour and detail for our ideas of "the life and activities of the middle and lower classes of Anglo-Saxon society, concerning which," as Garmonsway says, "Old English Literature is, in the main, silent." A final point: the reason that the boys don't care what they talk about and are prepared to be beaten so long as they are taught to speak Latin *recte* ("accurately") is that the oblates in a monastery were required to read aloud in the refectory as well as take part in the liturgical chants in church, and that faults in articulation were severely punished.

> PUPILS: Oh master, we children beg that you will teach us to speak correctly, because we are unlearned and speak badly.
>
> MASTER: What do you want to talk about?
>
> PUPILS: We don't care what we talk about, as long as it is accurate and useful conversation, and not frivolous or filthy.
>
> MASTER: Are you prepared to be beaten while learning?
>
> PUPILS: We would rather be beaten for the sake of learning than be ignorant. But we know that you are kind and unwilling to inflict blows on us unless we compel you to.
>
> MASTER: I ask you (*indicating a particular pupil*), what do you say to me? What is your work?
>
> "MONK": I am a professed monk, and every day I sing seven times with the brethren, and I am busy with reading and singing, but nevertheless, between-times I want to learn to speak the Latin language.
>
> MASTER: What do your friends do?
>
> "MONK": Some are ploughmen, some shepherds, some oxherds; some again, huntsmen, some fishermen, some fowlers, some merchants, some shoe-makers, salters, bakers.
>
> MASTER: What do you say, ploughman? How do you carry out your work?
>
> "PLOUGHMAN": Oh, I work very hard, dear lord. I go out at daybreak driving the oxen to the field, and yoke them to the plough; for fear of my lord, there is no winter so severe that I dare hide at home; but the oxen, having been yoked and the share and coulter fastened to the plough, I must plough a full acre or more every day.
>
> MASTER: Have you any companion?
>
> "PLOUGHMAN": I have a lad driving the oxen with a goad, who is now also hoarse because of the cold and shouting.
>
> MASTER: What else do you do in the day?

"PLOUGHMAN": I do more than that, certainly. I have to fill the oxen's bins with hay, and water them, and carry their muck outside.

MASTER: Oh, oh! It's hard work.

"PLOUGHMAN": It's hard work, sir, because I am not free.

MASTER: What do you say shepherd? Do you have any work?

"SHEPHERD": I have indeed, sir. In the early morning I drive my sheep to their pasture, and in the heat and in cold, stand over them with dogs, lest wolves devour them; and I lead them back to their folds and milk them twice a day, and move their folds; and in addition I make cheese and butter; and I am loyal to my lord.

MASTER: Oh, oxherd, what do you work at?

"OXHERD": Oh, I work hard, my lord. When the ploughman unyokes the oxen, I lead them to pasture, and I stand over them all night watching for thieves; and then in the early morning I hand them over to the ploughman well fed and watered.

(Swanton, *Anglo-Saxon Prose*, p. 108)

Pupils then take the parts of a Huntsman and a Fisherman (plenty of names of fish); then a Fowler.

MASTER: What do you say, fowler? How do you trap birds?

"FOWLER": I trap birds in many ways: sometimes with nets, sometimes with snares, sometimes with lime, by whistling, with a hawk or with a trap.

MASTER: Have you got a hawk?

"FOWLER": I have.

MASTER: Do you know how to tame them?

"FOWLER": Yes, I know how. What good would they be to me unless I knew how to tame them?

"HUNTSMAN": Give me a hawk.

"FOWLER": I will give you one willingly, if you will give me a fast dog. Which hawk will you have, the bigger one or the smaller?

"HUNTSMAN": Give me the bigger one.

MASTER: How do you feed your hawks?

"FOWLER": They feed themselves, and me, in winter; and in the spring I let them fly away to the woods; and in the autumn I take young birds and tame them.

MASTER: And why do you let those you have tamed fly away from you?

"FOWLER": Because I don't want to feed them in the summer, since they eat too much.

MASTER: Yet many feed the tamed ones throughout the summer, in order to have them already again.

"FOWLER": Yes, so they do. But I don't want to go to so much trouble over them, because I know how to catch others — not just one, but many more.

(Swanton, p. 111)

Play continues with the Merchant, Shoemaker, Salter, Baker and Cook, then back to the Monk:

MASTER: Oh monk, you who are speaking to me. Now, I have found that you have good and very necessary companions; and who are these I ask you?

"MONK": I have craftsmen: blacksmiths, a goldsmith, silversmith, coppersmith, carpenters and workers in many other different crafts.

MASTER: Have you got any wise counsellor?

"MONK": Certainly I have. How can our community be directed without a counsellor?

MASTER: What do you say, wise man? Which trade among these seems to you to be superior?

"COUNSELLOR": I tell you, to me the service of God seems to hold the first place among these crafts, just as it reads in the gospel: "Seek first the kingdom of God and his righteousness, and all these things shall be added unto you."

MASTER: And which among the secular arts seems to you to hold the first place?

"COUNSELLOR": Agriculture, because the ploughman feeds us all.

The "SMITH" says: Where does the ploughman get his plough-share or coulter or goad, except by my craft?

240

Where the fisherman his hook, or the shoemaker his awl, or the tailor his needle? Isn't it from my work?

The "COUNSELLOR" *answers*: What you say is in fact true. But we would all prefer to live with you, ploughman, than with you, because the ploughman gives us bread and drink. You, what do you give us in your smithy but iron sparks, and the noise of hammers beating and bellows blowing?

The "CARPENTER" *says*: Which of you doesn't make use of my craft, when I make houses and various vessels and boats for you all?

The "BLACKSMITH" *answers*: Oh, carpenter, why do you talk like that when you couldn't pierce even one hole without my craft?

The "COUNSELLOR" *says*: Oh, friends and good workmen, let us bring these arguments to an end quickly, and let there be peace and concord between us, and let each one of us help the others by his craft. And let us always agree with the ploughman, where we find food for ourselves and fodder for our horses. And I give this advice to all workmen, that each one pursue his trade diligently: for he who abandons his craft will be abandoned by his craft. Whoever you are, whether priest or monk or peasant or soldier, exercise yourself in this, and be what you are; because it is a great disgrace and shame for a man not to want to be what he is, and what he has to be.

(Swanton, p. 113)

The Counsellor's last line is the fundamental medieval social attitude; the boys' reaction to it indicates Aelfric's skill as a teacher.

MASTER: Oh, boys, how do you like this speech?

PUPIL: We like it well, but you talk very profoundly and use speech beyond our ability; but talk to us according to our comprehension, so that we can understand the things you say.

MASTER: I ask you, why are you so eager to learn?

PUPIL: Because we don't want to be like stupid animals, who know nothing but grass and water.

MASTER: And what do you want?

PUPIL: We want to be clever.

MASTER: With what kind of cleverness? Do you want to be subtle or cunning in deceit, crafty in speech, artful, wily, speaking good and thinking evil, given to bland words, nourishing guile within, just like a sepulchre, painted outside and full of a stink inside?

PUPIL: We don't want to be clever like that, because he who deludes himself with pretence is not clever.

MASTER: But how do you want to be?

PUPIL: We want to be sincere, without hypocrisy, and wise, so that we turn away from evil and do good. However, you are still questioning us more deeply than our years can take; so speak to us in our own way, not so deeply.

MASTER: I will do just as you ask. You, boy, what did you do today?

PUPIL: I did lots of things. Last night when I heard the ringing of the bell I got up from my bed and went to church and sang mattins with the brethren, after which we sang of all the saints and the morning hymns; after this the six o'clock service and the seven psalms with the litanies and the chapter-Eucharist. Then we sang the nine o'clock service and did the Eucharist for the day; after this we sang the midday service, and ate and drank and slept. And we got up again and sang the three o'clock service; and now we are here before you, ready to hear what you have to say to us!

MASTER: When are you going to sing evensong and compline?

PUPIL: When it's time!

MASTER: Have you been beaten today?

PUPIL: I haven't, because I behave myself carefully.

MASTER: And how about your friends?

PUPIL: Why do you ask me about that? I dare not reveal our secrets to you. Each one of us knows if he was beaten or not.

MASTER: What do you eat in the day?

PUPIL: I still enjoy meat, because I am a child living under instruction.

MASTER: What else do you eat?

PUPIL: I eat vegetables and eggs, fish and cheese, butter and beans and all clean things, with much gratefulness.

MASTER: You are very greedy if you eat everything that is in front of you.

PUPIL: I am not so great a glutton that I can eat all kinds of food at one meal.

MASTER: Then how so?

PUPIL: Sometimes I partake of this food and sometimes that, in moderation as befits a monk, not with greed, because I am no glutton.

MASTER: And what do you drink?

PUPIL: Ale if I have it, or water if I have no ale.

(Swanton, pp. 114–15)

The elementary teaching of Latin preceded the *Trivium* (grammar, rhetoric, and dialectic). This was followed, in the classical curriculum which was maintained in monasteries, by the *Quadrivium* (arithmetic, geometry, music, and astronomy). The first and last of these were useful for the Church's calendar, and music meant plain-song.

Aelfric had attended Aethelwold's school at Winchester before going to teach at Cernel in 987, much as Abbo had taught at Ramsey. The Reform was an education in the Rule, not simply the application of its rules. Indeed, all Aelfric's work can be called educational. His schoolbooks taught the new monks Latin, and his homilies expounded the basics of Christianity in a form so clear that the layman who heard them read could grasp them. Clarity is a constant quality of Aelfric's writing. He wrote two volumes of *Catholic Homilies*, forty in each cycle to be read over two liturgical years. Together they explain the Old Law and the New Law, concentrating on the Incarnation but also providing a Universal History from Creation to Doomsday. The homilies were completed by 992; and after a work on computing the calendar and his manuals of Latin, he turned to the *Lives of the Saints*, another cycle of forty. These were largely for private reading, unlike the homilies. While at Cernel, Aelfric also translated, at the request of a lay patron, Genesis 1–24, and parts of other early books of the Old Testament. He did this reluctantly, since he feared that the patriarchs might set an inappropriate example in modern times. Before going from Cernel to Eynsham as abbot in 1005, Aelfric wrote works on the Creation, on the duties of monks, and on the duties of the pastoral clergy; he also revised and reorganised his earlier collections of homilies. He had thus provided a modern Christian curriculum for the England of his day, and made a learned clergy practicable. At Eynsham, near Oxford, he confined his writing to a number of occasional works. Of no other early English writer does so much survive (there are over one hundred sermons extant, several of them in several copies). Though we know little of the author from external evidence, the works themselves allow a satisfactory chronology to be worked out for his writings.

Anglo-Saxonists have much studied Aelfric's prose style (comparing and contrasting it, of course, with that of Wulfstan). An ease in reading Old English is a prerequisite for the enjoyment of prose style—an ease which undergraduates do not attain; like Aelfric's pupils, in so far as they have to achieve a correct grasp of the elements of grammar, they tend not to care what they read. It can truthfully be said that Aelfric's is the only Old English prose that can always be read with some aesthetic pleasure. Alfred and Wulfstan have more personal moral weight in their writings, which excites admiration. But the king can be clumsy and the archbishop too indignant for extended reading; Aelfric is truly sweet to read, and this charm largely evaporates in translation. He is fluent, measured, has the elegance of learning while being perfectly unpedantic and unpretentious, and beautifully clear not only in sentence construction but in the articulation of paragraphs and the design of the whole. He wished to be orthodox, and drew only on authorities recognised by all Christians: Augustine, Jerome, Gregory, Bede, and some Carolingian commentators—because he meant to convey the essentials of Christian doctrine, as he says in preface to the *Catholic Homilies*, "which I thought might be enough for simple persons, for the amendment of their lives, in as much as laymen cannot take in all things, though they may learn them from the mouth of the learned" (Hurt, *Aelfric*, p. 58). He shares the Benedictine simplicity and *suavitas* (sweetness) with Bede, though less original and less outstanding in his day for his learning; but differs from Bede in writing principally for the layman. As the *Colloquy* shows, he has a fine sense of his audience. His homilies are called Catholic, which means universal, not for their orthodoxy but as designed to be read by all, lay as well as cleric.

II • AELFRIC'S HOMILIES

Something of this engaging simplicity appears in the opening of his *Martyrdom of St. Edmund, King and Martyr*, one of his *Lives of the Saints*, freely adapted from Abbo's *Passio Sancti Eadmundi* referred to above. Edmund had been martyred in 870; his example was particularly needed in these years of renewed Danish pressure on Ethelred's England, the years between the Battle of Maldon (991) and the martyrdom of Alphege. The change in style after the short prologue is noticeable even in translation.

In the time of King Æthelred a certain very learned monk came from the south over the sea from St. Benoît sur Loire [the monastery of Fleury] to Archbishop Dunstan, three years before he died; and the monk was called Abbo. Then they talked together until Dunstan told the story of St. Edmund, just as Edmund's sword-bearer had told it to King Athelstan when Dunstan was a young man and the sword-bearer was a very old man. Then the monk set down all the information in a book; and afterwards, when the book came to us a few years later, then we translated it into English, just as it stands hereafter. Then within two years the monk Abbo returned home to his monastery and was straightway appointed abbot in that very monastery.

The blessed Edmund, King of East Anglia, was wise and honourable, and by his noble conduct ever glorified Almighty God. He was humble and virtuous, and continued resolutely thus so that he would not submit to shameful sins, nor did he alter his conduct in any way, but was always mindful of that true teaching: "You are appointed ruler? do not exalt yourself, but be amongst men as one of them." He was as generous as a father to the poor and to widows, and with benevolence always guided his people towards righteousness, and restrained the violent, and lived happily in the true faith.

Then eventually it happened that the Danish people came with a pirate force, harrying and slaying widely throughout the land, as their custom is. In that fleet, united by the devil, were the very important leaders Ivar and Ubbi [sons of the Viking King, Ragnar Lothbrok], and they landed with warships in Northumbria, and wasted the land and slew the people. Then Ivar turned eastwards with his ships and Ubbi remained behind in Northumbria, having won victory with savagery. Then Ivar came sailing to East Anglia in the year in which prince Alfred (he who afterwards became the famous King of Wessex) was twenty-one years old; and the aforesaid Ivar abruptly stalked over the land like a wolf, and slew the people: men and women and the innocent children, and humiliated the honest Christians.

Then immediately afterwards he sent an arrogant message to the king that if he cared for his life, he should submit to do him homage. The messenger came to King Edmund and quickly announced Ivar's message to him: "Ivar our King, brave and victorious by sea and by land, has subdued many nations and now suddenly landed here with an army, so that he might take winter quarters here with his host. Now he orders you to divide your secret treasures and the wealth of your forbears with him quickly, and if you want to live, you will be his under-king, because you have not the power to be able to resist him."

Well, then King Edmund summoned a certain bishop who was very near at hand, and discussed with him how he should answer the savage Ivar. Then the bishop was afraid because of the unexpected disaster, and for the king's life, and said that he thought it advisable that he should submit to what Ivar commanded. Then the king was silent and looked at the ground, and then eventually said to him, regally: "Oh bishop! this wretched nation is humiliated, and I would rather fall in battle against him who might possess my people's land." And the bishop said: "Alas, dear king, your people lie slain, and you have not the forces to be able to fight; and these pirates will come and bind you alive, unless you save your life by flight, or save yourself by submitting to him thus." Then said King Edmund, very brave as he was: "This I desire and wish with my heart, that I alone should not be left, after my beloved thegns, who with children and wives were suddenly slain in their beds by these pirates. It was never my custom to take flight, but I would rather die for my own country if I must; and Almighty God knows that I would never turn away from his worship, nor from his true love, whether I die or live."

After these words he turned to the messenger that Ivar had sent to him and said to him unafraid, "You would certainly deserve death now, but I would not dirty my clean hands in your filthy blood, for I follow Christ who set us an example thus; and I will cheerfully be slain by you if God so ordains it. Go very quickly now and say to your savage lord: 'Edmund will never while living submit to the heathen war-leader, Ivar, unless he first submit in this land to Christ the Saviour in faith.'"

(Swanton, pp. 97–99)

Edmund offers no resistance to his enemies and is tortured like St. Sebastian and beheaded. Aelfric tells how a wolf miraculously guarded Edmund's severed head and how the head, which had been hidden by the Vikings in a thicket, called out to the Angles who were looking for it. The legendary and fairy-tale elements do not detract from Edmund's martyrdom. The king is credibly shown as a better shepherd to his people than was their prudent bishop, just as Aelfric was relaxed enough to show the boys in his school as capable of boredom—and as unwilling to tell tales on other boys. Although Aelfric was hospitable to the ideal of Germanic lordship and to romantic miracles, he was also critical of excesses in this line. He omits the more lurid tortures in his saints' lives just as he omits the more far-fetched allegorical interpretations in his homilies on scripture. This taste and commonsense in adapting sources in the direction of credibility is a constant tendency in Bede, Cynewulf, and Aelfric, which may testify to an

English moderation and preference for fact. (There are, of course, exceptions, especially as regards virgin martyrs, whose plight — real enough — plucked the heart-strings of celibate clerics into believing unreal imaginings.) Aelfric's artistry shows in his constant abbreviation of his hagiographic sources, and in his harmonic abilities: every piece he wrote (and he adapted from highly diverse sources) hangs together well.

Intellectually, the *Catholic Homilies* are naturally more impressive than the narratives of saints' lives, and there are few more pleasant medieval expositions of such Christian mysteries as the Incarnation, the Trinity, the Eucharist, and the Assumption of Our Lady than those made by Aelfric in these sermons for the chief feasts of the Church's year. Aelfric combines homeliness and plain sense with theological grasp and a warm devotion. It is an ecumenical irony that this gentle schoolmaster (he was known as Aelfric Grammaticus from the popularity of his Latin *Grammar*), the meticulous soul of orthodoxy, should have been resurrected at the Reformation as a proto-Protestant. His Easter Sermon on the Eucharist was printed by Elizabeth I's Archbishop Parker in 1567 with a preface by the anti-Catholic John Foxe, in which Foxe tries to show that the Anglo-Saxon Church did not believe in the Real Presence of Christ in the Eucharist, a dogma later defined as transubstantiation, the doctrine which much later was particularly objected to by Reformers. The following extract includes the passage which gave rise to Foxe's misinterpretation, one which suited the Church of England under Elizabeth.

Aelfric introduces his Easter sermon with an account of the original Passover in Egypt, a paraphrase of Exodus. He then explains the scripture (this is properly what is expected in a Homily) as follows:

Dearly beloved, you have frequently been told about our Saviour's resurrection, how on this present day he rose up in strength from death after his passion. Now, by the grace of God, we will explain to you about the holy Eucharist to which you must now go, both according to the Old Testament and according to the New; lest any doubt concerning the living food might harm you.

The Almighty God commanded Moses, the leader in the land of Egypt, that he should command the people of Israel on the night in which they left that country for the promised land to take a year-old lamb on each hearth and offer that lamb to God: and afterwards cut it up and make the sign of a cross on their door-posts and lintels with the blood of the lamb, and afterwards eat the lamb's flesh roasted, and unleavened loaves with wild lettuce.

God said to Moses: "Eat nothing of the lamb raw, nor boiled in water, but roasted in the fire. Eat the head and the feet and the entrails and let nothing of it be left until morning; if there is anything left, burn it. Eat it in this manner. Gird your loins, and be shod, have your staff in hand, and eat in haste; this time is God's passover." And on that night, in every house throughout Pharaoh's entire kingdom the first-born child was slain; and God's people Israel were delivered from that sudden death through the offering of the lamb and the marking with its blood. Then said God to Moses: "Keep this day in your remembrance, and celebrate it solemnly in your generations with eternal observance, and at this festival eat unleavened bread continually for seven days." After this deed, God led the people of Israel over the Red Sea with dry feet, and drowned in it Pharaoh, who had persecuted them, and all his host together; and afterwards fed the people of Israel for forty years with heavenly food, and gave them water out of the hard rock, until they came to the promised homeland. We have expounded part of this narrative elsewhere; we will now explain that part which appertains to the holy Eucharist.

Christian men may not now keep the old law bodily, but it behoves them to know what it signifies spiritually. The innocent lamb which the old Israel then slaughtered had the significance, in the spiritual sense, of Christ's passion, who innocent, shed his holy blood for our redemption; about which the servants of God sing at every mass: *Agnus dei; qui tollis peccata mundi; miserere nobis*. That is in our language, "Lamb of God, who takest away the sins of the world, have mercy upon us." The people of Israel were delivered from sudden death and from Pharaoh's slavery through the sacrifice of the lamb, which had the significance of Christ's passion, through which we are redeemed from eternal death and the power of the cruel Devil, if we believe properly in the true redeemer of all the world, Christ the Saviour. The lamb was sacrificed in the evening, and our Saviour suffered in the sixth age of this world; that age is considered the evening of this transitory world. With the blood of the lamb they marked a Tau, that is a sign of the cross, on their doors and lintels, and were thus protected from the angel who slew the first-born children of the Egyptians. And we should mark our foreheads and our bodies with the sign of Christ's cross, so that we may be saved from destruction, when we are marked both on the forehead and in the heart with the blood of the Lord's passion.

The people of Israel ate the flesh of the lamb at their Easter-tide, when they were delivered; and we now partake spiritually of Christ's body and drink his blood when with true faith we partake of the holy Eucharist.

(Swanton, pp. 89–90)

Later he asks how it is that the bread can be changed into Christ's body:

Now certain men have often questioned, and still frequently question, how the bread which is prepared from grain and baked by the heat of the fire, can be changed into Christ's body; or the wine, which is pressed out from many grapes, becomes changed, by any blessing, into the Lord's blood? Now we say to such men that some things are spoken of Christ figuratively, some literally. It is a true and certain thing that Christ was born of a virgin, and of his own will suffered death, and was buried, and on this day arose from death. He is called "bread" figuratively and "lamb" and "lion" and so forth. He is called "bread" because he is our life, and the angels'; he is called "lamb" on account of his innocence; a "lion" on account of the strength with which he overcomes the powerful devil. But nevertheless according to true nature, Christ is neither bread, nor lamb, nor lion. Why then is the holy Eucharist called Christ's body, or his blood, if it is not truly that which it is called? In fact the bread and the wine which are consecrated through the priests' mass, appear one thing to human understanding, from without, and cry another thing to believing hearts from within. From without they seem bread and wine, both in form and in taste, but after the consecration they are, through a spiritual mystery, truly Christ's body and his blood. A heathen child is baptized, but it does not alter its outward form, although it is changed within. It is brought to the font sinful because of Adam's transgression, but it is washed from all sins within although it does not change its outward form.

(Swanton, p. 91)

The rest of the sermon explains the theology of the sacrifice and elaborates further the allegorical significance of the original Passover ceremony. Much of Aelfric's doctrinal writing is concerned with explaining the Old Testament in terms of the New; his reluctance to translate the Old Testament stems from a concern that some foolish modern man might think that, like a patriarch, he might have more than one wife. Although a great populariser, Aelfric was keenly aware that the laity and the clergy had different needs.

The general effect of Aelfric's writings on the monastic culture of England was so widespread that it outlasted the Conquest, and entered into the bloodstream of the English Church; his homilies were copied through the twelfth century. The effect of his prose style itself cannot be traced beyond the currency of written Old English, though it may have faintly influenced the style and content of sermons, where the language continued. Aelfric's prose was designed to be read aloud, and it is frequently rhythmical, especially in the saints' lives. The narrative mode, naturally less cool than the exegetical, tended to declamation. And the theme of heroic martyrdom invited the emotive two-stress phrasing of the old heroic poetry, as can be seen, for example, in the *Martyrdom of St. Edmund*. Pulpit oratory today, what remains of it, often falls into a pattern of two-stress phrases, from "Dearly beloved" onwards. Rarely, however, does it run smoothly in Aelfric's balanced periods.

III • WULFSTAN

Leofe men ("Beloved men") is one of Wulfstan's favourite phrases. Wulfstan was much more of an evangelical preacher than Aelfric, at least in his famous *Sermo Lupi*. His style here is an agitated and emphatically heightened version of Aelfric's, and in its hammering effect is more reminiscent of Old English verse. Indeed, some writings of both men have sometimes, misleadingly, been printed by modern editors as if they were in verse. Although prose and verse are not distinguished in manuscripts, and there was both in Latin and English a tradition of rhythmical prose, Old English verse had strict rules that the homilists had no wish to observe. The tone and purpose of the *Sermo Lupi* (1014) is suggested by its opening:

> Beloved men, recognize what the truth is: this world is in haste and it is drawing near the end, and therefore the longer it is the worse it will get in the world. And it needs must thus become very much worse as a result of the people's sins prior to the advent of Antichrist; and then, indeed, it will be terrible and cruel throughout the world. Understand properly also that for many years now the Devil has led this nation too far astray, and that there has been little loyalty among men although they spoke fair, and too many wrongs have prevailed in the land. And there were never many men who sought a remedy as diligently as they should; but daily they added one evil to another, and embarked on many wrongs and unlawful acts, all too commonly throughout this whole nation.
>
> (Swanton, pp. 116–17)

Wulfstan, like the Chronicler of Hastings, sees the depredations of the Danes as a punishment for the sins of the English; and, here, as preliminary to Doomsday. The catalogue of crimes, sins, treasons, and abuses is horribly vivid and, although one-sided, believable. There is much lament, as might be expected, on the despoiling of sanctuaries, and on rape; more impressive, as testimony to Wulfstan's sense of civilised liberties, is his continual stress on legal rights, and their ground in Christian liberty:

> And it is shameful to speak of what has too commonly happened, and it is dreadful to know what many too often do, who practise that wretchedness that they club together and buy one woman in common as a joint purchase, and with the one commit filth one after another and each after the other just like dogs who do not care about filth; and then sell for a price out of the land into the power of enemies the creature of God and his own purchase that he dearly bought.
>
> (Swanton, p. 119)

Deeper outrage to Wulfstan's feelings is caused by faith-breach: the selling of kindred into slavery, and, worst, the betrayal of a lord. His catalogue of horrors culminates in the shame of Danegeld:

> And often ten or twelve, one after another, will disgracefully insult the thegn's wife, and sometimes his daughter or near kinswoman, while he who considered himself proud and powerful and brave enough before that happened, looks on. And often a slave will bind very fast the thegn who was previously his lord, and make him a slave through the wrath of God. Alas for the misery, and alas for the public disgrace which the English now bear, all because of the wrath of God! Often two pirates, or sometimes three, will drive herds of Christian men out through this people from sea to sea, huddled together as a public shame to us all, if we could in earnest properly feel any. But all the disgrace we often suffer we repay with honour to those who bring shame on us. We pay them continually, and they humiliate us daily. They ravage and they burn, plunder and rob, and carry away on

board; and indeed, what else is there in all these events but
the wrath of God clear and visible towards this nation?

(Swanton, p. 120)

The cause of all this is the neglect of God's love and service.
Despite a crescendo of indignantly listed sins, Wulfstan is not a
pessimist: he calls on the English to repent and defend themselves
lest they be defeated (and go to hell)—and here he cites Gildas,
and the parallel fate which had befallen the Britons at the hands
of the Anglo-Saxons centuries before.

Wulfstan wrote other homilies, some based on Aelfric's; on the
Benedictine office; on Edgar (for the *Chronicle*). But the *Sermo
Lupi* eclipses his other work, from a literary as from an historical
viewpoint. It is often seen as the climax of Old English prose, and
its well-marshalled indignation has a profound impact. As a document of Anglo-Saxon values in a national crisis it is uniquely
powerful: loyalty and Christianity are indistinguishable. Characteristically Anglo-Saxon, and reminiscent of *Beowulf*, is its final
implication that Doomsday, though hastening on, can be post-
poned by resolute common action. Yet Wulfstan's grandeur, like
Alfred's, is moral rather than literary. His concatenated thunder is
somewhat mechanical when its articulation is compared with
Aelfric's, especially in its repeated use of intensives. This is better
oratory than prose, although it is remarkably eloquent and effective and, for a historian and many a reader, will have much more
colour and fire than Aelfric. For the historian, too, the *Institutes of
Polity*, laying out the responsibilities and rights of every rank from
the king downwards, are of great interest, not least in Wulfstan's
strictures upon monastic abuses. It shows that England, despite
Ethelred and the Danes, saw itself as a Christian country, profoundly informed by civilised laws.

There are other homilies from this time, in the Vercelli Book
and, from somewhat earlier, the Blickling Homilies, one of which
has a vision of hell which echoes the landscape of the Mere in
Beowulf. But the chief remaining prose of literary interest is in the
Apollonius of Tyre. This is an eleventh-century translation of a
Latin version of a Greek romance, a story that was popular
throughout the middle ages and gave Shakespeare his marvellous
Pericles. The Greek east influenced Anglo-Saxon England from

the beginning—its monasticism, its learning, its hagiography and, above all, its art. The secular romance of *Apollonius* has a fantastic plot and sophisticated sentiment, and the Old English everywhere improves on its source: it is smooth and felicitous, and deals gracefully with romantic love, with blushes, and even with playful puns. It is a contradiction of all hirsute stereotypes and a reminder of kinds and ranges of literature that have been lost (see Greenfield, p. 53).

IV • VERSE OF THE TENTH CENTURY

Of the later Old English poems four are outstanding: *The Phoenix, Judith, Brunanburgh* and *Maldon*. *The Phoenix* was probably written in the later ninth century and stands almost as far away from the norms of Old English verse as does *Apollonius of Tyre* from those of prose. Like the romance, it is adapted from a Latin source (the *Carmen de ave phoenice* attributed to Lactantius, who died in about 340), itself inspired by exotic oriental traditions. The phoenix is first mentioned in Western literature in the Greek historian Herodotus (6th century BC). It is an Egyptian bird which every 500 years returns to Heliopolis on the death of its parent. Its uniqueness, its asexual rebirth from the ashes of its parent, its dying song, its perch in a palm in India, Arabia or Persia, its association with paradise and with spices—all these had gathered round this fabulous bird of glorious plumage in pre-Christian classical sources.

Christians immediately allegorised this myth of the sun into a parable of the resurrection, either of the body or of the immortal soul from the ashes of the body, identifying the bird's paradisal home as the New Jerusalem. The story was very popular both in itself and with allegorists. The first 380 lines of the Old English poem are an expansion of the 170-line *Carmen* of Lactantius; the remaining 297 lines offer an allegorisation which draws on the *Hexæmeron* of Ambrose and much of the same tradition.

The early part of the poem has been admired for the gorgeousness of its paradisal imagery, which stands out like an orchid against the grey stones of the rest of Old English verse. The mysterious appeal of the phoenix has since attracted Shakespeare, and D. H. Lawrence, Wallace Stevens, and James McAuley among modern poets. None, however, exceed the Old English poet in wonder.

> The groves are hung with growing fruit,
> Bright to look upon; the burden of those woods
> Favoured by heaven does not fail ever.
> Nor does blossom, the beauty of trees,
> Lie waste upon the ground; wonderfully rather,
> The branches of the trees bear always
> Perpetual plenty of fruit
> And stand out green above the grassy plain.
> It is the most glorious of groves, its gay adornment
> The work of the Holy One. The wood's canopy
> Is not to be broken, and it breathes out incense
> Through that happy land. This shall last unchanging
> For ever and ever, until the Ancient One
> Shall ordain an end to all He first created.
>
> Beautiful is the bird abiding in that wood,
> Fair and feathered strongly: Phoenix is his name.
> There he lives alone, looking out upon his homeland;
> Dauntless he surveys it. Death shall not touch him
> On that lovely plain, for as long as the world lasts.
>
> (71–89)

The Christian kernel of allegory is of greater intellectual import to the poet than this husk of beauty — which we should, so Augustine tells us in *On Christian Doctrine*, discard. It is hard, however, to prefer to this description the poet's appended explanation of the phoenix as Christ, however impressively developed. A genuine taste for elaborate posterior analytics is hard to acquire, especially when the poet has set the initial fable in a firmly Christian and heroic Germanic perspective, so that we are from the outset fully aware that the phoenix is symbolic, and so that the application, however grave, is more than we need. Modern taste in poetry prefers the inexplicit.

Taken together, *The Phoenix* and *Apollonius of Tyre* are works of an accomplishment and character that English medieval literature was not to exceed until the days of *Pearl* and Chaucer's and Gower's romances. Although wholly naturalised in Old English, they are clearly works of European rather than merely Germanic origin. Europe itself, including Rome, had repeatedly been Germanised, however, and Christianity has oriental origins.

The tenth-century poem *Judith*, found in the *Beowulf* manuscript, is the most straightforwardly successful of the Anglo-Saxon adaptations of a Bible story, a heroic narrative without allegorical complication. The book of Judith (canonical in the Vulgate but apocryphal in the Authorised Version) tells an Old Testament tale of the tribe that in its essentials scarcely needed transposition. The daring beauty who decapitates Holofernes in his tent and inspires the Israelites to victory over the Assyrian foe must have seemed a peculiarly appropriate heroine to Dane-endangered England, a symbol of national resistance against cruel odds. David's defeat of Goliath has a universal appeal, in which the element of bloody tribal vindication is easier to forget than in the case of Judith. The Old English poet relishes the scenes of triumph with the zest displayed in the near-contemporary poem *Brunanburh*. At Brunanburh some of Athelstan's foes were Christians, whereas the Vikings at Maldon (991) are called "the heathen" by the poet of *The Battle of Maldon*. His battle is one between Christians defending their homeland and pagan raiders who are fiends as much as Danes. This is very like the feeling of the Israelites in their struggles with the Philistines or Assyrians.

In such a religious perspective, the sex of the hero of *Judith* is a bonus: virgin martyrs were the pin-ups of the persecuted Church (witness Cynewulf's St. Juliana or Aelfric's Agatha). The Vulgate Judith is a widow rather than a virgin, but in Old English tradition she is a virgin, and when she brings back, Beowulf-like, the head of her persecutor, she is a potent symbol indeed—if not quite in the class of Joan of Arc, who was both a triumphant heroine and a virgin martyr. There had been powerful women in Anglo-Saxon England, such as Alfred's daughter Aethelflæd, the Lady of the Mercians; nor would the Danes, from what Wulfstan tells us of them in *Sermo Lupi*, have respected virtuous widows. But the evident energy of *Judith* was generated not by actual parallels, however emotive, but by the way the religious and the military-heroic frames of reference could here exactly coincide. Aelfric's

Martyrdom of St. Edmund and the poem on Maldon show how very close these two traditions had grown by the tenth century. In the earlier poem *Andreas*, the apostles were roundly presented as a commando unit; no such incongruity afflicts *Judith*.

To turn from the Vulgate to the Old English version is a startling lesson in how to dramatise. The poet drops the "history" and reduces the cast of named characters to two, Judith and Holofernes; what we have of the story consists only of the high points, isolated but heightened and elaborated. *Judith* now opens with an encomium of Judith's faith (something—perhaps not much—is lost at the beginning of the poem) but immediately moves to Holofernes holding a feast, and the arrival at it, on its fourth day, of Judith, "a woman as beautiful as an elf." The drunkenness of Holofernes is magnificently barbaric:

> When the wine
> Rose in him their chieftain roared and shouted
> With triumph, bellowed so loud that his fierce
> Voice carried far beyond
> His tent, his wild pleasure was heard
> Everywhere. And he demanded, over and over,
> That his men empty their cups, drink deep.
> Thus the evil prince, haughty
> Giver of rings, soaked his soldiers
> In wine, the whole day through, drenched them
> till their heads swam
> And they fell on the ground, all drunk, lay as
> though death had struck them
> Down, drained of their senses.
> (17–32; trans. Raffel; Greenfield, p. 163)

Danish drinking was notorious, as in *Hamlet*; but in *Beowulf* only Unferth is said to be drunk. The realism of this Germanic feast is maintained in the detail that it takes Judith two blows to cut off the tyrant's head, even after she has moved his drunken body into the right position. The combination of northern heroic norms with an eye for practical detail (and the impossibility of turning the result into modern English prose) is illustrated by a sentence which Gordon translates as follows:

Then the wise maiden swiftly brought the warrior's head all bloody in the bag in which her servant, a fair-cheeked woman of excellent virtue, had fetched thither the food for them both, and Judith then gave it all gory into her hand, to her attendant, the prudent woman, to bear home.

(*Anglo-Saxon Poetry*, p. 322)

The poet then freely invents a magnificent battle, in which the Hebrews, encouraged by Judith's returning speech and the sight of Holofernes' head, smite the Assyrians. In the Vulgate the Assyrians flee at dawn when they discover the death of Holofernes, and there is no battle. But in *Judith* the "earls," though hard-pressed, wait all day before anyone dares to go in to Holofernes' pavilion. They stand outside it: "All supposed that the prince of men and the fair maid were together in the beautiful tent, Judith the noble and the lecher, terrible and fierce" (Gordon, p. 322). Finally, "the earls wished to waken their friendly lord; they did not succeed" (Gordon, p. 325). One ventures in — horror! — and the resultant ignoble panic and flight must have been extremely satisfying to the audience, as well as to the beasts of prey, which are as ever in attendance. Anachronism is rife: Judith prays to the Son as "the Glory of the Trinity," and at the end (like the beginning) she is said never to have doubted in her eternal reward. In the tenth century *Judith* was a modern story and is all the better for it. Its artistic success is not due to any stylistic refinement but to a bold cutting and reordering of the original in accordance with narrative tradition; the result is well-knit, vivid, and convincing.

Brunanburh and *Maldon* are the last heroic poems in Old English, but the first in the *Chronicle* and the first to describe actual battles on English soil: the new literary verse was more literal-minded than that of the oral tradition. Brunanburh in 937 was a great national victory, Maldon in 991 a minor local defeat. The battle of Brunanburh was one of the most clinching demonstrations of the power of the West Saxon dynasty: Athelstan and his successor Edmund were truly kings and masters of the whole of England; as late as 972 Edgar was rowed on the river Dee by six kings. But by 991 the Danes had the English on a slippery slope. The defeat at Maldon gave rise to the more satisfactory and more Christian poem.

Brunanburh is nevertheless splendid: it deploys the repertory of time-honoured heroic phrases, somewhat stiffly but in a correct versification, and with a sustained use of the prized variation which makes it especially difficult to translate, as will be seen from the version below. Tennyson made a free adaptation of this poem, and a close translator would need some of his musical skill to bring out the distinction of *Brunanburh*'s composition.

Brunanburh is the sole entry for the year 937 in four of the seven manuscripts of the *Chronicle*: after this, verse entries occur several times: *The Capture of the Five Boroughs, The Coronation of Edgar, The Death of Edgar,* and so forth. Each of these pieces is more feeble in content than the last, and the verse itself finally crumbles into prose adulterated with rhyme. *Après Brunanburh le déluge.* This brings home several truths about the procession of Old English verse: *Brunanburh* is the first royal panegyric, the first court poem, the first heroic poem to mention the reading of books, and the last example of correct versification. All of which makes the appearance of the provincial *Maldon* all the more remarkable.

Brunanburh is a place in the north-west of England no longer identifiable, possibly Bromburgh, Cheshire, on the Wirral shore of the river Mersey. In this place, the West-Saxon Athelstan, king of England, and his sixteen-year-old brother Edmund defeated the combined invading forces of King Constantine III of Scotland, King Owen of Strathclyde, and, the prime mover, Olaf of Dublin, leader of the Norsemen of eastern Ireland and of the Norsemen whom Athelstan had driven out of Northumbria. The West Saxons with Mercian help defeated the Scots and Picts, the Strathclyde Welsh, and the Vikings. Foreign annals confirm that the defeat was annihilating and mention the same casualties as the English poem. The historicality of *Brunanburh* does not, however, extend to the meaner details which make *Maldon* so specific and local. *Brunanburh* is the old heroic poetry converted with artistry into a war-praise: the brothers were worthy of their ancestry, they broke the board-wall, the foemen fled, the West Saxons pursued, the fallen were many and noble, the beasts of battle feasted well. It is all there in all its terrible pride, lofty economy, skill and effectiveness; yet it was all about to disappear.

Athelstan the King, captain of men,
Ring-giver of warriors—and with him his brother
Edmund the Atheling—unending glory
Won in that strife by their swords' edges
That there was about Brunanburgh. The board-wall
      they cut through,
Cleft the lindens with the leavings of hammers,
Edward's offspring, answering the blood
They had from their forebears: that in the field they
      should often
Against every foe defend their land,
Hoard and homes. The hated ones fell,
The people of the Scots and the shipmen too,
Fell as was fated. The field was running
With the blood of soldiers from the sun's rise
At the hour of the morning when that marvellous star
God's bright candle, glided over the lands,
To the time when the creature of the eternal Lord
Sank to rest. Then sated with battle
And weary lay many there, men of the Northerners
Shot above their shields, and Scots men likewise
Wasted by spears. The West Saxons
Rode in troop right through the day
Hard on the heels of the hated peoples,
Pursuing hewed fiercely at the fleeing warriors
With mill-sharpened swords. The Mercians did not refuse
The hard hand-play to any hero among those
Who with Anlaf over the ocean's courses
In the bosom of a ship had sought our land
And their doom in that flight. There were five kings
Who in their youth lay low on that battlefield,
Slain by the sword; and seven earls
Of Anlaf's also; others without number
Of shipmen and Scots. With a scant retinue
The prince of the Northmen was put to flight
By stark need to the stern of his craft:
The long ship drove out across the dark waters;
The king slipped away, saved his life.
The old king likewise came away also,

The grey-haired campaigner, Constantine, fled
To the North he knew. He had no need to rejoice
In that meeting of swords where he was shortened of
    kinsmen
And deprived of friends on the field of assembly,
Plucked on the battlefield: on that place of slaughter
He left his son brought low by wounds,
The young man in war.

                                    (1–44)

Virtually all the images and phrases employed are traditional
and so is the skill of their disposition, if more awkwardly managed
in translation. Two points may be taken to show that the poet
understood his art: the West Saxons' day-long pursuit, and the loss
of Constantine's son. Old English poetry is at its most characteristic in setting human action against the larger natural world, and
here the length of the day's slaughter is enforced in the epic
periphrasis of the transit of the sun. The natural perspective
makes the killing both more terrible and less important.

               The field was running
With the blood of soldiers from the sun's rise
At the hour of the morning when that marvellous star,
God's bright candle, glided over the lands,
To the time when the creature of the eternal Lord
Sank to rest ....

This periphrasis for "during daylight" is not an accident of the
oral-formulaic roulette-wheel, but a choice of a collocation
found in that tradition. (A similar panoramic effect is introduced
in both the *Brunanburh* and *Maldon* by the motif of the birds and
beasts of battle.) The sun is traditionally a sign of victory and of
God's blessing, as in *Beowulf* and in one version of the account of
the Emperor Constantine's vision of the cross. As for King Constantine III of Scots, and his young son, the father's loss comes
with more of a shock after the deliberately misleading introductory statement that he had been "deprived of kinsmen" in general. This is wholly traditional: understatement leading to tension of

opposites. As (in imagination) West-Saxon readers of the *Chronicle*, we both rejoice in the lesson that has been served on the old
fox and feel the hard chance of an enemy who has to leave his son
unburied on the place of slaughter and defeat. *Brunanburh* ends:

No worse slaughter
In this island has ever yet
Before these days befallen a people
By the edge of the sword—so say the books,
The wise men of old—since from the east came
Angles and Saxons up to these shores,
Seeking Britain across the broad seas,
Smart for glory, those smiths of war
That overcame the Welsh, and won a homeland.

(65–73)

This claim to the greatness of the battle of Brunanburh is based
on the books of historians, not on "as I have heard." Hearsay, however, is still the authority of the poet of *The Battle of Maldon*, and
so convincing does his account of the battle seem that many readers have believed him a witness; it is clear enough that he knew
the men and places he mentions. The value we have come to
place on historical actuality makes *Maldon* the most accessible to
newcomers of all Old English poems. Only when it is compared
with *Beowulf* or even *Brunanburh* does the grip of the heroic ethos
and of narrative convention become clearly apparent. Battles
could be conceived and perceived in no other way.

V   •   *THE BATTLE OF MALDON*

Although Maldon was not a major battle, it was a milestone in
that after it the English decided for the first time to pay Danegeld.
Two versions of the *Chronicle* mention this:

Parker Chronicle

993 [991]. In this year came Anlaf with ninety-three ships to
Folkestone, and harried outside, and sailed thence to Sand-

A HISTORY OF OLD ENGLISH LITERATURE

wich, and thence to Ipswich, overrunning all the country-
side, and so on to Maldon. Ealdorman Byrhtnoth came to
meet them with his levies and fought them, but they slew
the ealdorman there [10 August] and had possession of the
place of slaughter.

Laud Chronicle

In this year it was decided for the first time to pay tribute to
the Danes because of the great terror they inspired along the
sea coast. On this first occasion it amounted to ten thousand
pounds.

(Garmonsway, pp. 126–27)

The author of the poem apparently did not know the identity of
the enemy leader, but the Anlaf of the *Chronicle* was probably the
great Viking saga hero Olaf Trygvasson, who was soon after converted, won the crown of Norway, and in five years converted five
peoples to Christianity. The leader of the East Saxon levy was
Byrhtnoth, the veteran Ealdorman of Essex. The Viking host had
sailed up from Ipswich and beached their long ships on an island
in the tidal estuary of the River Blackwater ("Panta"); this island,
Northey, is linked to the shore by a causeway ("bridge").

The beginning and end of the poem are lost and the text survives only through a transcript of the year 1725 made shortly
before a fire destroyed the manuscript (and others in the Cotton-
ian collection now in the British Museum). It now opens with
two actions which have definite symbolic implication, and may
also have been part of what might have been observed near Maldon on 10 August 991. The Ealdorman ("Earl") drives far the
horses; the young warrior looses his hawk. No retreat: no more
time for play.

> Then he bade each man let go bridles
> Drive far the horses and fare forward,
> Fit thought to hand-work and heart to fighting.

> Whereat one of Offa's kin, knowing the Earl
> Would not suffer slack-heartedness,

Loosed from his wrist his loved hawk;
Over the wood it stooped: he stepped to battle.
By that a man might know this young man's will
To weaken not at the war-play: he had taken up weapons.

(2–10)

The Earl draws up his troop on the shore and hears the Viking
spokesman shout out across the water their demand for tribute.
These taunting speeches match each other in sarcasm.

Then Bryhtnoth dressed his band of warriors,
From horseback taught each man his task,
Where he should stand, how keep his station.
He bade them brace their linden-boards aright,
Fast in finger-grip, and to fear not.
Then when his folk was fairly ranked
Bryhtnoth alighted where he loved best to be
And was held most at heart — among hearth-
        companions.
Then stood on strand and called out sternly
A Viking spokesman. He made speech —
Threat in his throat, threw across the seamen's
Errand to the Earl where he stood on our shore.

"The swift-striking seafarers send me to thee,
Bid me say that thou send for thy safety
Rings, bracelets. Better for you
That you stay straightaway our onslaught with tribute
Than that we should share bitter strife.
We need not meet if you can meet our needs:
For a gold tribute a truce is struck.

Art captain here: if thou tak'st this course,
Art willing to pay thy people's ransom,
Wilt render to Vikings what they think right,
Buying our peace at our price,
We shall with that tribute turn back to ship,
Fare out on the flood, and hold you as friends."

265

Bryhtnoth spoke. He raised shield-board,
Shook the slim ash-spear, shaped his words.
Stiff with anger, he gave him answer:

"Hearest thou, seaman, what this folk sayeth?
Spears shall be all the tribute they send you,
Viper-stained spears and the swords of forebears,
Such a haul of harness as shall hardly profit you.

Spokesman for scavengers, go speak this back again,
Bear your tribe a bitterer tale:
That there stands here 'mid his men not the meanest of
        Earls,
Pledged to fight in this land's defence,
The land of Aethelred, my liege lord,
Its soil, its folk. In this fight the heathen
Shall fall. It would be a shame for your trouble
If you should with our silver away to ship
Without fight offered. It is a fair step hither:
You have come a long way into our land.

But English silver is not so softly won:
First iron and edge shall make arbitrement,
Harsh war-trial, ere we yield tribute."

(17–61)

The causeway across the ford to Northey is passable only at low
tide, and this exchange took place when the tide was in.

He bade his brave men bear their shields forward
Until they all stood at the stream's edge,
Though they might not clash yet for the cleaving waters.
After the ebb the flood came flowing in;
The sea's arms locked. Overlong it seemed
Before they might bear spear-shafts in shock together.

So they stood by Panta's stream in proud array,
The ranks of the East Saxons and the host from the ash-
        ships,

266

Nor might any of them harm another
Save who through arrow-flight fell dead.

The flood went out. Eager the fleet-men stood,
The crowding raiders, ravening for battle....

(62–73)

Bryhtnoth (spelled thus in the translation) places three men on
the causeway: an arrow kills the first Dane (all Scandinavians are
"Danes") who steps on the stonework. The enemy have already
shrewdly appealed to Bryhtnoth's pride, and honour; baulked at
the "bridge," they now do so again.

When the hated strangers saw and understood
What bitter bridge-warders were brought against them
        there,
They began to plead with craft, craving leave
To fare over the ford and lead across their footmen.

Then the Earl was overswayed by his heart's arrogance
To allow overmuch land to that loath nation:
The men stood silent as Brighthelm's son
Called out over the cold water.

"The ground is cleared for you: come quickly to us,
Gather to battle. God alone knows
Who shall carry the wielding of this waste ground."

The war-wolves waded across, mourned not for the
        water,
The Viking warrior-band; came west over Pant,
Bearing shield-boards over sheer water
And up onto land, lindenwood braced.

Against their wrath there stood in readiness
Bryhtnoth amid his band. He bade them work
The war-hedge with their targes, and the troop to stand
Fast against foe. Then neared the fight,
The glory-trial. The time grew on

267

When there the fated men must fall;
The war-cry was raised up. Ravens wound higher,
The eagle, carrion-eager; on earth — the cry!

Out flashed file-hard point from fist,
Sharp-ground spears sprang forth,
Bows were busy, bucklers flinched,
It was a bitter battle-clash. On both halves
Brave men fell, boys lay still.

(84–112)

Bryhtnoth enters the battle, kills one man, laughs and thanks
God; he is wounded by a spear throw; he kills another Viking
who comes to take his armour, but in the process is mortally
wounded. So he pays the penalty for his excess of spirit. His
dying speech is the prayer of a Christian soldier.

"I give Thee thanks, Lord God of hosts,
For I have known in this world a wealth of gladness,
But now, mild Maker, I have most need
That Thou grant my ghost grace for this journey
So that my soul may unscathed cross
Into Thy keeping, King of angels,
Pass through in peace: my prayer is this,
That the hates of hell may not harm her."

(173–80)

One Godric mounts Bryhtnoth's horse and escapes, with his
brothers; some East Saxons follow him.

This Offa had told him on an earlier day
At the council-place when he had called a meeting,
That many gathered there who were making brave
        speeches
Would not hold in the hour of need.
And now the folk's father had fallen lifeless,
Aethelred's Earl. All the hearthsharers
Might see their lord lying dead.

(198–204)

The remaining third of the poem describes the resistance of the remaining Saxons. Before advancing to their deaths a series of men make formal speeches, all similar to the speech of Wiglaf at the end of *Beowulf*. The noble Aelfwine spoke first:

> "Remember the speeches spoken over mead,
> Battle-vows on the bench, the boasts we vaunted,
> Heroes in hall, against the harsh war-trial!
> Now shall be proven the prowess of the man.
> I would that you all hear my high descendance:
> Know that in Mercia I am of mighty kin,
> That my grandfather was the great Ealhelm,
> Wise Earl, world-blessed man.
> Shall the princes of that people reproach Aelfwine
> That he broke from the banded bulwark of the Angles
> To seek his own land, with his lord lying
> Felled on the field? Fiercest of griefs!
> Beside that he was my lord he was allied to me in blood."
>
> (212–24)

The next speech, that of the second-in-command, explains the cause for the imminent defeat.

> Offa spoke, shook his ash-spear:

> "In right good time dost thou recall us to
> Our allegiance, Aelfwine. Now that the Earl who led us
> Lies on the earth, we all need
> Each and every thane to urge forth the other
> Warriors to the war while weapon lives
> Quick in a hand, hardened blade,
> Spear or good sword. Godric the coward,
> The coward son of Odda, has undone us all:
> Too many in our ranks, when he rode away
> On Bryhtnoth's big horse, believed it was the Earl,
> And we are scattered over the field. The folk is split,
> Shield-wall shattered. Shame on that defection
> That has betrayed into retreat the better half of the army!"
>
> (230–43)

There follow speeches by Leofsunu of Sturmer; Dunnere, a simple churl; Edgelaf, a noble hostage; Edward the Tall; and Aetheric. The companions advanced:

> Board's border burst asunder,
> Corselet sang its chilling song.
> How they beat off the blows!
>   At the battle's turn
> Offa sent a seafarer stumbling to the ground;
> But crippling strokes crashed down
> And Gadd's kinsman was grounded also.
>
> Yet Offa had made good his given word,
> The oath undertaken to his open-handed lord,
> That either they should both ride back to the burg's
>   stockade,
> Come home whole, or harry the Danes
> Till life leaked from them and left them on the field.
> Thane-like he lay at his lord's hand.
>
> Then was a splintering of shields, the sea-wolves
>   coming on
> In war-whetted anger. Again the spears
> Burst breast-lock, breached life-wall
> Of Weird-singled men. Wistan went forth,
> That Wurstan fathered, fought with the warriors
> Where they thronged thickest. Three he slew
> Before the breath was out of Offa's body.
>
>   (284–302)

Each of these speeches and the actions which follow them is different, but each teaches the same lesson.

> Then Byrhtwold spoke, shook ash-spear,
> Raised shield-board. In the bravest words
> This hoar companion handed on the charge:
> "Courage shall grow keener, clearer the will,
> The heart fiercer, as our force grows less.
> Here our lord lies levelled in the dust,

The man all marred: he shall mourn to the end
Who thinks to wend off from this war-play now.
Though I am white with winters I will not away,
For I think to lodge me alongside my dear one,
Lay me down by my lord's right hand."

(309–19)

The first two lines of this speech were once the most celebrated in Old English—the equivalent of the epitaph of Simonides upon the heroes of Thermopylae, though their consequence was quite otherwise. The transcript breaks off shortly afterward.

The plain and spartan quality of *Maldon* makes it suitable for extensive quotation in translation; the translator has so much less to bring across than with *Beowulf*. Though more straightforwardly an heroic poem, and more evidently successful within its narrower limits, than *Beowulf*, *Maldon* is much less of a poem. The pious dying speech of Byrhtnoth, affecting though it is, is perhaps its only naive feature, conventional where the rest of the poem is traditional; but the stuff of which *Maldon* is made is thin when compared with the bronze of *Beowulf*. It is, interestingly, both more prosaic and, in a purely visual way, more vivid than the older poem. Changes in the English language—such as the breaking down of the grammatical functions expressed by inflections into small separate words—put the economy of the traditional versification under strain. Several lines of *Maldon* have too many syllables, often definite articles which are strictly unnecessary but are allowed in by a poet who could not have known in his bones the purpose of such strictness. Likewise the old poetic diction is wanting, as is the solemn variation; and although enough of the old tradition guides the composition, it comes here as something of a surprise when the poet introduces the birds of battle or panoramic overviews of the field. Finally, though the narrative construction by type-scene is similar in kind to that of *Beowulf*, in *Maldon* we have a simple linear progression like that of the Bayeux Tapestry or of the *Song of Roland*. Coherent, yet lacking the epic scope of *Beowulf* (which is almost ten times as long), it lacks too its weight of general implication, its grave completeness. The theme of heroic defeat, and the tragic quality of Bryhtnoth's magnanimous error and its consequence, inevitably summon up thoughts of *Beowulf*, no other Old English poem so directly invokes this punishing comparison. It must also be granted that, weakened though it is in *Maldon*, the understanding of life persisting in the forms of heroic verse is more compelling in its expression than that to be found in any Old English prose, even Alfred's *Preface to the Soliloquies* or Wulfstan's *Sermo Lupi*.

The spirit of what may now be called national resistance, felt in *The Martyrdom of St. Edmund*, in *Judith*, and in *Sermo Lupi*, made Maldon, and *Maldon*, possible. After this, Danegeld and prose became the rule.

TEN : AFTERWARDS

AFTER the death of Wulfstan of York in 1023, Old English writing of any very distinct literary interest is to be found only in the prose of the *Anglo-Saxon Chronicle*, and only occasionally. Old English poetry that is more than merely verse ends with *Maldon*, not, as might be supposed, with the Norman Conquest. It seems unlikely, from the quality of the specimens surviving in the *Chronicle*, that verse of much interest will turn up from the eleventh century; *Durham*, a pleasant encomium of that city of relics, is an exceptionally late survivor, dating from the twelfth century, yet its charm is antiquarian: it is a pious exercise correctly performed. *Brunanburh* was already the ghost of the old tradition.

The composition of Old English verse was an art originally oral and martial, although it had been adapted to literary and religious purposes with considerable success by a number of poets composing between Cædmon and the authors of *Judith* and *The Phoenix*. The conversion of verse-making to a writing process was an effect of the conversion of the Anglo-Saxons. Physically, there is no writing in Old English which is not Christian, even *Waldere*, *Widsith*, *Deor*, *The Wife's Complaint*, and the Charms, which are largely pagan in sentiment. Yet with the strengthening of English literacy, especially in prose, came a weakening of the impulse to make verse. Everything after *Maldon* is a memorial, official or panegyric, metrically crumbling into the Chronicler's prose which it so much resembled. It has been said that after *Beowulf* Old English verse shows a steady decline; yes, but we do not know how much of it was written after *Beowulf*. By the time of Cynewulf the tradition had been tamed into a literary orthodoxy; Cynewulf is the Aelfric of Old English verse — a scholar, a stylist, an artist, but as inferior in power to the author of *Exodus* as William Cowper was to John Milton. The circumstances which gave rise to *Finnsburh*, or to Cædmon, had disappeared. Latin literacy carried all before it and the art of Cynewulf was precisely an art appreciated by a clerisy. When Latin monastic learning failed and English prose attempted to take over many of its functions, the two chief functions it fulfilled — chronicle-keeping and sermon-writing — were kept up far from the hearth of the mead-hall where the poet had traditionally been heard. Alfred, and the *Chronicle* of his reign, make an exception; but the later *Chronicle* is clearly composed in cloisters and not at the court. As for the sermon or homily, the more it articulated communal feelings, the more it relied upon a rhetoric and rhythm which had previously been formalised more strictly and for other purposes. The emphatic rhythms of some of Aelfric's sermons, and especially of Wulfstan's *Sermo Lupi*, borrow the thunder of Old English verse. The alliterative phrase and the rhythmical balance so characteristic of Old English sacred oratory spring from the same expressive forces in the Old English language which earlier had crystallised in verse-composition. Professor Angus McIntosh distinguished at least five distinct stylistic genres in the English writings of the tenth century, only the most formal of which has the metrical regularity of true verse. The three genres intervening between true verse and simple prose are all cannibalisations, more or less, of the repertory of effects proper to verse — but without the system of rules of versification which turned the old phrases into gold and their movement into a dance.

I • OLD AND MIDDLE

The most practical and determining of the factors which led to the end of Old English verse is the series of changes in the nature of the language itself, amounting to the transformation eventually marked by the change of name from Old to Middle English, conventionally dated at the year 1100. These changes were only partly brought about by the imposition of Norman French. The Conquest led to hybridisation of French and English, but English was already changing both structurally and locally, and these changes were accelerated by the Conquest.

Old English was originally a language with a full system of inflections. In the spoken language, in its various dialects, these inflections began to reduce in number, especially in the Danelaw, a region of Danish settlement and intermarriage, for the language of the incomers was similar but had rather different inflections, and confusion led to disuse of such inflections. As the endings of words simplified it became necessary to adhere to a more restricted word order to make it more rapidly clear which word was subject and which object, and which was the verb. The modern order of subject-verb-object began to dominate. Another reason why the inflection system simplified is the fixing of the main stress, which primitively had been mobile, upon the first syllable of a word; this led eventually to a blurring of the distinction between similar case-endings. Prepositions were then needed to express certain relationships previously implicit in inflections. Although in every part of England Old English was spoken differently, in accent and vocabulary, these structural changes affected each dialect.

The Norman Conquest revealed this diversity by replacing the official West Saxon by Norman French. It then became clear that the standard language of administration and of literature, as it had been written from Alfred's day to Aelfric's, was very different from the way the language had been developing outside Wessex, especially in its spoken forms. Even inside Wessex the language had changed much more than its standard written form had suggested. Once the conservative and centripetal force of a standard literary form of English had been removed, the dialects raced away from each other, so that, when they were widely written once more in the thirteenth and fourteenth centuries, dialects differed more one from another than they had in the eighth or the eleventh centuries. This differentiation of dialects makes non-Chaucerian Middle English initially more bewildering than Old English.

The influence of a literary standard language is conservative. But the Old English poetic dialect was not so much conservative as radically archaic. Even in *Beowulf* there are a few traditional words which the author, or later scribes, seem not fully to understand. This dialect had crystallised and its terms and gestures became archaic; as times changed the diction of poetry did not change. It absorbed its Christianity, whereas Old English prose was largely made by Christianity. Aelfric, for example, shows considerable facility in coining words to express theological concepts new to Old English, whereas the religious verse is most successful when it renders Christian narratives in heroic terms. It will be readily understood, then, that changes in the language itself could not be accommodated, beyond a certain point, in the rigid system of Old English verse: normal English usage had come to prefer a word order, an accidence, and a proliferation of small relational words which were difficult to fit in to the old metrical limitations and made the old economy of gesture less easy. Gradually the skill of composition, which had been sustained by social transmission and by social needs now old-fashioned, became rarer and less appreciated; it finally collapsed. In the twentieth century the same sort of process was visible, from the point of view of the audience, in the abandonment for general purposes of Church Latin and of the Authorised Version of the Bible.

Before passing to the fate of Old English prose, two popular misconceptions about the posterity of Old English verse may be corrected. It is commonly supposed that Middle English alliterative verse, such as is found in Layamon's *Brut* and in *Piers Plowman*, is the heir of Old English alliterative verse, and has the same quality and character. But the later verse, although it has an Old English ancestry, is so loose in its prosodic organisation that the discipline and force of Old English verse are quite lacking. Old English verse is governed by stress, and takes the form of a limited number of variations upon stress-unstress, stress-unstress, caesura, stress-unstress, stress-unstress. This pattern is pointed by alliteration, but alliteration is incidental, relatively speaking, and stress-pattern fundamental. Middle English alliterative verse has a variety of measures, often found within the same work; the number of stressed and unstressed syllables varies widely and the caesura is not uniform. The symmetry of stresses is weakened, and is less prominent than alliteration. This alliteration is epidemic rather than measured, and such verse may indeed be called alliterative. If there is a rule, it sometimes seems to be the more alliteration the better. The effect is often so rough and irregular, and the old diction is so broken and transformed that — to adapt what Robert Frost said about writing free verse — the composing of alliterative verse, compared with that of Old English verse, is like playing tennis without a net. This is not at all to deny the achievements of that wide tradition — the virtuosity of the *Gawain*-poet, the colloquial vigour and variety of Langland, the rude force of the alliterative *Morte Arthure*—but to point out that, as a verse tradition, it is a bastard tradition, its vocabulary mixed with French and with popular elements, and its spirit one of Gothic ornamentation and encyclopaedic excess rather than the selection, dignity, and restraint of Old English verse.

The second misconception is more strange, recent, and active: it is that the closest thing to Old English verse in modern verse is the verse of Gerard M. Hopkins. On the contrary, Old English verse is impersonal, unidiosyncratic, unexperimental, and unenthusiastic: the impulse of the *scop*, schooled by a time-honoured tradition was not, like Hopkins, "to admire and to do otherwise," but to carry on. The pith and thew of native English, so much sought after by Saxonisers throughout Modern English from Ascham to William Morris, is present in Old English but is not self-conscious; it is far from the vivid particularity sought by Hopkins, and shuns the unique. Only in some early passages of *The Dream of the Rood* is there any stylistic resemblance to Hopkins, the Hopkins of *The Wreck of the Deutschland*.

The true posterity of Old English verse is the persistence of its four-beat stress pattern within the five-foot line adapted by English poets from Chaucer onwards. Many of the famous lines in Shakespeare have four rather than five main stresses: "To *be*, or *not* to be, *that* is the *question*." This unconscious persistence has sometimes changed, since the rediscovery of Old English, to conscious imitation, as by Ezra Pound and W.H. Auden. The greatest debt of modern English literature to Old English is, however, inalienable — it is the stock of the language itself, the record and expression of the experience of the generations.

A final sample of late Old English verse may be given for comparison with the not dissimilar opening of the Middle English *Piers Plowman. Judgement Day II* is a poetic expansion of a Latin original; it begins:

> Lo! I sat alone   in a leafy bower
> Deep in a wood   and sheltered in shade
> Where welling waters   wandered and murmured
> In the midst of meadow,   all as I tell.
> There pleasant plants   were budding and blooming
> In a throng together   in that gay expanse;
> The trees of the wood   were tossing and sighing
> In a storm of wind;   the heavens were stirred,
> And my sad spirit   was sorely troubled.
>   Then all suddenly,   fearful and sad,
> I commenced to sing   those mournful verses,
> All as you said.
>
> (trans. Kennedy; Greenfield, p. 134)

Kennedy's version accurately suggests the increase in looseness: "all as I tell" and "All as you said" are just the sort of "minstrel" tags found in later medieval literature. Four centuries later Langland begins his poem:

	In a somer seson whan soft was the sonne,
dressed / clothes/shepherd	I shope me in shroudes as I a shepe were,
hermit / secular	In habite as an heremite unholy of workes,
hear	Went wyde in this worlde wondres to here.
But / hills	Ac on a May mornynge on Malverne hulles,
wonder	Me byfel a ferly of fairy, me thoughte;
tired of walking	I was wery forwandered and went me to reste
stream's	Under a brode banke bi a bornes side,
leaned	And as I lay and lened and loked in the wateres,
sounded	I slombred in a slepyng, it sweyved so merye.

The opening of the dream vision is metrically more regular, and composed with more care, than the bulk of *Piers Plowman.* Through Kennedy's translation of *Judgement Day II* above it can be seen that the Old English poem, itself directly based on a similarly conventional opening, is in a broken style — weighty traditional phrases with hollow amplifications. The comparison shows that Langland had available to him an English which had settled down into a staple style, more casually conversational in its easy pace, but also more assured, than the final stages of Old English verse.

II • LATE PROSE

If Middle English verse of the alliterative type is the descendant, after some generations of French intermixture, of Old English verse, the same may be said of the way prose evolved. Though the transition in prose may be traced more continuously, there is a similar gap in the twelfth century, after the Peterborough continuation of the *Chronicle* ends in 1154. In prose the same changes, which are changes in the language itself, occurred more gradually, unimpeded by archaic traditions of prosody and of diction. The mainstream of Norman and Angevin literary culture flowed, however, through Latin prose, where the intellect of Anselm or of John of Salisbury on the one hand and the voluminous competence of chroniclers such as William of Malmesbury on the other, knew no rivals in the native language. As a result of the Benedictine Revival, there was in existence in 1066 an established clerical class which made the forced transition to continental models with ease; for in Latin the differences were not profound. As Auden wrote of the non-national culture of Christendom, in "Memorial for the City":

the sword, the local lord
Were not all; there was home and Rome;
Fear of the stranger was lost on the way to the shrine.

The *Anglo-Saxon Chronicle* was continuously kept up at Winchester from Alfred's time until the year 1001 by a succession of ten scribes. In 891 it had been copied at other centres, and thereafter three of the other six extant versions were virtually independent. The seven surviving versions of the Alfredian *Chronicle* have a historical interrelationship too complex to summarise. Eventually, however, the four major versions reflected local as well as national interests, and were kept from the point of view of particular monastic houses at Winchester, Abingdon, Worcester and Medehamstead (Peterborough). The interest of the later *Chronicle* is uneven but often high, though extended quotation would necessitate many footnotes. Its revival had coincided with the Benedictine Revival in the late tenth century, and its different versions record vividly, if patchily, the chief events of the reigns of Ethelred II and his successors up to the reign of William and his sons.

The Laud or Peterborough *Chronicle*, for example, was written at Peterborough, under a Norman abbot, from 1121 to 1154. (For the period before 1121, it is based on a lost Canterbury chronicle itself based on northern and West Saxon sources.) The twelfth-century continuation is famous for its description of the baronial anarchy of King Stephen's reign. To historians of the language it is famous as exhibiting the beginnings of Middle English.

For a single example of the later *Chronicle*, however, part of the Peterborough entry of 1085 is chosen, for its thoroughly clerical note, so characteristic of the professional scribe and so different from the entries for Alfred's reign.

The king spent Christmas with his councillors at Gloucester, and held his court there for five days, which was followed by a three-day synod held by the archbishop and the clergy. At this synod Maurice was elected bishop of London and William bishop of Norfolk and Robert bishop of Cheshire: they were all chaplains of the king.

After this the king had important deliberations and exhaustive discussions with his council about this land, how it was peopled, and with what sort of men. Then he sent his men all over England into every shire to ascertain how many hundreds of "hides" of land there were in each shire, and how much land and live-stock the king himself owned in the country, and what annual dues were lawfully his from each shire. He also had it recorded how much land his archbishops had, and his diocesan bishops, his abbots and his earls, and—though I may be going into too great detail—and what or how much each man who was a landholder here in England had in land or in live-stock, and how much money it was worth. So very thoroughly did he have the inquiry carried out that there was not a single "hide," not one virgate of land, not even—it is shameful to record it, but it did not seem shameful to him to do—not even one ox, nor one cow, nor one pig which escaped notice in his survey. And all the surveys were subsequently brought to him.

(Garmonsway, p. 216)

Though less famous now than the Domesday Book which it scorns here, the *Anglo-Saxon Chronicle* is a remarkable cultural achievement, unique among the vernaculars of the Europe of its age for its very existence, let alone its quality and range. It is a pity that literature, as studied at universities in the early twenty-first century, is divided into three parts—poetry, drama, and fictional prose. Except by new historicists wishing to put literature into a particular political context, nonfictional prose, the medium of political, social, intellectual, and religious life, has been neglected. Nor can literary history properly represent non-fictional prose by quoting from translations.

After the Conquest, English of course continued to be spoken by all except the small class of new rulers. Officials employed by the Normans had, at some level, to speak English in order to be understood. This level moved downwards for some time then upwards again until it included the king. The rulers were soon bilingual and their scribes often trilingual. By the early thirteenth century, Archbishop Peckham of York directed his clergy to preach in English—indicating that they did not usually or always do so. But some parish priests must have continued to preach in the English they spoke. And there is a stream of continuous evidence, mostly in small quotations in the text or the margins of works in Latin, for a continuing popular oral tradition of minstrel poetry and song. There are also many old stories of oral and English origin in the Latin chronicles, as of Hereward the Wake or of Alfred burning the cakes. Before the end of the twelfth century there were accomplished works in a literary English verse and prose—*The Owl and the Nightingale* and the *Ancrene Wisse*—which lies outside the boundary of this history.

English survived the Conquest, then, without any difficulty not only as a spoken language but as a language used for preaching, entertainment, and all forms of popular culture, notably the romance. The continuity claimed for English prose by R.W. Chambers, however, seems to consist chiefly in the continuity of spoken English and of the English language. A continuing tradition of prose style, as a qualitative entity separable from the continuity of the spoken language itself, is elusive. The desire to trace such a continuity is a patriotic thing and natural enough, although it has sometimes served insular and particularist ends, either party-political or sectarian, and tends to be self-confirming. That such a continuity must exist—if not on some special terms—is as evident as the impossibility of defining it satisfactorily. So many of our institutions are descended from Anglo-Saxon times—not Christianity itself, nor our legal institutions only, but verbal institutions like the names of the days of the week; of persons and places; and of mother and father, son and daughter, husband and wife; and perhaps most of the words in a book such as this. On the other hand, a retrospective search for desirable national "vernacular" characteristics is bound to be successful. Those who wrote in Latin were, however, just as English as those who dug the ditches and wrote and read no language. The first known English poet was an illiterate cowherd with a Celtic name—known to us only through a Latin writer, who was an Angle rather than an Englishman. It is tempting to find elements of the English character in Old English literature. Perhaps the Anglo-Saxons really were more melancholy, stoic, loyal, Christian, fair-minded, modest, steady, noble, and true to their word, as has been claimed, than their neighbours—or than their descendants. It is pleasant to think that most Englishmen were like King Edwin or King Alfred. They were not, however, instinctive village-green democrats, as some Victorians were led to believe.

There is today undoubtedly a direct linguistic inheritance from Old English, but it is thoroughly interbred with French, not to mention earlier Scandinavian and later Latin contributions; and the modern language is very different. It has been said that Modern English differs as much from Old English as French does from Latin, and more than any other European language does from its own first-known state. Whatever the value of such estimates, it

The Harrowing of Hell

would be strange to regret the enrichment of the language.

Is there a specifically literary inheritance from Old English literature? If so, the evidence lies too deep for analysis, for it is chiefly rhythmical and structural, that is, linguistic. It would be difficult to nominate an element more fundamental or distinctive to any society than its language. There is a persistence of Old English metre in the classic English pentameter line. There are turns of phrase in the modern language, phrases like "heaven and earth," which are "Anglo-Saxon"; so, no doubt, are recently coined alliterative doublets like "Guinness is good for you." The words of the Anglican marriage service, recently adopted by the Catholic Church—"to have and to hold ... for better for worse"—are based on an Anglo-Saxon formulaic oath which survived the Conquest. But the posterity of Old English verse, as distinct from prose, is lost. It would have been lost even if Harold had won the Battle of Hastings. Thanks to scholars we can enjoy it again—a privilege not permitted to Shakespeare.

APPENDIX : A NOTE ON DEOR

Deor seems an invented character, but the examples of wrongs endured with which he makes his consolation bear famous Germanic names. Wayland (or Weland) was the smith of the gods, the northern Vulcan. He was captured by Nithhad and hamstrung. He escaped, nevertheless, having killed Nithhad's two sons and turned their skulls into bowls. He can be seen on one side of the Franks Casket (see p. 49) presenting such a bowl to Nithhad as an example of his art. On the right of this scene is a figure who may represent Beadohild, whom Wayland ravished. The offspring of this union was Widia, a famous hero; later his parents were reconciled. The story behind the third strophe cannot be identified, though it seems that the woman's sorrow may, again, turn to something sweeter. Theodoric might be either the Ostrogoth who ruled Merano for only thirty years before being exiled by Eormanric; or the Frank who was exiled to Merano and ruled it unhappily for thirty years. Eormanric (in the fifth strophe) was the king of the Goths who died in 375; in legend he was a tyrant. Finally, Deor himself has been discarded by King Heoden in favour of Heorrenda, a singer and harper with the skill to win the heart of the beauty Hild for his new master.

NOTES ON PLATES

tispiece **Sutton Hoo Helmet:** a re-creation. The original survives only in small corroded fragments, which can be seen in the British Museum. It has an iron crest and visor, with iron cheek-pieces and neck-guard. The iron was covered with bronzed and tinned plates which repeat three subjects: a mounted warrior riding down a fallen warrior; two dancing warriors; and an animal interlace. The crest terminates at each end in a gilt-bronze dragon head with garnet eyes. The front dragon is nose-to-nose with a third dragon with wings which are also the bronze and silver eyebrows of the visor; a body which is the gilt-bronze nose-piece; and a tail which is the gilt-bronze moustache of the visor. The eyebrows are underlined with garnets and terminate in bronze boars.

p.20 **Offa's Penny:** The silver penny introduced by Offa in about 780, standardised at twenty-two grains in weight, was the best currency in Europe; it was copied in England until Henry III. Obverse: +OFFA REX MERCIOR—. Reverse: EADHVN (Moneyer's name). 17mm diameter (actual size).

p.25 **Sutton Hoo Spoons:** these two spoons are of a late-classical type. The Greek inscriptions read Paulos (Paul) on the lower and

287

Saulos (Saul) on the upper. As a pair that could be used for baptismal presents, they would allude to the conversion of Saul. The upper inscription is unskilfully done, and the reading Saulos has been queried. Length 26.7cm.

p.26 **Sutton Hoo Silver Bowls:** two of the set of ten light silver bowls, between 8 and 9 inches in diameter. The inside of the bowl is inscribed with the Greek Christian motif of the equal-armed cross. Of late sixth-century, provincial Byzantine manufacture.

p.27 **Sutton Hoo Shoulder-Clasp:** one of a pair of gold shoulder-clasps found in the buried treasure. The gold pin fastening the clasp at the hinge (here withdrawn) is about 6cm long. The clasp would have been stitched by staples at the back onto a two-piece leather coat, the halves joining at and sitting on the shoulders. The rectangular panels are filled in a carpet pattern with red garnets in *cloisonné*, alternating with blue and white *millefiori* glass. The gold border is decorated with animal interlace *cloisonné* in garnet. The round ends are formed by the crested backs of two intersecting boars, in large cloisons of garnet, with blue *millefiori* shoulder-joints and tusks.

p.29 **Sutton Hoo Sceptre:** a bar of fine-grained stone 2 feet in length, tapered at each end to a terminal knob, each of the four sides ending in a carved human face. One knob is attached by a bronze clasp to a bronze saucer which acts as base. Missing from the other end was the bronze terminal which held the bronze pedestal, base of the iron wire ring on which a bronze stag is mounted. This bar, now recognised as a sceptre, was formerly described as a ceremonial whetstone; the stag was formerly exhibited as part of the iron standard.

p.29 **Sceptre: a detail:** the base of the sceptre, showing three faces, two in profile. The face shown in full is bearded; others are moustached; others seem to be women's faces. All eight faces are grave, intent and severely stylised within their frames.

p.33 **The Ruthwell Cross:** front view of the reassembled cross as it now stands in the parish church at Ruthwell, Dumfriesshire. The cross (discussed on pp. 216-27) stands 5.5m high; this was originally the south face. It shows six scenes. At the bottom (defaced) the Crucifixion; then (behind the rails) the Annunciation; the healing of the man born blind; Mary Magdalen wiping the feet of Christ; the Visitation; an archer shooting at (above the modern crosspiece) a bird. The inscriptions identifying the scenes they enclose are in Latin, in Roman letters, except for that around the Visitation which is in runes. The Old English text of *The Dream of the Rood* borders the narrower sides of the cross.

p.37 **Lindisfarne Gospels: St. Matthew's Incipit:** the opening words are *Liber generationis* ... (the book of the genealogy of Jesus Christ son of David son of Abraham). The first three letters of *Liber* form one grand polychrome initial, the central "I" brandishing Celtic terminals of fantastic exuberance. Next to the head of the "I" the tiny Old English gloss *boc* (book) can just be distinguished.

p.38 **Lindisfarne Gospels: a Carpet Page:** according to Alfred of Chesterle-Street, who later inserted an interlinear Old English gloss on the text, this Gospel Book was written for God and St. Cuthbert by Eadfirth, who in 698 became bishop of Lindisfarne. This carpet page, at the beginning of St. Mark's Gospel, has a most complex double-stranded interlace pattern running between panels. The central medallion and the narrow border panels contain a stepped design similar to that in the Sutton Hoo shoulder-clasps (p. 27). The triangular panels contain animal interlace, as do the excrescences at the corners and sides of the "carpet." The other rectangular panels contain Celtic spirals. The principal colours are red, yellow, blue, and green. Length 34.5cm.

p.39 **Lindisfarne Gospels: St. John:** the Evangelist sits magisterial on a bench, his scroll across his knees, his right hand over his heart. His name and title are given in Greek, written in Latin letters: O AGIOS (the holy) IOHANNES. The image of an eagle, his symbol, emerges from his halo, identified in Latin (*aquilae* is mis-

289

spelled, perhaps for reasons of symmetry). The iconography is based on Latin and Greek models. Main colours as in 11 above, with brown for the eagle.

*p.*43 **St. Lawrence, Bradford-on-Avon, Wiltshire:** built by Aldhelm, bishop of Sherborne 705-09. Restored and enlarged in the late tenth century, when the upper arcading was added. Rediscovered in 1859, re-dedicated and restored. External length 14.6m.

*p.*49 **The Franks Casket:** a small carved whalebone box presented to the British Museum by Sir Augustus Franks in 1867. The Old English runic inscription on the front (shown here) reads: "This is whale bone. The sea cast up the fish on the rocky shore. The ocean was troubled where he swam aground onto the shingle." The front panel shows (right) the Adoration of the Magi and (left) Wayland the Smith. He offers to Nithhad a cup made of the skull of one of Nithhad's sons, whose body lies at Wayland's feet. Behind Nithhad's back stands Beadohild (see note on *Deor*, p. 298). Behind her Aegil, Wayland's brother, catches birds. On the top of the casket Nithhad's men besiege Aegil. On the left side, Romulus and Remus. Other scenes show Sigurd; and the capture of Jerusalem by Titus in A.D. 70. Length 23.3cm. Dated to early eighth century. Northumbrian?

*p.*101 **The Exeter Book: Folio** 103a. A page of this MS written on parchment in a large half-uncial script, probably in the third quarter of the tenth century. Text shows end of riddle 7 and beginning of riddle 10, with riddles 8 and 9 complete. For 8 (*Hraegl min swigath*) see p. 100-02. Nine (*Ic thurh muth sprece*) is referred to on p. 69-70.

*p.*163 **The Alfred Jewel:** found near Athelney, Somerset, in 1693. Made of gold with a *cloisonné* enamel portrait of a man holding two sceptres, set under crystal. The sides of the jewel read *Aelfred mec heht gewyrcan* (Alfred commanded me to be made). The animal head terminal below, is gold filigree, holds a cylindrical socket (see p. 180). Length 7.4cm.

p.230 **Christ and St. Dunstan:** the later inscription at the top says that the picture and writing are both from the hand of St. Dunstan himself, who is seen kissing the hem of Christ's robe. There is no reason to doubt this. The red and black pen drawing would then have been added in Glastonbury, in about 960, to an MS of Ovid written about 900.

p.232 **Edgar's New Minster Charter:** King Edgar granted the Charter of the New Minster at Winchester in 966. This is the title page of a rich version of the foundation charter painted in the early eleventh century. The King between the Virgin and St. Peter offers the charter to a Christ who is seated above in a mandorla, flanked by angels. The acanthus border in blue, green, red, purple, and gold is Carolingian in origin but its exuberance is English, as is the unimperial sprightliness of the king. Length 20.5cm.

p.233 **Aethelwold's Benedictional: Entry into Jerusalem:** from the most splendid of the Winchester MSS, painted between 971 and 984. A Latin poem opening the Bishop's Benedictional says of its decoration that the Saint "commanded also to be made in this book many frames well adorned and filled with various beautiful colours and with gold." There are twenty-eight "filled" pages, of which this is one, and twenty-one other decorated pages. The iconography, of the buildings for example, is Byzantine in origin, but the vitality of the branches and their cutters is native. Length 19cm.

p.283 **The Harrowing of Hell:** from an eleventh-century psalter, Cotton MS Tiberius C.vi, damaged by fire, pen drawing on vellum. Christ stands at the door raising the souls of the just from Hell, represented by the jaws of a huge beast, and trampling upon the Devil who is bound hand and foot. Beneath the Devil is a dragon. Written space 21.6 x 12.4cm.

BIBLIOGRAPHY AND FURTHER
READING

GENERAL

Campbell, James, ed. *The Anglo-Saxons*. Oxford: Phaidon, 1982;
Harmondsworth and New York: Viking Penguin, 1991.
Greenfield, Stanley B. *A Critical History of Old English Literature*.
New York: New York University Press, 1965; London:
University of London Press, 1966.
Mitchell, Bruce. *An Invitation to Old English and Anglo-Saxon
England*. Oxford: Blackwell, 1995. [though chiefly linguistic,
Mitchell's book has an annotated bibliography for the
beginning student]
Raw, Barbara C. *The Art and Background of Old English Poetry*.
London: Edward Arnold, 1978.
Shippey, T.A. *Old English Verse*. London: Hutchinson, 1972.
Wrenn, C.L. *A Study of Old English Literature*. London: Harrap,
1967.

Recent scholarly publications can be followed in *The Year's
Work in English Studies* (Oxford University Press, annually
since 1921); *Old English Newsletter* (Binghamton, NY: for the
Modern Language Association of America by the Center for
Medieval and Early Renaissance Studies, State University of

New York at Binghamton, twice yearly since 1967); and *Anglo-Saxon England* (Cambridge University Press, annually since 1970).

LANGUAGE

Davis, Norman. *Sweet's Anglo-Saxon Primer*. Oxford: Clarendon Press, 1953.
Mitchell, B., and F.C. Robinson. *A Guide to Old English*. 5th ed. Oxford: Blackwell, 1994.
Quirk, R., and C.L. Wrenn. *An Old English Grammar*. 2nd ed. London: Methuen, 1963.

EDITIONS

Collected editions
Krapp, G.P., and E.V.K. Dobbie. *The Anglo-Saxon Poetic Records*. 6 vols. New York: Columbia University Press; London: Routledge, 1931–54.
Pope, John C. *Seven Old English Poems*. 2nd ed. New York: Norton, 1981.
Whitelock, Dorothy. *Sweet's Anglo-Saxon Reader*. Oxford: Clarendon Press, 1970.

Beowulf
Alexander, Michael. *Beowulf: A Glossed Text*. Penguin English Poets. Harmondsworth and New York: Penguin, 1966; rev. ed., 2000.
Davis, N. *Beowulf*. A facsimile with facing transcriptions. The Early English Text Society. London: Oxford University Press, 1966.
Jack, George, ed. *Beowulf, A Student Edition*. Oxford: Clarendon Press, 1994.
Kiernan, Kevin S., ed. *Electronic* Beowulf *on CD-ROM*. London: British Library, 2000.
Klaeber, F. *Beowulf and the Fight at Finnsburg*. Ed. with introduction, bibliography, notes, glossary, and appendices. 3rd ed. with two supplements. Boston: D.C. Heath; London: Harrap, 1950.

Mitchell, B., and F. Robinson, eds. *Beowulf: An Edition*. Oxford: Blackwell: 1998.

Swanton, Michael, ed. *Beowulf*. Manchester: Manchester University Press, 1978.

Wrenn, C.L., ed. *Beowulf*. 3rd ed., rev. W.F. Bolton. Exeter: Exeter University Press, 1973.

Other editions
From Methuen's Old English Library (London):
Aelfric's Colloquy. Ed. G.N. Garmonsway. 2nd ed., 1947.
Cynewulf's Elene. Ed. P.O.E. Gradon, 1958.
Deor. Ed. Kemp Malone. 3rd ed., 1961.
Finnsburh: Fragment and Episode. Ed. D.K. Fry, 1974.
Judith. Ed. B.J. Timmer. 2nd ed., 1961.
The Seafarer. Ed. I.L. Gordon, 1966.
Sermo Lupi Ad Anglos. Ed. Dorothy Whitelock. 3rd ed., 1963.
The Wanderer. Ed. T.P. Dunning and A.J. Bliss, 1969.
The Battle of Maldon. Ed. E.V. Gordon, with a supplement by D.G. Scragg. Manchester: Manchester University Press, 1976.
The Dream of the Rood. Ed. Michael Swanton. Manchester: Manchester University Press; New York: Barnes and Noble, 1970.
The Phoenix. Ed. N.F. Blake. Manchester: Manchester University Press, 1964.
Widsith. Ed. R.W. Chambers. Cambridge: Cambridge University Press, 1912.

TRANSLATIONS

Alexander, Michael. *The Earliest English Poems*. 3rd ed. Harmondsworth: Penguin: 1991.
—. *Beowulf, A Verse Translation*. 2nd ed. Harmondsworth: Penguin, 2001.
—. *Old English Riddles from the Exeter Book*. London: Anvil Press Poetry, 1980; 1984.
Bradley, S.A., ed. and trans. *Anglo-Saxon Poetry*. London: Dent, 1982; Boston: Charles E. Tuttle, 1991.
Clark Hall, J., and C.L. Wrenn. *Beowulf and the Finnesburg Fragment*. A translation into Modern English prose, with

Prefatory Remarks by J.R.R. Tolkien. 2nd ed. London: Allen and Unwin, 1950.

Garmonsway, G.N. *The Anglo-Saxon Chronicle*. London: Dent, 1953; New York: Dutton, 1954.

Garmonsway, G.N., and J. Simpson. *Beowulf and its Analogues*. London and New York: Dent, 1968.

Gordon, R.K. *Anglo-Saxon Poetry*. Rev. ed. London: Dent; New York, Dutton, 1954.

Heaney, Seamus. *Beowulf: A New Translation*. London: Faber, 1999.

Kennedy, Charles W. *Early English Christian Poetry*. London: Hollis and Carter, 1952.

Liuzza, R.M. *Beowulf: A New Verse Translation*. Peterborough, ON: Broadview Press, 2000.

Raffel, Burton. *Poems from the Old English*. Lincoln: University of Nebraska Press, 1960.

Swanton, Michael. *Anglo-Saxon Prose*. London: Dent; Totowa, NJ: Rowman and Littlefield, 1975.

Whitelock, Dorothy. *English Historical Documents*. Vol. 1: 500–1042. 2nd ed. London: Eyre Methuen, 1972.

—. *The Anglo-Saxon Chronicle*. With David C. Douglas and Susie I. Tucker. London: Eyre and Spottiswoode, 1961.

CRITICISM

Beowulf

Bjork, Robert E., and John D. Niles. *A Beowulf Handbook*. Lincoln: University of Nebraska Press, 1997.

Bonjour, A. *The Digressions in Beowulf*. Oxford: Blackwell: 1950.

Brodeur, A.G. *The Art of Beowulf*. Berkeley and Los Angeles: University of California Press, 1959.

Chambers, R.W. *Beowulf, an Introduction*. 3rd ed., with a supplement by C.L. Wrenn. Cambridge: Cambridge University Press, 1959.

—. "*Beowulf* and the Heroic Age in England." *Man's Unconquerable Mind*. London: Cape, 1939.

Chase, C., ed. *The Dating of Beowulf*. Toronto: University of Toronto Press, 1981.

Clark, G. *Beowulf*. Boston: Twayne, 1990.

Irving, E.B., Jr. *A Reading of Beowulf.* New Haven: Yale University Press, 1968.
—. *Rereading Beowulf.* Philadelphia: University of Pennsylvania Press, 1989.
Nicholson, L.E., ed. *An Anthology of Beowulf Criticism.* Notre Dame: University of Notre Dame Press, 1963.
Niles, J.D. *Beowulf: The Poem and its Tradition.* Cambridge, MA: Harvard University Press, 1983.
Robinson, F.C. *'Beowulf' and the Appositive Style.* Knoxville: University of Tennessee Press, 1985.
—. *The Tomb of Beowulf and other essays on Old English.* Oxford: Blackwell, 1993.
Shippey, T.A. *Beowulf.* London: Edward Arnold, 1978; Boston: Charles River Books, 1979.
Sisam, K. *The Structure of Beowulf.* Oxford: Clarendon Press, 1965.
Tolkien, J.R.R. "Beowulf: The Monsters and the Critics." *Proceedings of the British Academy* 22. London: Oxford University Press, 1936. pp.245-95; included in Nicholson (above).
Whitelock, D. *The Audience of Beowulf.* 2nd ed. Oxford: Clarendon Press, 1958.

CONTEXTS, LITERARY AND HISTORICAL

Allen, Michael J.B., and Daniel G. Calder. *Sources and Analogues of Old English Poetry: The Major Latin Texts in Translation.* Cambridge: D.S. Brewer; Totowa, NJ: Rowman & Littlefield, 1976.
Attwater, Donald. *Penguin Dictionary of Saints.* Harmondsworth, 1965.
Bede. *Bede's Ecclesiastical History of the English People,* etc. Ed. D.H. Farmer. Trans. L. Sherley-Price. Rev. ed. Harmondsworth: Penguin, 1990.
—. *The Ecclesiastical History of the English Nation.* Trans. J. Stevens, rev. J.A. Giles. London: Dent, 1965.
Blair, Peter Hunter. *An Introduction to Anglo-Saxon England.* Cambridge: Cambridge University Press, 1965.
—. *The World of Bede (Studies in Anglo-Saxon England).* New York: Cambridge University Press, 1990.

Bolton, W.P. *A History of Anglo-Latin Literature 597-1066.* Vol. I: 597-740. Princeton: Princeton University Press, 1967.

Brown, Peter. *The World of Late Antiquity.* London: Thames & Hudson, 1971.

Bruce-Mitford, R.L.S., et al. *The Sutton Hoo Ship Burial.* London: British Museum, 1975-83; New York: W. Sessions (UK)/State Mutual Book and Periodical Service, 1988.

Chadwick, H.M., and Nora K. Chadwick. *The Ancient Literature of Europe.* Vol. I of *The Growth of Literature.* Cambridge: Cambridge University Press, 1932; New York, 1986.

Chadwick, Nora. *The Celts.* Harmondsworth: Penguin, 1970.

Chambers, R.W. *Man's Unconquerable Mind.* London: Cape, 1939.

—. *On the Continuity of English Prose.* London: Oxford University Press for the Early English Text Society, 1932.

Clancy, Joseph P. *The Earliest Welsh Poetry.* London: Macmillan; New York: St. Martin's Press, 1970.

Elliot, Ralph W.V. *Runes.* Manchester: Manchester University Press, 1959.

Finberg, H.P.R. *The Formation of England 550-1042.* London: Hart-Davis, MacGibbon, 1974; Paladin, 1976.

Henderson, George. *Early Medieval.* Harmondsworth: Penguin, 1972.

Hurt, James. *Aelfric.* New York: Twayne, 1972.

Jackson, Kenneth Hurlstone. *A Celtic Miscellany.* Rev. ed. Harmondsworth: Penguin, 1971.

Ker, W.P. *The Dark Ages.* London: 1904; Hyperion, CT, 1979.

—. *Epic and Romance.* London, 1896; New York: Dover, 1957.

Keynes, S., and M. Lapidge, eds. *Alfred the Great.* Harmondsworth: Penguin, 1983.

Knowles, Dom David. *The Monastic Order in England.* 2nd ed. Cambridge: Cambridge University Press, 1963.

Lapidge, M., J. Blair, S. Keynes, and D. Scragg, eds. *The Blackwell's Encyclopaedia of Anglo-Saxon England.* Oxford and Malden, MA: Blackwells, 1999.

Lapidge, M., and M. Godden, eds. *The Cambridge Companion to Old English Literature.* Cambridge: Cambridge University Press, 1991.

Lord, A.B. *The Singer of Tales.* Cambridge, MA: Harvard University Press, 1964; New York: Atheneum, 1965.

Mitchell, Bruce. *An Invitation to Old English and Anglo-Saxon England*. Oxford: Blackwell, 1995.

Nordenfalk, Carl. *Celtic and Anglo-Saxon Painting*. London: Chatto and Windus, 1977.

O'Connor, Frank. *Kings, Lords and Commons*. New York: Knopf, 1959; London: Macmillan, 1961.

Page, R.I. *Life in Anglo-Saxon England*. London: Batsford, 1970.

Parry, Milman. *The Making of Homeric Verse*. Ed. Adam Parry. Oxford: Clarendon Press, 1971.

Rice, David Talbot. *English Art 871-1100*. Oxford: Clarendon Press, 1952.

Stanley, E.G., ed. *Continuations and Beginnings*. London: Nelson, 1966.

Stenton, Sir Frank. *Anglo-Saxon England*. 3rd ed. Oxford: Clarendon Press, 1971.

Tacitus, Publius Cornelius. *Germania*. Trans. H.S. Mattingly. *Tacitus on Britain and Germany*. Harmondsworth: Penguin, 1950.

Whitelock, Dorothy. *The Beginnings of English Society*. Harmondsworth: Penguin, 1960.

Williams, Margaret. *Word-Hoard*. London: Sheed & Ward, 1946.

Wilson, David M. *The Anglo-Saxons*. Rev. ed. Harmondsworth: Penguin, 1971.